SAVED BY GRACE

SAVED BY GRACE

The Holy Spirit's Work in Calling and Regeneration

Herman Bavinck

Edited, with an Introductory Essay by J. Mark Beach
Translated by Nelson D. Kloosterman

Reformation Heritage Books
Grand Rapids, Michigan

© 2008 by Nelson D. Kloosterman and J. Mark Beach

Published by
REFORMATION HERITAGE BOOKS
2965 Leonard St., NE
Grand Rapids, MI 49525
616-977-0599 / Fax 616-285-3246
e-mail: orders@heritagebooks.org
website: www.heritagebooks.org

Paperback edition published 2013
ISBN 978-1-60178-281-6

Printed in the United States of America

Originally published in Dutch as *Roeping en Wedergeboorte*
(Kampen: G. Ph. Zalsman, 1903).

This is a REFORMED EXPLORATIONS monograph,
commissioned by the faculty of Mid-America Reformed Seminary

The Library of Congress has cataloged the hardcover edition as follows:

Bavinck, Herman, 1854-1921.
  [Roeping en wedergeboorte. English]
  Saved by grace : the Holy Spirit's work in calling and regeneration /
by Herman Bavinck ; edited, with an introduction by J. Mark Beach ;
translated by Nelson D. Kloosterman.
    p. cm.
  Includes bibliographical references and index.
  ISBN 978-1-60178-052-2 (hardcover : alk. paper)
  1. Regeneration (Theology) 2. Grace (Theology) 3. Reformed
Church--Doctrines. I. Beach, J. Mark (James Mark) II. Title.
  BT790.B3813 2008
  234--dc22
                        2008030170

From 29 March 1901 through 2 May 1902, some forty articles were published in *De Bazuin* [*The Trumpet*], essays which sought to communicate greater clarity concerning the doctrine of immediate regeneration. These articles now appear separately under a somewhat modified title. May they, also in this form, ensure that difference of insight does no injury to the unity of the Confession and to the peace of the churches.

Herman Bavinck

CONTENTS

Part IV: The Relation between the Immediate Operation of the Holy Spirit and the Means of Grace

INTRODUCTORY ESSAY[1]

HERMAN BAVINCK was born December 13, 1854, at Hoogeveen, the Netherlands. His father, J. Bavinck (1826–1909), was a prominent minister in the church of the Secession, which had seceded from the National Dutch Reformed Church (*De Hervormde Kerk*) in 1834. Herman was an extraordinarily gifted student, studying first at the Theological School of the Secession churches in Kampen, but transferring to Leiden University in order to become acquainted first hand with the modernist theology of J. H. Scholten and A. Kuenen and their more scientific approach to the discipline of theology. He earned a doctorate from Leiden in 1880, whereupon he was offered a teaching post at the newly founded Free University of Amsterdam. He declined that appointment and entered the pastorate at Franeker for a year, before accepting the appointment to teach at Kampen. Here he was to spend the next twenty years of his life, in spite of the Free University of Amsterdam again offering him a teaching position in the theological faculty in 1889. Finally, in 1902 Bavinck came to the Free University to occupy the chair of dogmatics vacated by Dr. Abraham Kuyper. He labored at the Free University until his death in 1921.[2]

Bavinck is often contrasted with his great contemporary and senior, Abraham Kuyper (1837–1920). We may briefly observe, as has been noted by others, that whereas Kuyper was a man of broad vision and sparkling ideas, Bavinck was a man of sober disposition and clear concepts. Whereas Kuyper was more speculative, tracing out intuitively grasped thoughts, Bavinck was a more careful scholar and built on and from historical givens. While Kuyper is notable for his efforts to bring reform to the church and society, applying the principles of Calvinism to the social and political concerns of his time, even helping to orchestrate the first Christian political party in the Netherlands (the Antirevolutionary Party), Bavinck's strengths resided in examining some of the inadequacies of old answers and so demonstrating the need to press forward with new proposals. Finally, while Kuyper was mainly deductive, Bavinck

---

[1] A different version of this essay, at some points abridged and at various points much expanded, can be found under the title "Abraham Kuyper, Herman Bavinck, and the Conclusions of Utrecht 1905," in *Mid-America Journal of Theology* 19 (2008).

[2] The most notable biography of Bavinck is R. H. Bremmer, *Herman Bavinck en zijn tijdgenoten* (Kampen: J. H. Kok, 1966); also see V. Hepp, *Dr. Herman Bavinck* (Amsterdam: W. Ten Have, 1921). For an analysis of aspects of Bavinck's life and especially his relationship to Abraham Kuyper, as well as the Ethical and Modernist theology that flourished in the Netherlands during the time that he labored, see Rolf Hendrik Bremmer, *Herman Bavinck als Dogmaticus*, Academisch Proefschrift, Vrije Universiteit te Amsterdam (Kampen: J. H. Kok, 1961), 1–147.

was mainly inductive.³ Without question, Kuyper was the more controversial of the two men, for Kuyper excelled at polemics and directed most of his theological work to a more popular audience. Bavinck, on the other hand, sought to gain a hearing for classic Reformed theology within the modern academic context, though he did write his share of popular works aimed at pastors and the laity.

In reference to Bavinck's writing, his chief work was his *Gereformeerde Dogmatiek* in four volumes, first published in 1895–1901, with a second and expanded edition issued in 1906–11. (The English publication of this work is now complete under the title *Reformed Dogmatics* [2003–2008], translated by John Vriend, edited by John Bolt.) Bavinck also subsequently penned two abbreviated dogmatic works. The first, *Magnalia Dei: Onderwijzing in de Christelijke Religie naar Gereformeerde Belijdenis* [The Wonderful Works of God: Instruction in the Christian Religion according to Reformed Confession] (1909), was a one volume, compressed dogmatics (659 pages), and was translated into English in 1956, and is still in print under the title: *Our Reasonable Faith*. The second dogmatic work that Bavinck wrote was *Handleiding bij het Onderwijs in den Christelijken Godsdienst* [Manual for Instruction in the Christian Religion] (1913), a short compendium of the previously mentioned work, consisting of some 251 pages. Other notable writings from Bavinck's pen include,⁴ first from his time as professor at Kampen: *De Katholiciteit van Christendom en Kerk* (1888)⁵; *De Algemeene Genade* (1894)⁶; *Beginselen der Psychologie* (1897); *Schepping of Ontwikkeling* (1901); *De Offerande des Lofs* (1901)⁷; *De Zekerheid des Geloofs* (1901)⁸; and then from his years as professor at the Free University: *Godsdienst en Godgeleerdheid* (1902); *Hedendaagsche Moraal* (1902); *Christelijke Wetenschap* (1904); *Christelijke Wereldbeschouwing* (1904); *Paedagogische Beginselen* (1904); *Het Christelijk Huisgezin* (1908); *The Philosophy of Revelation* (1908), which comprises the Stone Lectures he delivered at Princeton Theological Seminary in that year; *Calvin and*

---

³ See T. Hoekstra, *Gereformeerde theologisch tijdschrift* 22 (1921): 101; also see Bremmer, *Herman Bavinck als Dogmaticus*, 13–64; Jan Veenhof, *Revelatie en inspiratie* (Amsterdam: Buijten & Schipperheijn, 1968), 130–133; Louis Praamsma, *The Church in the Twentieth Century: Elect from Every Nation*, vol. 7., trans. the author (St. Catherines, Ontario: Paideia Press, 1981), 25–28.

⁴ For a complete and detailed bibliography of Bavinck's writings, see Bremmer, *Herman Bavinck als Dogmaticus*, 425–53.

⁵ In English, "The Catholicity of Christianity and the Church," trans. John Bolt, in *Calvin Theological Journal* 27 (November 1992): 220–251.

⁶ In English, "Common Grace," trans. Raymond C. Van Leeuwen, in *Calvin Theological Journal* 24 (April 1989): 35–65.

⁷ In English, *The Sacrifice of Praise: Meditations before and after receiving access to the Table of the Lord*, 2nd ed., trans. John Dolfin (Grand Rapids: Louis Kregel, 1922).

⁸ In English, *The Certainty of Faith*, trans. Harry der Nederlanden (St. Catherines, Ontario: Paideia Press, 1980).

Common Grace (1909)[9]; and also *Modernisme en Orthodoxie* (1911); *De Opvoeding der Rijpere Jeugd* (1916); *Bijbelsche en Religieuse Psychologie* (1920). Many of Bavinck's articles were collected after his death and published under the respective titles *Verzamelde Opstellen* (1921)[10] and *Kennis en Leven* (1922). The volume here translated for the first time, *Roeping en Wedergeboorte* [Calling and Regeneration] (1903), was composed during Bavinck's initial years at the Free University.

Bavinck's Book on Calling and Regeneration

This last mentioned work, to which we have given the English title, *Saved by Grace: the Work of the Holy Spirit in Calling and Regeneration*, offers in a more popular form Bavinck's treatment of God's gracious work in bringing fallen sinners to new life and salvation. This book, therefore, takes up questions with which every new generation of Reformed writers must grapple. Indeed, in dealing with the work of the Holy Spirit in the heart of sinners, and in dealing with the means or instruments that the Spirit employs in order to accomplish His sovereign work, Reformed theologians have had to chart their way through a thicket of errors. On the one side is the error of undervaluing the use of means—of any kind—with the result that, in protecting God's sovereignty in performing the work of salvation, Word and sacrament, and the church's role in administering Word and sacrament, are denigrated and "the *means* of grace" becomes an empty phrase. On the other side is the error of overvaluing the use of means—the means of both Word and sacrament—with the result that divine agency in the work of salvation is transferred to means and the *means* of grace comes actually to denote the *agents* of grace.

The practical effect of each error is not difficult to predict or trace. In the first case people become passive, introspective, given to mysticism and quietism—as one waits for God to do his work; in the second case people forget that salvation is truly God's gracious work; Arminianism or semi-Pelagianism lurk nearby, and with it the temptation to treat Word and sacrament in a kind of *ex opere operato* fashion, i.e., by the mere faithful performance of the preaching of the gospel and the administering of baptism or the Supper, people are saved. This in turn breeds a kind of objectivism and sterile formalism, where *means* of grace accomplish, in themselves, the *work* of grace. The call to genuine faith and repentance can easily be shortchanged or ignored altogether.

---

[9] This essay was composed in English, first printed in *The Princeton Theological Review* (1909) and subsequently published with a collection of three other essays in *Calvin and the Reformation*, ed. William Park Armstrong (London: F. H. Revell, 1909; repr., Grand Rapids: Baker Book House, 1980), 99–130.

[10] In English, *Essays on Religion, Science, and Society*, ed. John Bolt, trans. Harry Boonstra and Gerrit Sheeres (Grand Rapids: Baker Academic, 2008).

Bavinck's little book seeks to protect the church from both sets of errors. The volume itself was, as Bavinck himself explains in his short preface, first a series of forty short articles published in the periodical *De Bazuin* [*The Trumpet*] from 29 March 1901 through 2 May 1902. In taking up the question of *immediate* or *unmediated* regeneration, Bavinck was not needlessly or fruitlessly burdening the church with a technical topic of obscurantist theology. He was seeking to bring unity to the recently formed church body, The Reformed Churches in the Netherlands (*De Gereformeerde Kerken in Nederland*, the *GKN*). The formation of these churches came about in 1892 through the union of two distinct reformatory movements from within the Dutch State Reformed Church (*De Hervormde Kerk*), namely the *Afscheiding* of 1834 and the *Doleantie* of 1886.[11]

The Churches of the Secession

The *Afscheiding* (or Secession) can be characterized as an ecclesiastical movement that attempted to effect reform within the State Reformed Church (*De Hervormde Kerk*) but came to exist as a separate denomination apart from it. The occasion for this effort to reform the church is a story in itself. For our purposes it is sufficient to assert that, fundamentally, this effort at reform sought to re-establish the church upon the foundations of the fathers, i.e., to affirm the Three Forms of Unity (the Heidelberg Catechism, the Belgic Confession, and the Canons of Dort) as a living and authoritative confession of the church, and that these standards govern the church along with the old Dort Church Order. More broadly and generally, the *Afscheiding* sought to thwart the decaying effects of doctrinal liberalism and to reassert biblical authority in the face of its denial by liberal critics. The acids of the Enlightenment had eaten away at the vitality and purity of the churches. The *Afscheiding* sought to bring healing and reform to what was left. In so doing, it was concerned that a genuinely reinvigorated piety mark the church in its life and fellowship.

---

[11] See L. Knappert, *Geschiedenis der Hervormde Kerk onder De Republiek en Het Koningrijk der Nederlanden*, 2 vols. (Amsterdam: Meulenhoff & Co., 1911–12), II, 37–41, 298–313, 342–46; D. H. Kromminga, *The Christian Reformed Tradition: from the Reformation to the Present* (Grand Rapids: Eerdmans, 1943), 79–98; Henry Beets, *De Chr. Geref. Kerk in N. A.: zestig jaren van strijd en zegen* (Grand Rapids: Grand Rapids Printing Company, 1918), 18–50, 327ff.; idem, *The Christian Reformed Church* (Grand Rapids: Baker Book House, 1946), 24–37; James D. Bratt, *Dutch Calvinism in Modern America: A History of a Conservative Subculture* (Grand Rapids: Eerdmans, 1984), 3–33; Hendrik Bouma, *Secession, Doleantie, and Union: 1834–1892*, trans. Theodore Plantinga (Neerlandia, Alberta: Inheritance Publications, 1995); J. Veenhof, "Geschiedenis van theologie en spiritualiteit in de gereformeerde kerken," in *100 Jaar Theologie: aspecten van een eeuw theologie in de Gereformeerde Kerken in Nederland (1892–1992)*, ed. M. E. Brinkman (Kampen: J. H. Kok, 1992), 9–27.

Among the principal leaders of this movement were Hendrik De Cock (1801–1842) and Anthony Brummelkamp (1811–1888).[12] Turbulent years were to follow for the Seceders, for they were persecuted from without by the state authorities and subject to disagreement and division from within by a series of doctrinal and practical disputes. In 1854 these churches reached a strong measure of concord; and that same year they founded a theological school at Kampen for the training of ministers. Herman Bavinck was appointed professor of Dogmatics at Kampen in 1882.

The Churches of the Grieving

The *Doleantie* (or the Grieving) on the other hand represented the churches that had been ousted from the State Reformed Church after failing to bring reform to that ecclesiastical body during the period leading up to the mid 1880s. It was organized under the leadership of Abraham Kuyper (1837–1920), and Kuyper's personality was very much woven into the identity of that group of churches. The *Doleantie* is perhaps best characterized as a second Secession. Both movements attempted reform within the State Church; and both failed to achieve the desired remedy.

Kuyper had founded the Free University of Amsterdam in 1880, besides pursuing his own ministerial labors in the State Reformed Church, working hard in publishing articles in both the ecclesiastical and political press, and working to bring doctrinal renewal in the *Hervormde Kerk* in the face of modernism and unbelief. The *Doleantie* itself emerged from the practical question whether those who denied the Reformed faith could be admitted to membership in the State Church. When the Amsterdam Consistory (the consistory having jurisdiction over all the churches in Amsterdam and its vicinity) refused to comply with the provincial board's decision that ordered acceptance of such members, some 80 members of the consistory were deposed from office, Kuyper among them. This episode took place in 1886, and brought about the formation of a new ecclesiastical body of *Doleerende Kerken* [Grieving Churches]. This movement soon spread far beyond Amsterdam.

The Union of 1892 and the Problems Leading to the Conclusions of Utrecht 1905

The union of 1892 between the *Afscheiding* and the *Doleantie* was preceded by suspicion and difficulties. Some members of each group looked askance at the other, and some leaders in the *Afscheiding* distrusted Kuyper and disliked elements of his theology. Of particular concern in the union talks was the status of the theological school at Kampen and the theological faculty at the Free University of Amsterdam. Each

---

[12] Other leaders included Hendrik Peter Scholte, Simon Van Velzen, Albertus C. Van Raalte, and G. F. Gezelle.

school was allowed its place and its identity, and students could be trained for ministry at either school. The union was accomplished in 1892 and adopted the name *De Gereformeerde Kerken in Nederland* (*GKN*) [The Reformed Churches in the Netherlands]. This union, unfortunately, proved to be less than harmonious from the start. Immediately some ministers and congregations of the *Afscheiding* left the union, returning to the churches that had not joined the merger, namely the *Christelijk Gereformeerde Kerk* [The Christian Reformed Church]. Meanwhile, within a decade of the union, some particular theological views of Kuyper had created enough disagreement and ecclesiastical rankling as to move Bavinck to enter the fray.

Bavinck's book, written shortly after he had taken up the chair of dogmatics at the Free University of Amsterdam in 1901 (as Kuyper's successor) was a mildly "anti-Kuyperian" work—that is, Bavinck stands, if ever so gently, against Kuyper on this particular point. (Bavinck had also previously completed the first edition of his *Reformed Dogmatics* in four volumes [1895–1901].) The controversy, surrounding some features or accents of Kuyper's theology on regeneration and baptism, escalated. For example, L. Lindeboom, Bavinck's colleague at Kampen, asserted that Kuyper taught views not demanded by the Reformed confessions. It became clear that the matter would require synodical adjudication. In 1905 the Synod of Utrecht offered what might be termed "compromise" declarations or "pacifying" conclusions on four issues under discussion, though in each case Kuyper's particular views, far from being vindicated, are mildly censured.[13]

The committee that took up this matter included members of each group, "A" churches and "B" churches (*Afscheiding* and *Doleantie* respectively).[14] The presider of the committee was H. H. Kuyper, a fervent advocate of his father's views. That Utrecht sought to maintain unity among the churches is reflected in the committee's explanation of its work—two quotations in particular illuminate the mind-set of the committee, wherein they recommend that Synod not offer a definitive judgment on the disputed points. They explain that such was

---

[13] For an English translation of the Conclusions of Utrecht, see the Appendix.

[14] This divided mindset of "A" churches and "B" churches continued to plague the *GKN* in its subsequent history, culminating in theological controversy that ended in the fracturing of those churches in 1944, with the deposition of Klaas Schilder and others. At the risk of over simplifying the matter, "A" churches, in general, wanted to preserve the theological heritage of the Secession, though doctrinal disagreement on covenant and baptism marked that heritage, while "B" churches, reflecting Kuyper's theological accents, emphasized the theological heritage of prominent strands of seventeenth-century Dutch Reformed theology. The Conclusions of Utrecht 1905, sought to argue that both camps were within confessional boundaries and each "side" ought to guard against one-sidedness and allow the full revelation and accents of Scripture to be given their due. See the appendix for the full text of the Conclusions of Utrecht 1905; cf. E. Smilde, *Een Eeuw van Strijd over Verbond en Doop*, met een woord vooraf van Prof. Dr. K. Dijk (Kampen: J. H. Kok, 1946), 279–319.

... neither necessary nor desirable, because the differences involved, provided one guards carefully against all exaggeration, do not touch on a single essential point of our confession, a single fundamental dogma of our Church, but only concern a difference of understanding, a difference of presentation, a difference in terminology. Your committee regrets that some strong expressions, the use of unusual terms, and the emphasis on certain doctrinal formulations have given occasion for the action which presently disturbs our church. But it regrets equally that the impression is given to our church that this is a struggle against an actual departure from the precious confession made by our fathers, by which purity of doctrine is endangered and a new doctrine introduced into the Church. But for anyone who knows history it is plain that the disputed points may be found wholly or in part in the leading teachers of our Church, such as Calvin, Beza, Ursinus, de Brès, Gomarus, Voetius, Comrie, Holtius, etc., and that our churches in the golden age of Reformed theology never dreamed of accusing these men of departure from the Confession. . . .

The committee was of the conviction that the different views and the ensuing debate on the disputed points reflected a human trait to veer off into one-sidedness, which reveals a failure to maintain Scripture's full portrait.

If on the one hand men lay more emphasis on the sovereignty of God, on the eternity and immutability of God's decrees, on the omnipotent working of God's grace, and on the stability of the Covenant of Grace; while on the other hand men fix their attention more on the guilt of man, on the application of God's decrees in time, on the means which God uses in the work of grace, and on the personal appropriation of the blessings of the Covenant; both presentations find their ground in Scripture, they serve to complement each other in warding off all one-sidedness, and the elimination of one of these lists of propositions in the interests of the other would do damage to the knowledge of God, to the salvation of our souls, and to the practice of piety. Our Reformed Churches have therefore at all times and in all lands maintained *libertas profetandi* with respect to these differences. Thereby they have demonstrated how, in the defense of the Confession, a breadth of insight and approach serves to guard the churches against one-sidedness and to keep the way open to further developments in theology.[15]

The Four Issues in Dispute at Utrecht 1905

Specifically, four issues were in dispute: (1) the debate between supralapsarianism versus infralapsarianism; (2) justification from eternity; (3) immediate regeneration; and (4) presupposed regeneration (vis-à-vis infant baptism).

---

[15] Both quotations are taken from John Kromminga, *Christian Reformed Church History (Class notes)* (Grand Rapids: Calvin Theological Seminary, n.d.), 29–30. The copy I am quoting from was issued in 1983.

In order to better understand Bavinck's contribution to the discussion on immediate regeneration (which he set forth just a couple of years before the Conclusions of Utrecht 1905), we do well to linger here briefly to glimpse Kuyper's specific stance on each of these issues, and then consider Bavinck's formulations which often modulate his predecessor's views.

Supralapsarianism versus Infralapsarianism

Regarding the debate between supralapsarianism and infralapsarianism, Kuyper, while having sympathies to certain features of the infralapsarian position, embraced supralapsarianism. Indeed, certain features of his theological thinking appeared to be consequential of this stance. But before we explore that avenue, it is important not to caricature Kuyper. He embraces supralapsarianism with some reserve, for he offers his own criticisms against it, which are direct and pointed. A dangerous construct is easily put upon the supralapsarian scheme, Kuyper warns, so that sin is deduced from God's decree and God is rendered culpable for human depravity. Supralapsarianism also evokes the idea that God creates a part of humankind for the express purpose of damning millions of souls to hell and destroying them eternally. Kuyper recoils from these conceptions and regards them as incompatible with God's "love" and "inscrutable mercies."[16] Nonetheless, Kuyper believes that infralapsarianism is plagued with similar problems, for it relies on a kind of divine foreknowledge such that God knows what is in store for the humans he decrees to create, yet, God decrees to create them just the same.

Kuyper offers an illustration: Suppose there is a shipping company, and the owner has a ship with a crew of one hundred. He wants to send this ship to sea, but the night before doing so he gets a vision giving him certain knowledge that while at sea explosive cargo on the ship will ignite a fire and all the sailors will perish unless he take precautionary measures to protect or rescue his seamen. And, so, equipped with that certain knowledge and foresight, the ship-owner sends the ship to sea with its explosive cargo; but he resolves to make provision by giving life-jackets to ten of the sailors, concluding that the rest of the sailors will have to perish in the flames.

Kuyper argues that we are quick to judge such a man as barbaric, inhumane, and monstrous. We would all say about the ship-owner (since he knows that the cargo would explode and cause such a destructive fire, even if the sailors are at fault) is responsible to prevent such a tragedy; he

---

[16] Abraham Kuyper, *E Voto Dordraceno: Toelichting op den Heidelbergschen Catechismus*, 4 vols. (Amsterdam: J. A. Wormser, 1892–95), II, 170–171. Also see Kuyper's "De Deo Operante" (Het Werken Gods) in *Dictaten Dogmatiek: College-Dictaat van een Studenten niet in den Handel*, met een woord vooraf van Dr. A. Kuyper, 5 vols. (Kampen: J. H. Kok, n.d.), I, 114ff.; "Locus De Ecclesia" in IV, 38–44.

may not send the ship to sea with that cargo, or, at the very least, he must provide life-jackets to the entire crew.[17]

Infralapsarianism, then, Kuyper maintains, does not get us one step closer than supralapsarianism to solving the mystery surrounding the fall and God's decree. God knows with perfect certainty that if he creates man, he will fall—i.e., Adam and all his posterity; and God knows with perfect certainty whom he will save according to his good pleasure and inscrutable mercy. Thus, for Kuyper, we must leave unexplained what Scripture leaves unexplained, and the relation between God's eternal decree and the fall into sin, with its terrible repercussions, is impenetrable for us. This means that we cannot deduce the fall from God's decree, since that removes human guilt; nor can we deduce the decree from the fall, for then God's decree no longer exists and, in the end, we lose God as well.[18] "All schemes that have tried to find a solution for this mystery end either with a weakening of man's consciousness of sin and guilt, or with a weakening of the sovereignty and self-sufficiency of God."[19] Thus, given that dilemma, Kuyper takes up supralapsarianism as simply being more in line with the truth of Scripture, not as the solution to an impenetrable mystery. Scripture everywhere constrains us to recognize that the salvation of the elect is the fruit and result of God's eternal love, and that by virtue of election they are created, by virtue of election they are formed, and by virtue of election they shall be saved. The way of election—and this is what we must hold fast—precedes the fall and precedes the creation.[20]

Kuyper's followers generally adhered to the supralapsarian position, and if supralapsarianism is prone to fall into a doctrinal temptation, it is to so over-accent divine sovereignty as to minimize or under-accent or otherwise slight the use of means in the work of salvation.

Bavinck treats this topic at length in his *Reformed Dogmatics* under a chapter entitled "The Divine Counsel." He believes that this debate cannot be resolved by an appeal to Scripture. Both views are grounded finally on the sovereign good pleasure of God. The difference rests in this: the infralapsarian position seeks to follow a historical, causal order of the decrees, while the supralapsarian position follows the ideal, teleological order. Each view ends up needing aspects of the other, and neither view captures the whole truth of Scripture.[21] Thus, although the infralapsarian

---

[17] Kuyper, *E Voto Dordraceno*, II, 171–72.

[18] Kuyper, *E Voto Dordraceno*, II, 172.

[19] Kuyper, *E Voto Dordraceno*, II, 172.

[20] Kuyper, *E Voto Dordraceno*, II, 172. Also see Kuyper's *De Vleeschwording des Woords* (Amsterdam: J. A. Wormser, 1887), 202–24.

[21] Bavinck, *Reformed Dogmatics,* ed. John Bolt, trans. John Vriend, 4 vols. (Grand Rapids: Baker Academic, 2003–2008), II, 384–92. Also see Louis Berkhof, *Systematic Theology,* 4th ed. (Grand Rapids: Eerdmans, 1939, 1941), 118–25; G. C. Berkouwer, *Divine Election,* Studies in Dogmatics, trans. Hugo Bekker (Dutch edition, 1955) (Grand Rapids: Eerdmans, 1960), 254–277; B. B. Warfield, *The Plan of Salvation,* revised ed. (1915, repr.; Grand Rapids: Eerdmans, 1977), 23–29; 87–104; A. A. Hodge, *Outlines of Theology,* 2nd

view seems less harsh and more modest, more gentle and fair, in fact it cannot account for reprobation as a matter of sin and unbelief; rather, infralapsarians must view reprobation, like election, as founded upon the inscrutable good pleasure of God. Moreover, in placing the decree of reprobation after the fall, infralapsarians face the difficulty of specifying the nature of the fallen sinners who are rejected, namely, as those reckoned in Adam and infected with original sin. Or also as individuals with all of their actual sins accumulating to them as well.[22]

Meanwhile, the supralapsarian view faces its own set of problems, chief of which is that it conceives of election and reprobation in abstract terms, and makes the objects of the same "non-beings"—that is, "not specific persons known to God by name."[23] Although this view does not try to justify God, and it forthrightly and immediately sets itself upon the good pleasure of God, it does so in a way that threatens to make election in Christ exactly parallel to reprobation for sin. That is,

> it makes the eternal punishment of reprobates an object of the divine will in the same manner and in the same sense as the eternal salvation of the elect; and further, that it makes sin, which leads to eternal punishment, a means in the same manner and in the same sense as redemption in Christ is a means toward eternal salvation.[24]

Bavinck commends supralapsarianism for holding to the unity of the divine decrees, so that all things serve and are coordinated for an ultimate goal; and he lauds infralapsarianism for differentiating the divine decrees with respect to their distinct objects, so that not only a teleological but also a causal order is discerned. But he also observes that neither view can really capture God's perspective, since God views the whole scene of the created order and its history in a single intuition; indeed, all things are "eternally present to his consciousness." This means that "His counsel is one single conception, one in which all the particular decrees are arranged in the same interconnected pattern in which, *a posteriori*, the facts of history in part appear to us to be arranged now and will one day appear to be fully arranged."[25] In short, the interrelationship and diversity of connections is so "enormously rich and complex" that our ordering of the divine decrees cannot replicate it. Moreover, the idea of predestination does not encapsulate the counsel of God, for God's counsel is much richer than the eternal destiny of his rational creatures. Bavinck proposes that "common grace" be given a much more central place

---

ed. (1879; repr. Edinburgh: The Banner of Truth Trust, 1972), 200–13; 230–36; K. Dijk, *De strijd over Infra- en Supralapsarisme in de Gereformeerde Kerken in Nederland* (Kampen: J. H. Kok, 1912); A. G. Honig, *Handboek van de Gereformeerde Dogmatiek* (Kampen: J. H. Kok, 1938), 262–71.

[22] Bavinck, *Reformed Dogmatics*, II, 385–86.
[23] Bavinck, *Reformed Dogmatics*, II, 387.
[24] Bavinck, *Reformed Dogmatics*, II, 387.
[25] Bavinck, *Reformed Dogmatics*, II, 392.

in connection with the divine decrees and God's counsel, for this involves the whole of cosmic history and enables us to understand that the creation is to be viewed "as a systematic whole in which things occur side by side in coordinate relations and cooperate in the furthering of what always was, is, and will be the deepest ground of all existence: the glorification of God." Bavinck likens the scope and compass of the divine decree pertaining to the world as a "masterpiece of divine art," in which every part, every detail, is organically interconnected and serves its purpose according to the eternal design of its sovereign author.[26]

It is interesting to note that in the second edition of his *Reformed Dogmatics* (published after the Conclusions of Utrecht 1905), Bavinck supplements his discussion of the first edition, where he treats the inadequacy of supralapsarianism and infralapsarianism, with two telling footnotes that reference Kuyper. In the first of these footnotes, Kuyper acknowledges that from a *human perspective* infralapsarianism seems preferable and inevitable, election being interpreted as election from the mass of fallen sinners, while from a *divine perspective* supralapsarianism seems preferable and inevitable, election being interpreted as election before creation and fall and governing the ordinance of creation. In fact, Kuyper himself admits that

> all the polemics conducted by the two parties over this issue have not helped the church to take a single step forward, for the simple reason that both parties started out from opposing positions. The one stood squarely on the level ground below; the other loftily looked at the issue from a mountain summit. No wonder the two failed to understand each other. For that reason as well, it is absurd to say that a theologian of our time would be called a 'supralapsarian,' or to take the opposite point of view as the self-styled 'infralapsarian.' This is simply inconceivable, if for no other reason than that in our time this profound issue has assumed a very different form.[27]

Bavinck then refers to the decision taken by the Synod of the *GKN* at Utrecht in 1905 on this matter.[28]

A little later in this same discussion Bavinck appeals to Kuyper again in order to bolster his argument against making predestination to refer too narrowly to the election and reprobation of humans and angels. Over against this narrow perspective, Bavinck maintains that predestination pertains to all of world history, and world history may not be discarded after the consummation; on the contrary, it continues to have fruits for

---

[26] Bavinck, *Reformed Dogmatics*, II, 392.

[27] Herman Bavinck, *Reformed Dogmatics,* II, 388–89, fn. 148. The quotation from Kuyper is taken from his *Gemeene Gratie*, 3 vols. (Amsterdam: Höveker & Wormser, 1902–1904), II, 95–96. Note: these remarks, first printed in *De Heraut*, and then published with all the articles in the series in book form, predate the Synod of Utrecht 1905.

[28] See the appendix.

eternity.[29] Kuyper lends support to this view and asserts that earlier Reformed theologians did not adequately accent God's concern for all of creation, even as they neglected the use of common grace in constructing the doctrine of predestination itself.

If nothing else, whatever problems vexed theologians, pastors, and laypersons prior to the synodical decisions of Utrecht 1905, Kuyper's views ought not to be caricatured, and Bavinck, editing and revising his *Dogmatics* after Utrecht (the second edition appearing from 1906–1911), actually appeals to Kuyper to demonstrate the inadequacies of both supralapsarianism and infralapsarianism, when each stand alone.

The Conclusions of Utrecht acknowledge that infralapsarianism is the presentation that the Three Forms of Unity follow, though supralapsarianism was never condemned; yet the warning is offered that "such profound doctrines, which are far beyond the understanding of the common people, should be discussed as little as possible in the pulpit, and that one should adhere in the preaching of the Word and in catechetical instruction to the presentation offered in our Confessional Standards."

Justification from Eternity

As for justification from eternity, here Kuyper took up a clearly minority position within the history of Reformed theology. Here also is where his supralapsarianism had indeed "gone to seed" (something that can be traced in certain other Reformed supralapsarians as well). Simply stated, justification from eternity means that "the sinner's justification need not wait until he is converted, nor until he has become conscious, nor even until he is born."[30] Whereas sanctification depends upon our faith, has to do with "the quality of our being," and cannot be "effected outside of us," justification depends "only upon the decision of God, our Judge and Sovereign" and is "effected outside of us, irrespective of what we are...." Kuyper judges this point to be essential for rightly understanding justification, for the justification of the sinner is never on the basis of the sanctification of the sinner.[31] Thus, since justification does not depend upon any virtue or merit or good work in the sinner, and since God is free and sovereign in his engagements with his human creatures, God is therefore free to declare one justified at any moment he pleases. "Hence the Sacred Scripture reveals justification as an *eternal* act of God,

---

[29] Bavinck, *Reformed Dogmatics*, II, 390, fn. 152. Bavinck references Kuyper's *Gemeene Gratie*, II, 91–93.

[30] Abraham Kuyper, *Het Werk van den Heiligen Geest*, 2nd ed. (Kampen: J. H. Kok, 1927), 462; in English, *The Work of the Holy Spirit*, trans. Henri De Vries; with explanatory notes by Henri De Vries, with an introduction by Benjamin B. Warfield (New York: Funk & Wagnalls, 1900), 369. Both sources will be cited throughout this essay, first the original, followed by the pagination of the English translation in square brackets [ ]. Quotations are from the English translation unless otherwise indicated.

[31] Kuyper, *Het Werk van den Heiligen Geest*, 460 [367–68].

i.e., an act which is not limited by any moment in the human existence."32 Kuyper even more strongly writes, "It should openly be confessed, and without any abbreviation, that justification does not occur when we become conscious of it, but that, on the contrary, our justification was decided from eternity in the holy judgment-seat of our God."33 Justification, then, is not something that depends upon the believing sinner's awareness or knowledge in order to take effect in him; rather, it takes place "at the moment that God in His holy judgment-seat declares him just."34 Kuyper hastens to add that "this publishing in the consciousness of the person himself *must necessarily follow,*" which is the Holy Spirit's work; he reveals to God's elect, in the way of faith, the divine verdict of justification regarding them, i.e., he "causes them to appropriate it to themselves."35

Kuyper does not deny, but affirms, that Christ, as Son of God, prepares the way of salvation in his work of incarnation and resurrection, and so "brings about justification," and God the Father acts as the judiciary who justifies the ungodly on that basis. Meanwhile, God the Holy Spirit unveils this justification to God's chosen people. Thus, for Kuyper, Scripture teaches two positive truths, which on the surface appear to contradict one another, namely (1) that God "has justified us in His own judgment-seat *from eternity*; and (2) that we are justified *by faith* "only in conversion."36

In his commentary on the Heidelberg Catechism Kuyper again addresses this topic, and again argues that the way of redemption, including justification, is grounded in the eternal counsel of God. The elect are *destined* to justification; and since God's counsel is eternal the elect are justified, according to God's counsel, from eternity. From eternity, in his eternal "telic-vision" (*eindaanschouwing*), they stand before him as righteous or justified.37

Kuyper acknowledges that in a certain sense justification is not an entirely accomplished fact so long as it is not appropriated by the individual; and since this appropriation only comes by way of faith, it can be said that God first brings about the justification of persons when he awakens them to faith. Nonetheless, this imparting of faith and subsequent declaration and appropriation of justification does not change what has always been the case according to God's eternal decision, namely, that justification is from eternity.38 Thus, from God's point of view, the believer is justified from eternity, according to God's own sovereign and eternal counsel. From the point of view of the objective ac-

---

32 Kuyper, *Het Werk van den Heiligen Geest,* 462 [369].
33 Kuyper, *Het Werk van den Heiligen Geest,* 462–63 [370].
34 Kuyper, *Het Werk van den Heiligen Geest,* 463 [370].
35 Kuyper, *Het Werk van den Heiligen Geest,* 464 [371].
36 Kuyper, *Het Werk van den Heiligen Geest,* 463–64 [370–71].
37 Kuyper, *E Voto Dordraceno,* II, 333–34.
38 Kuyper, *E Voto Dordraceno,* II, 338.

complishment of the basis for justification for all the elect, then justification is accomplished at Christ's resurrection. And from the believer's
point of view, when justification begins to be worked in him or her personally, then justification is when God places his hand of preparatory
grace upon that person. But if the question is when do believers come to
know themselves as justified, then the answer is when they believe, that
is, when faith is effectuated in them. Finally, if it is inquired when the
justification of believers will become a reality and known before the uni-
verse, then the answer is at the last judgment.[39] Kuyper thus articulates
five senses in which we may conceive of justification.[40] Eternal justification, then, is the first sense that grounds all the others, since it has to do
with the justification of the sinner in God's eternal decree.

In addressing this topic, Bavinck agrees that *in a sense* the sinner's
justification has already taken place in the counsel of election.[41] He observes that this is a "precious truth" that no Reformed person will deny.
However, he also asserts that that truth does not mean it is advisable to
speak of an eternal justification, for "Scripture nowhere models this usage."[42] The Reformed have almost unanimously contested this doctrine.
To be sure, justification is decreed from eternity, but that same sort of
truth applies to everything that transpires in time; everything in the concrete history of this creation is decreed from eternity. There is nothing
that escapes God's eternal counsel.[43]

Bavinck explains that the Reformed were compelled, in their opposition to neonomianism and antinomianism, to examine justification in a
more conceptually penetrating way so as to avoid both of those errors.
Thus they came to distinguish between an active and passive justification. The Reformed warded off neonomianism by arguing that faith is not
a work that accomplishes forgiveness; and they fended off antinomianism in that they "almost unanimously rejected the doctrine of eternal justification."[44] Bavinck elaborates on the latter point:

> Thus they commonly assumed that, even if one could with some warrant
> speak of a justification in the divine decree, in the resurrection of Christ,
> and in the gospel, active justification first occurred only in the internal
> calling before and until faith, but the intimation of it in human con-
> sciousness (in other words, passive justification) came into being only
> through and from within faith.[45]

---

[39] Kuyper, *E Voto Dordraceno*, II, 340.

[40] For Kuyper's further elaboration on each of these, see *E Voto Dordraceno*, II,
340–46.

[41] Herman Bavinck, *Our Reasonable Faith: A Survey of Christian Doctrine*, trans.
Henry Zylstra (1956; repr., Grand Rapids: Baker Book House, 1977), 459.

[42] Bavinck, *Reformed Dogmatics*, IV, 216

[43] Bavinck, *Reformed Dogmatics*, IV, 216

[44] Bavinck, *Reformed Dogmatics*, IV, 202–03; also see III, 583. 590—91.

[45] Bavinck, *Reformed Dogmatics*, IV, 203.

To demonstrate the cold reception that the doctrine of eternal justification received by most Reformed writers, Bavinck first references the Westminster Confession of Faith, chapter 11, art. 4, which states that "God did, from all eternity, decree to justify all the elect, and Christ did, in the fullness of time, die for their sins, and rise again for their justification: nevertheless, they are not justified until the Holy Spirit doth, in due time, actually apply Christ unto them." Bavinck also cites various renowned seventeenth-century Reformed theologians who opposed the doctrine. But, interestingly, the Reformed writers who propagated the doctrine of an eternal justification, such as A. Comrie, J. J. Brahe, and Nicolaus Holtius, come from the eighteenth century, after the rise of pietism.[46] Antinomians were most prone to accept this doctrine and use it in their opposition to the neonomians. In any case, Bavinck refers to numerous Reformed writers who opposed this teaching, and to various Reformed confessions that make clear that justification is *by faith*, without conceiving of faith as a work that contributes to or cooperates with the verdict of justification.[47]

Bavinck explains that the Reformed were generally united in opposing neonomianism, but they disputed the nomenclature of a justification from eternity. Indeed, in the counsel of peace Christ offered himself from eternity to be our surety, to take our guilt upon himself, and to secure righteousness before God on our behalf and in our stead, to be appropriated by the means God ordains. However, to title this aspect of the divine decree "justification" involves an unacceptable equivocation of terms, for that accords to justification "a very different meaning than that which it had from ancient times...." Moreover, in doing this, proponents of eternal justification have "lost sight of the difference between the decree and its execution, between the 'immanent' and the 'objectivizing' act."[48]

> Furthermore, even when it is considered in the decree, the satisfaction of Christ for his own is undoubtedly logically anterior to the forgiveness of their sins and the imputation of the right to eternal life. After all, those who reversed this order would in fact make Christ's satisfaction superfluous and go down the road of antinomianism. . . . Even those among Reformed theologians who accepted a kind of eternal justification never claimed that the exchange between Christ and his church in the pact of redemption [i.e., the *pactum salutis*] already constituted full justification. But they considered it its first component and expressly stated that this justification had to be repeated, continued, and completed in the resurrection of Christ, in the gospel, in the calling, in the testimony of the Holy Spirit by faith and from its works, and finally in the last judgment. Accordingly, not one of them treated or completed [the doctrine of] justification in the locus of the counsel of God or the

---

46 Bavinck, *Reformed Dogmatics*, IV, 203, fn. 98.
47 Bavinck, *Reformed Dogmatics*, IV, 203, fn. 99.
48 Bavinck, *Reformed Dogmatics*, III, 590–91.

covenant of redemption, but they all brought it up in the order of salvation, sometimes as active justification before and as passive justification
after faith, or also completely after faith.[49]

In spite of these weighty criticisms, Bavinck adds these words, lest
readers misunderstand his point:

> It is of the greatest importance, nevertheless, to hold onto the Reformed
> idea that all the benefits of the covenant of grace are firmly established
> in eternity. It is God's electing love, more specifically, it is the Father's
> good pleasure, out of which all these benefits flow to the church.[50]

Bavinck, then, keeps in place the importance of grounding all the
works of redemption in God's eternal counsel without advocating a full-
blown doctrine of eternal justification.

Unfortunately, let it be observed, to speak of an "already" in relation
to time and eternity and in connection with the divine decree is not properly speaking apropos, for the divine decree is not subject to temporal
categories, like "already" and "to come." God's decree is his eternal and
ever-present and active will, not merely a "whence" or a "back when"; it is
his eternal will. Thus, while it is permissible to distinguish our justification as objectively pronounced in the resurrection of Christ and in the
preaching of the gospel (Rom. 4:25; 2 Cor. 5:19) from our justification as
subjectively appropriated in internal calling and the act of faith (as it is
likewise permissible to speak of our justification as an eternal and gracious decision of God regarding his elect in time through Christ's righteousness in the way of faith), it is not helpful to accent the eternal aspect
in any manner that renders time superfluous or treats the sinner's appropriation of Christ's righteousness by faith as anticlimactic. Such an
error has Platonic tendencies.[51]

It is not difficult to see that to posit an actual justification from eternity (or eternal justification), without qualifying comments, is to commit
a category mistake—the difference between God's decree and its execution. To be sure, the believing sinner's justification is decreed from eternity, even as the gift of faith wrought in God's elect is decreed from eternity, even as Christ's incarnation and the procurement of salvation are
decreed from eternity. Indeed, everything that exists in time is decreed

---

[49] Bavinck, *Reformed Dogmatics*, III, 591.

[50] Bavinck, *Reformed Dogmatics*, III, 591. Cf. Bavinck's comments in his book *Our
Reasonable Faith*, 459.

[51] Cf. Bavinck's comments in his book *Our Reasonable Faith*, 459. It should be noted
that holding to a supralapsarian position does not require an affirmation of justification
from eternity. See, for example, Geerhardus Vos, *Systematische Theologie: Compendium*
(Grand Rapids, 1916), 24, 98, who, though a supralapsarian, denies eternal justification.
Thus concerning the question whether justification is from eternity, Vos offers a negative
reply and says that while the decree concerning justification is from eternity, justification
itself is not eternal. He offers specific arguments in rebuttal of eternal justification (pp.
98–99).

from eternity. Should we therefore speak of creation from eternity over against the believer's conscious faith that the cosmos is the work of God as creation? Or should we insist that the Son of God became incarnate from eternity (or was eternally incarnate) in distinction from the Son of God becoming incarnate in time or in distinction from the child of God believing in Christ as the incarnate One? Should we argue for an eternal atonement for sins before Christ atones for sins on the cross or before the believer has faith in Christ and his cross, that in distinction from having Christ's atoning work applied to us by the Holy Spirit in the way of faith? Finally, are we to speak of an eternal fall into sin—we were eternally sinners—in distinction from our sinning in time? Need we next maintain that the faith wrought in fallen sinners is an eternal faith?

All of this is clearly mistaken, and it is due to a category mistake or otherwise a radical voluntarist and nominalist commitment that makes the forgiveness of sins a matter of arbitrary divine fiat rather than a matter of the satisfaction of God's justice by means of the incarnation of the Son of God and his sacrificial death for the atonement of sin. In fact, the decree of God does not displace history; on the contrary, it gives us history. It does not make the events of history eternal—if they were eternal they would not be historical events in time—but it does mean that the temporal events of history are grounded in the divine will and dependent upon God's providence, ordinary and extraordinary, in order to come into existence and reach their end.

Indeed, it is necessary to say—given God's eternal decree—in whatever sense the language of an eternal justification can be pressed into a mold that has some semblance of orthodoxy, it is not particularly helpful; nor is it according to a Scriptural pattern of speaking. What is more, it is not even clear that it is necessary. What problem is remedied by speaking of an eternal justification? From Kuyper's own broader theological project, it is evident that he wants to make room for the justification of covenant children who depart this life as infants, such that though they never had come to any knowledge or consciousness of their justification, nonetheless they participate in God's forgiveness and acceptance prior to this being impressed upon their consciousness or their obtaining an experience of it. Justification is not dependent upon a human appropriation of it; rather, it is a reality because God, from his holy judgment-seat, sovereignly declares his elect justified, and so it is not dependent in any way upon anything in the sinner, neither conversion, the act of faith, or spiritual rebirth.[52] The consequence of this view, or the potential and feared consequence, was that the call to covenant obedience and the appropriation of Christ by faith would be short-changed or ignored altogether.

Let it be noted that to affirm Christ's eternal suretyship is one thing, eternal justification another; and to acknowledge that Christ objectively

---

[52] Kuyper, *Het Werk van den Heiligen Geest*, 463, 462 [370, 369].

obtained for his own their justification through his redemptive work in history is very different from rendering history itself, and Christ's salvific work in history for the sinner's justification, secondary and anticlimactic, if not unnecessary. The demand and call to faith unto justification is part of the divine decree, i.e., it is part of God's eternal will, to be effected in history.[53] It is simply mistaken to evacuate history of significance *in order to* inflate the divine decree with a priority of importance.

As for Kuyper's oft repeated concern, within the broader context of his theology, that believing parents ought not to doubt the salvation and election of their covenant children who die in infancy, prior to their coming to a conscious act of faith and so also prior to their being conscious of their justification, we may offer an alternative remedy that surmounts the weaknesses of a doctrine of eternal justification—namely, that the children of believing parents are heirs of all the salvific blessings of the covenant of grace according to the divine promise, and therefore we need not wait for covenant children to reach maturity, and come to conscious faith, before reckoning them the recipients of God's saving work. On the contrary, on the basis of the divine promise, believing parents may properly regard their children, especially those who die in infancy, as God's elect and that God applies the saving work of Christ to them for eternal life (see Canons of Dort, I, art. 17).[54]

The Conclusions of Utrecht concede that aspects of this doctrine are confessionally permissible, yet they warn against two errors: (1) the error, in opposing this doctrine, that calls into question "Christ's eternal suretyship for His elect"; and (2) the error, in affirming this doctrine, that calls into question "the requirement of a sincere faith to be justified before God in the tribunal of conscience." Implicit in the first warning is that Christ "actually paid the ransom for us" in his suffering and death; and implicit in the second warning is that "we personally become partakers of this benefit only by a sincere faith."

---

[53] It should be noted that there have been a few Reformed writers who endorsed eternal justification, such as Alexander Comrie, *Brief over de regtvaardigmaking des zondaars: door de onmiddelyke toereekening der borggerechtigheit van Christus* (Amsterdam: Nicolaas Byl, 1761), 92–94; 106ff., idem, *Verhandeling van eenige eigenschappen des zaligmakenden geloofs: zynde een verklaaring en toepassing van verscheide uitgekipte texten des O. en N. Testaments* (Leiden: Johannes Hasebroek; Amsterdam: Nicolaas Byl, 1763), 64, 75; nonetheless, it has always been a dubious position among the Reformed and can easily be exposed as confused. See, e.g., Francis Turretin's discussion and critique of eternal justification in his *Institutes of Elenctic Theology*, ed. James T. Dennison, Jr., trans. George Musgrave Giger, 3 vols. (Phillipsburg, NJ: P&R Publishing, 1992–1997), XVI.ix. Also see the cogent critique of this notion as found in Louis Berkhof, *Systematic Theology*, 519–20.

[54] See Cornelis P. Venema, "The Election and Salvation of the Children of Believers Who Die in Infancy: A Study of Article I/17 of the Canons of Dort," *Mid-America Journal of Theology* 17 (2006): 57–100.

Presupposed Regeneration as the Ground for Infant Baptism

Leaving aside, for now, Kuyper's views on immediate regeneration, his views on the fourth issue, namely *presupposed* or *assumed regeneration* (*onderstelde wedergeboorte*)—often translated as presumed or presumptive regeneration—had to do principally with the ground for infant baptism.[55] Kuyper argued that a principal ground for administering the sacrament of baptism to the infants of believers is that we may presuppose their regeneration on the strength of God's promise to them. Kuyper posited this idea, it seems, in order to combat what he regarded to be two errors, namely the error surrounding the idea of a *volkskerk* or national church on the one hand, which breeds presumption and religious formalism, producing congregations of baptized but unsaved persons; and the error of a certain type of Reformed pietism, where Methodistic tendencies prevail, such that the baptized are reckoned lost until they come to a conversion experience in their early adult years or later in life and can testify of that experience, offering a narrative of grace.

Kuyper's doctrine of an assumed or a presupposed regeneration, an assumption that forms the principal ground for the administration of baptism to infants, sought to run parallel with the assumption the church makes in administering baptism to adult converts, for the church baptizes adults with the assumption of their regeneration, certainly not with the assumption of their non-regeneration. What is more, in presenting this view, Kuyper departs from a view that he first presented in his work on the divine covenants (*De Leer der Verbonden*), published in 1885. In that work Kuyper uses an older writer as an authority, whom he describes as "discerning" or "perceptive," namely Johannes Conradus Appelius (1715–1798).[56] Appelius certainly did not teach a presupposed

---

[55] Note: the Dutch words Kuyper uses are *veronderstelling*, *onderstelling*, *veronderstellen*, *onderstellen* and are best rendered into English as presuppose or assume, rather than to presume, inasmuch as the last term has more of a negative edge, rendering the wrong connotation. Also it should be strongly noted that a doctrine of "presupposed regeneration" is not at all an endorsement of, nor does it entail, a doctrine of "baptismal regeneration." On baptismal regeneration, see Berkhof, *Systematic Theology*, 477.

[56] Appelius was an eighteenth-century Dutch Reformed theologian, who served four pastorates, the first at Jukwert, the second at Appingedam, where he also served as the rector of the Latin school, the third at Uithuizen, and then at Zuidbroek, where he spent the majority of his years, from 1751/2 till his death in 1798. H. H. Kuyper explains why Kuyper appealed to Appelius in this connection: inasmuch as most of the older Dutch Reformed theologians wrote in Latin, and most of their works were no longer readily available, Kuyper looked to those writers who wrote in Dutch and whose writings were of more recent vintage. Thus theologians like Wilhelmus à Brakel (1635–1711), Alexander Comrie (1706–1774), and J. C. Appelius presented themselves as writers familiar to the popular audience Kuyper was addressing, and whose works the common people could read. What is more, Appelius, more than the others, treated at length the doctrine of the covenant of grace and, with that doctrine, he also had a fulsome discussion of the sacraments, baptism being understood as a sign and seal of the covenant of grace (see *Kuyper-Bibliographie*, ed. J. C. Rullmann, 3 vols. [Kampen: J. H. Kok, 1929], II, 118–119; also G. Kramer, *Het Verband van*

regeneration; to the contrary, Appelius vigorously argued that the covenant itself was sealed only to the church in general, and the church consisted only of true believers. Thus the sacrament of baptism is sealed only
to believers, and until a baptized person becomes a believer in the way of
faith and repentance, he has no part of the promises. The promises belong to the baptized only *in becoming believers.* Appelius therefore
taught that the ground for baptism is the promise of God, but he also
taught that God does not seal the promise to the baptized child in baptism, nor is the promise sealed to the parents of the child; rather, the
promise is sealed to "the church with which God has made his covenant
concerning her seed." This allowed for the idea of an empty baptism or
an invalid baptism *with respect to the baptized child,* though baptism
was always a valid baptism for the whole body of the saved, the church.
Baptism, then, for Appelius, was a sacrament for the church in general,
not for any covenant child in particular. Infant baptism likewise was not
for the strengthening of the faith of the baptized child, for the child does
not present him- or herself for baptism; instead, the church desires baptism and receives baptism in the body of that child. In this way Appelius
made the faith of the church the ground of baptism; and in this way he
could advocate a broad baptismal practice, yet baptism itself is not valid
or applicable, in a sealing sense, to all the baptized.[57]

It was such sentiments that Kuyper, in the early 1880s, reproduced
verbatim from Appelius, covering some ten pages. However, writing ten
years later, he repudiates that position. Kuyper explains that the light
concerning the mystery of baptism began to shine for him first in 1890
and he rejects his earlier naïve appeal to Appelius. He explains that he
was nurtured in Ethical theology and had no teachers to direct him in the
Reformed way. He had to venture on his own; and in addressing some
practical matters on baptism in that earlier work, he too hastily used Appelius as a guide.[58]

Thus, when Kuyper was writing his commentary on the Heidelberg
Catechism, later published as *E Voto Dordraceno,* 4 vols. (1892–95), he
had abandoned his strict adherence to Appelius's views and now advocated his doctrine of presupposed regeneration as the ground of infant
baptism. This is reflected in his devotional book *Voor een Distel een Mirt*
(1891), which treats the two sacraments, baptism and the Lord's Supper,

---

Doop en Wedergeboorte: nagelaten dogmenhistorische studie [Breukelen: "De Vecht",
1897], 351–354).

[57] The quoted pages of Appelius can be found in A. Kuyper's *De Leer der Verbonden:
Stichtelijke Bijbelstudien (Uit het Woord–Vijfde Bundel)* (1885; repr. Kampen: J. H. Kok,
1909), 198–207.

[58] See C. Veenhof, *Predik het Woord: Gedachten en beschouwingen van Dr A. Kuyper
over prediking* (Goes: Oosterbaan & Le Cointre, n.d.), 243–44, and 315 fn. 222. Veenhof
cites Kuyper's comments as recorded in "De Bazuin," 15 November, 1895.

and public profession of faith.[59] Let it be observed, in Kuyper's advocacy of presupposed regeneration we need to distinguish between God's perspective and the human perspective, for God does not make assumptions; that is a human trait. We also need to distinguish between human assumptions based upon false information and human assumptions based upon reliable testimony or divine promise—Kuyper has the latter in mind. As such, presupposed or assumed regeneration (that being the believing parents' and the church's disposition and response to God's promise) is not making an ontic claim about the regenerative status of a baptized person or of a covenant child. Rather, assumed regeneration has to do with the posture that the church and believing parents take toward covenant children in light of God's promise unto them. This is a subjective disposition and a kind of epistemological posture.

Thus, given the divine promise, Kuyper believes that God is already efficaciously working salvation in the life of a covenant child; and this is why he insists that faith is the only proper reply to God's Word of promise. So, inasmuch as little infants are incapable of manifesting the evident signs of the new life and rebirth, the church proceeds to administer baptism to them with the assumption—a faith assumption—that God is already working regeneration in them, which is God's initial salvific work of blessing, and which subsequently, in time, blossoms forth into manifest faith and repentance.[60]

In Kuyper's view, for the church to baptize covenant infants without this assumption of faith is both mistaken and disobedient. Indeed, if believers trust God's promise and embrace the meaning of what is signified and sealed in baptism, they may not take an agnostic posture toward the salvific status of a covenant infant presented for baptism—neither affirming nor denying that God is working new life in that child. For, from Kuyper's perspective, it is nothing less than sinful, a form of unbelief, to fail to trust that God is already acting to effect salvation in the covenant infant—and that according to the content of the divine promise and the symbolic meaning of baptism itself. Consequently, and worse, for believing parents to present their covenant child for baptism, and for the church to baptize such a child, with the assumption that this child, in spite of the divine promise, is dead in sin and under the wrath of God, having no communion with Christ and no part in the washing of regeneration by the Holy Spirit, is a presumption of non-regeneration, and is tantamount to presenting an unbeliever for baptism. Therefore, intentionally to present any person for baptism who has no part of Christ is perverse, for baptism is the mark and sign of salvation, that one is a member of Christ, participating in the salvation he bestows, signifying

---

[59] A. Kuyper, *Voor een Distel een Mirt: Geestelijke Overdenkingen bij den Heiligen Doop, het Doen van Belijdenis en het Toegaan tot het Heilig Avondmaal* (Amsterdam: Höveker & Wormser, 1891), 69, 72.

[60] See Kuyper, *E Voto Dordraceno*, III, 9–12.

and sealing forgiveness, rebirth, union with Christ, etc. For Kuyper, to baptize anyone, including covenant children, without the posture of faith and therefore the assumption of the recipient's regeneration is to baptize with a posture and disposition of unbelief—he wants nothing to do with it. Indeed, this is the cardinal point—Kuyper asserts that if we will not baptize our children under this assumption, then we ought to abandon the practice of infant baptism.[61]

Kuyper believes that the assumptive posture has practical benefits. He offers the illustration of a person who has two gems, but he does not have absolute certainty whether one or both of them are valuable diamonds or cheap glass. Without such certainty, he does well to regard both of them as expensive diamonds and to treat them accordingly—and so he protects them and keeps them safe from thieves, etc. Assuming both stones to be genuine diamonds means that the owner will not treat them as little, valueless pieces of glass. No, he will handle them as diamonds should be handled. Says Kuyper, likewise covenant children—although we do not have absolute certainty whether any given covenant child is a diamond or glass (elect or reprobate), we should regard them as diamonds and assume that the Holy Spirit is already working his regenerative grace in them and so take care of them accordingly.[62]

In expositing his view of presupposed regeneration, Kuyper employs the language of the Belgic Confession, art. 34, which teaches that the sacrament of baptism uses an outward washing with water to signify an inward cleansing through the blood of Christ, and that whereas ministers give us the sacrament and what is visible, the Lord gives what baptism signifies—namely the invisible gifts and graces; washing, purifying, and cleansing of our souls of all filth and unrighteousness; renewing our hearts and filling them with all comfort, etc.[63] However, Kuyper proceeds to assert explicitly that where these two features of the sacramental rite are not conjoined—that is, where God does not impart the thing signified as symbolized in the outward act of the minister, there we see the sacrament in *appearance* rather than in *reality*. This is simply to say, without the thing signified only an outward and visible sign is set forth, not the spiritual, invisible reality of Christ and his saving benefits.[64] When that is

---

[61] Kuyper, *E Voto Dordraceno*, III, 50, 67. Also see his *Het Werk van den Heiligen Geest*, 386–89 [299–301].

[62] Kuyper, *E Voto Dordraceno*, III, 12. Kuyper also emphasizes the practical benefit for parents whose children die in infancy or at a tender age. Given the high infant mortality rate at the time in which Kuyper lived, this was a very relevant pastoral issue. See his comments in *E Voto Dordraceno*, III, 6–7.

[63] See Kuyper, *E Voto Dordraceno*, II, 534–35, 538.

[64] Kuyper, *E Voto Dordraceno*, II, 535. This is not to be confused with his earlier view, which he subsequently repudiated, of *invalid baptism*. In fact, Kuyper's point here is standard Reformed theology, though Kuyper's terminology is less than felicitous. The Reformed have always distinguished "the sign" from "the thing signified," though they are not to be separated from each other. No less in baptism than in the Lord's Supper, without faith and the Holy Spirit applying the thing signified to the heart, the recipients of the sacraments

the case, says Kuyper, then baptism has become "a lamp without light, a hearth without fire, a lung without breath, a heart without a beat."[65] In short, if God does not act in the sacrament, the minister imparts nothing that has a spiritual benefit for the recipients—the water of baptism and the bread and wine of communion do not nurture anything to their souls. For only the Lord can nurture our souls with his grace, a fact that applies also to the preaching of the Word. Indeed, unless the Holy Spirit performs the inner, spiritual proclamation within our hearts, the outward preaching is impotent as to any saving benefit for the hearers. What all of this comes to, for Kuyper, is not difficult to sum up: the essence of a sacrament consists in this joint activity of both the outward rite performed by the minister and the inward grace imparted by the Lord himself.[66]

For his part, Kuyper believes that we ought to trust that God is acting in the sacrament, for sacraments function to nurture and confirm us in faith. Thus when the minister acts in administering the sacrament, we should believe that the Lord is likewise administering grace to the soul of the baptized child.[67] Moreover, Kuyper believes that his doctrine is a faithful interpretation of the Form for Baptism, has ancient Reformed pedigree, and offers a much needed remedy to the blind ritualism that plagues the national church idea (*volkskerk*) out of which he came.[68]

---

receive the form or shell or husk or outward dimension of the sacraments, but not their substance, matter, truth, and salvific blessing, i.e., Christ and all his saving benefits. See Bavinck, *Reformed Dogmatics*, IV, 477–90, 533–35; G. C. Berkouwer, *The Sacraments*, Studies in Dogmatics, trans. Hugo Bekker (Dutch edition, 1954) (Grand Rapids: Eerdmans, 1969), 149–153. Cf. Belgic Confession, art. 35. Jan Rohls observes, *Reformed Confessions: Theology from Zurich to Barmen*, trans. John Hoffmeyer (Louisville: Westminster John Knox Press, 1998), 211–12, 214, that the *Genevan Catechism* states that unbelievers "make it [i.e., the grace offered through baptism] of no effect by their perversity," so that "none but believers feel its efficacy." Likewise the Bremen Consensus says that children of Christian parents are not "to be regarded as unbelieving like the children of Jews and Turks, but as believing. For they believe according to their measure: that is, they have a seed of faith though the secret working of the Holy Spirit before, in and after baptism. Holy baptism seals and increases this seed of faith (M 770, 16–20)."

[65] Kuyper, *E Voto Dordraceno*, II, 535. This applies to the Lord's Supper as well.

[66] Kuyper, *E Voto Dordraceno*, II, 535.

[67] Kuyper, *E Voto Dordraceno*, II, 535.

[68] See Kuyper, *E Voto Dordraceno*, III, 51–53; 56–60. Also see Kuyper's foreword to G. Kramer's work *Het Verband van Doop en Wedergeboorte* (1897), a work that seeks to demonstrate the pedigree of Kuyper's views by examining the views of numerous Reformed thinkers on this topic. Kuyper argues in his foreword that the Reformed doctrine of baptism cannot be understood without grasping also the views of their opponents, particularly the Roman Catholics and the Lutherans, each arguing for doctrines of baptismal regeneration, as well as the Anabaptists, who denied infant baptism altogether and conceived of baptism only as a believer's testimony of faith. Calvin is the first and most authoritative voice for the Reformed in this regard, but subsequent Reformed authors had to wage further polemics against various opponents. In the course of time, Kuyper asserts, a certain stripe of pietism infected the Reformed tradition, corrupting both the doctrine of the church and of baptism, which stand or fall together. Thus the Reformed view that was forged in the sixteenth and seventeenth centuries was compromised and lost in the eighteenth and nineteenth centuries through the pietist onslaught.

It seems rather obvious that one of the weaknesses in Kuyper's doctrine of presupposed regeneration, as it stands, is that he makes a human response to the divine promise, which is necessarily subjective, *the ground* of infant baptism. The proper ground for infant baptism is principally the objective divine promise itself, along with the implicit command contained in that promise—namely, that the children of believing parents, as members of the covenant, ought to receive the sign and seal of the covenant, and ought to be baptized.[69] We could easily multiply both biblical and theological sources that confirm this point.[70] Suffice it to say that, for the Reformed, the ground for baptism (including infant baptism), in decreasing order of importance, is typically and principally (1) the command of Christ (Matt. 28:19, 20; Acts 16:15, 33; 18:8; 1 Cor. 1:16); (2) the divine promise of the covenant of grace (Gen. 17:7; Acts 2:39; 10:47); (3) the analogy derived from circumcision (Col. 2:12); (4) the fact that covenant infants belong to the kingdom of heaven (Matt. 19:13; Luke 18:15); (5) the importance of the biblical affirmation that covenant children are holy (1 Cor. 7:14; Acts 10:47); (6) that no legitimate reason exists to prevent their baptism; and (8) that the church fathers confirm infant baptism.[71]

As for Bavinck, although he does not always mention Kuyper by name, he clearly opposed his predecessor's doctrine of presupposed regeneration *as the ground of baptism*. The right to baptism, for both adults and children, is derived from the covenant of grace, to which they are parties. "Not regeneration, faith, or repentance, much less our assumptions pertaining to them, but only the covenant of grace" forms the ground for baptism. There is "no other, deeper, or more solid ground" for baptism.[72] This does not preclude, however, that covenant infants can possess "the disposition (*habitus*) of faith." As Bavinck explains, the Reformed used a rich terminology to refer to this, such as: "the seed, the root, the inclination, the potency, the disposition, or the principle of faith, or the seed of regeneration, and so forth." In any case, the Reformed were in complete agreement on this matter, though the terminology varied. Key texts were Jeremiah 1:5 and Luke 1:35, both of which demonstrated that God can perform the work of regeneration from in-

---

[69] Hence the language of the Form for Baptism used by most Reformed churches in the Dutch tradition: ". . . [covenant] children should be baptized as heirs of the kingdom of God and of His covenant. . . ."

[70] For example, the Belgic Confession, art. 34, where we confess the following: "We believe our children ought to be baptized and sealed with the sign of the covenant, as little children were circumcised in Israel on the basis of the same promises made to our children"; also Heidelberg Catechism, Q/A 74; Berkhof, *Systematic Theology*, 637–40.

[71] Such is the order of presentation as set forth by Turretin, *Institutes of Elenctic Theology*, XIX.xii.2–11.

[72] Bavinck, *Reformed Dogmatics*, IV, 525.

fancy, even in the womb. The Reformed championed this doctrine and used it against the Anabaptists.[73]

The differences that emerged among the Reformed came, says Bavinck, when they began to reflect on the implications of the covenant membership of small children.

Since this has been such a disputed idea in Reformed theology, and since there is so much confusion about this matter, we do well to quote Bavinck's analysis at length. As he explains:

> There were those who sought as long and as closely as possible to maintain the unity of election and covenant. They asserted, accordingly, that all children born of believing parents had to be regarded—according to the judgment of charity—as regenerate until in their witness or walk they clearly manifested the contrary, or that at least the elect children were usually regenerated by the Spirit of God before baptism or even before birth (à Lasco, Ursinus, Acronius, Voetius, Witsius, et al.). But others, noting the problems of experience, which so often tells us that baptized children grow up without showing any sign of spiritual life, did not dare to construe this regeneration before baptism as being the rule. They all without exception acknowledged that God's grace is not bound to means and can also work regeneration in the heart of very young children, but they left open the question whether in the case of elect infants that regeneration occurred before, during, or also, sometimes even a great many years, after baptism (Calvin, Beza, Zanchius, Bucanus, Walaeus, Ames, Heidegger, Turretin, et al.). This view won the day when the church [subsequently], by its neglect of discipline, fell into decay. Election and church, the internal and external side of the covenant, concepts formerly held together as much as possible but increasingly differentiated since the days of Gomarus, moved ever farther apart. In the church (ecclesia) one saw the formation of the conventicle (ecclesiola). Gradually, therefore, baptism was totally separated from regeneration, and, since people nevertheless wanted to continue this sacrament for their children, it was understood in one of the following ways: (1) conceived and justified as a sacrament of the church and a pledge of the children of believers in general; (2) as a confirmation of the objective conditional promise of the gospel; (3) as proof of participation in the external covenant of grace; (4) as a guarantee of an amissible rebirth—not one that was inseparable from salvation but one that was later to be confirmed by a personal faith; (5) as a pedagogical device that at a larger age spurs the baptized on toward genuine repentance.[74]

---

[73] Bavinck, *Reformed Dogmatics*, IV, 525. Cf. John Calvin, *Institutes of the Christian Religion* (1559). 2 vols., ed. John T. McNeill, trans. Ford Lewis Battles, Library of Christian Classics (Philadelphia: The Westminster Press, 1960), IV.xvi.17–22.

[74] Bavinck, *Reformed Dogmatics*, IV, 511. Lest Bavinck's point be misunderstood, he is not asserting that the view proposed by Calvin, Beza, Zanchius, etc. constituted a neglect in ecclesiastical discipline or led to it; he is only saying that when discipline waned in the church, this view more easily conformed to experience, and the other view (as defended by Voetius, etc.) created greater theological problems. As editor, I have inserted the "subsequently" in square brackets into Bavinck's text for clarity. Also see Herman Witsius, *Disquisitio Modesta et Placida de Efficacia et Utilitate Baptismi in Electis foederatorum Paren-*

According to Bavinck, whereas it is necessary for the church to exercise "a judgment of charity" in baptizing both adults and children, inasmuch as it is impossible to make "an infallible pronouncement" concerning the salvific status of all the baptized, nonetheless the "basis for baptism is not the assumption that someone is regenerate, nor even that [there is] regeneration itself, but only the covenant of God."[75]

In Bavinck's view, the doctrine of presupposed regeneration makes the ground of baptism a "subjective opinion." Rather than rest baptism upon an opinion, the church must administer baptism "in accordance with the revealed will of God and the rule of his Word."[76] Moreover, we must admit that baptism is often administered to those who fail to show the fruits of faith and repentance and do not walk in the way of God's covenant. There is chaff among the wheat, vessels of clay amidst vessels of silver and gold; indeed, not all is Israel that is called Israel. Assuming the regeneration of all covenant infants does not make it so, and their regeneration cannot be proved in any case.[77]

> In the Christian church, therefore, there is always room for the preaching of the gospel, of regeneration, faith, and repentance. The prophets, John the Baptist, and Jesus all came to their people with that message, a people that after all was God's own possession. The apostles too administered the Word not only to bring to expression the hidden life of faith; they also preached it as the seed of regeneration and as a means of making that faith effective.[78]

It is not Bavinck's aim to deny that the Holy Spirit may regenerate covenant infants at His discretion and according to His sovereign mercy, but he does oppose making this assumption concerning the Spirit's possible preceding operation as *the ground* for baptizing infants. He certainly affirms, in the language of the Form for Baptism, that just as the children of believers are without their knowledge conceived and born in sin, subject to eternal damnation, likewise without their knowledge "they can be regenerated by the Holy Spirit and endowed with the capacity to believe" (what Kuyper calls the seed or faculty of faith), and so likewise "they can also without their knowledge be strengthened in that capacity by the same Spirit."[79] But when the Form for Baptism calls the children

---

tum Infantibus (Utrecht, 1693), xxiv–lv; translated into English by William Marshall, edited and revised translation, with an Introduction by J. Mark Beach, "On the Efficacy and Utility of Baptism in the Case of Elect Infants Whose Parents Are under the Covenant of Grace," *Mid-America Journal of Theology* 17 (2006): 121–190

[75] Bavinck, *Reformed Dogmatics*, IV, 531.

[76] Bavinck, *Reformed Dogmatics*, IV, 531.

[77] Bavinck, *Reformed Dogmatics*, IV, 531.

[78] Bavinck, *Reformed Dogmatics*, IV, 531.

[79] Bavinck, *Reformed Dogmatics*, IV, 532. See Kuyper, *E Voto Dordraceno*, II, 543; idem, *Het Werk van den Heiligen Geest*, 382 passim [295 passim]. The Hungarian Confession speaks of a "seed of faith" (*semen fidei*) in children (M 422, 3ff.), as does the Bremen Consensus; see Rohls, *Reformed Confessions*, 214.

of believers "sanctified in Christ," which is found in the first question put to the presenting parents, Bavinck disputes Kuyper's view that this refers to an "internal renewal by the Holy Spirit."[80] Instead, Bavinck argues for a covenant sanctification at this point, yet he simultaneously disputes how the Reformed doctrine of baptism was to devolve among the Reformed churches under the influence of pietism, a devolution that Kuyper attempted to remedy by ascribing a special grace to baptism—namely a disposition to seek the fellowship or communion of the saints as body of Christ.[81]

In fairness to Kuyper, however, the above criticisms should be modulated a bit inasmuch as Kuyper himself would not dispute the above mentioned arguments. As J. C. Rullman has observed, when controversy first emerged concerning Kuyper's little book *Voor een Distel een Mirt* (1891), generating action at the General Synod of Middelburg in 1896, Kuyper subsequently clarified his view pertaining to the ground of baptism in *De Heraut* on 4 October 1896, in an article entitled "De Grond" ("The Ground"). Here Kuyper distinguishes four ways of thinking about the ground for baptism.[82] (1) If we speak of the ground upon which parents have the right (*het recht*) to request baptism for their children, then naturally for the parents the ground clearly rests in the divine ordinance of the covenant of grace. (2) If we speak of the ground upon which rests the right and duty of the church to administer baptism to the infants of its members, then the ground can only be, as before, God's ordinance as set forth in the covenant of grace (3) If, however, we speak of the ground upon which the ordinance in God's name rests, then naturally the ground cannot be the covenant of grace, which God Himself established; rather, the ground can only be His sovereign good pleasure. And finally (4) if we speak of the ground upon which rests the spiritual reality of baptism administered to an infant (as we have done), then naturally the only answer can be that the spiritual reality of baptism rests on nothing other than *regeneration*.[83]

Thus Kuyper clearly affirms that the legal ground (*rechtsgrond*), as distinguished from a sacramental and a spiritual ground, for infant baptism rests in God's covenant alone, for parents cannot know infallibly whether their child is regenerate. The church can judge only whether the child is born of believing parents and *in this fact alone*—that the child is

---

[80] Bavinck, *Reformed Dogmatics*, IV, 511. See Kuyper, *E Voto Dordraceno*, II, 541 ff.; III, 51. Also see Francis Turretin, *Institutes of Elenctic Theology*, XIX.xx.9, where he maintains that the holiness referred to in 1 Cor. 7:14 is a "federal holiness," which means they are regarded as "Christians and belonging to the church)"—that in contrast to heathen children.

[81] Bavinck, *Reformed Dogmatics*, IV, 512–13. See Kuyper, *E Voto Dordraceno*, II, 463, 541, 553ff. Also see Berkouwer, *The Sacraments*, 82–89; Berkhof, *Systematic Theology*, 637–642.

[82] J. C. Rullman, *Kuyper-Bibliographie: Deel I (1860–1879); Deel II (1879–1890); Deel III (1891–1932)* (Kampen: J. H. Kok, 1923, 1929, 1940), III, 39–44, especially 43–44. Also see Smilde, *Een Eeuw van Strijd over Verbond en Doop*, 113–117.

[83] Rullman, *Kuyper-Bibliographie*, III, 44.

included in the covenant promise of God as seed of believers—the legal ground for the baptism of infants is established for the church; and this rests upon nothing other than the rule of the covenant.[84]

Unquestionably, Kuyper's accent upon a presupposed regeneration as the ground for the baptism of infants was driven by a concern to safeguard the truth that the infants of believing parents are the objects of God's saving mercies, even though they are not yet capable of the manifest signs of faith and conversion; and so, should they die at a tender age, believing parents may rest in the assurance that Christ's work of salvation is for them, as baptism itself testifies.

The Conclusions of Utrecht reply to the Kuyperian doctrine of presupposed regeneration by saying that while it is correct to view the seed of the covenant as regenerated and sanctified in Christ, until they demonstrate the contrary, it is "less correct to say that baptism is administered to the children of believers on the ground of their presumed regeneration, since the ground of baptism is found in the command and promise of God."

Immediate (or Unmediated) Regeneration

Finally, turning now to the question of immediate regeneration, and its relationship to divine calling—the chief subject of Bavinck's book—Kuyper carefully staked out and vigorously argued for this view.

All the Reformed agreed that regeneration is God's saving, sovereign work, and is effectuated within the life of an elect person at God's gracious initiative and according to the Holy Spirit's irresistible power. The dispute focused upon whether in performing this saving work in a spiritually dead person God acted with the use of means—*mediate* regeneration—or without the use of means—*immediate* or *unmediated* regeneration, i.e., unmediated by anything else, including the means of Word and sacraments (those instruments commonly called "the means of grace").

Kuyper treats this topic at length in his book on the Holy Spirit; so we will focus our attention on that work, but also glimpse at his commentary on the Heidelberg Catechism.

In expositing his doctrine of immediate or unmediated regeneration, Kuyper is careful to set forth a number of distinctions in an effort to clarify his view and protect it from misunderstanding. First Kuyper differentiates regeneration defined in the narrower sense and regeneration defined in the wider sense. The former refers to God's exclusive act of quickening, whereby God "translates us from death into life, from the kingdom of darkness into the kingdom of His dear Son." This is regeneration understood as "*a starting-point.*" Here God "plants the principle of a new spiritual life" in the soul, and one is born again. The latter refers to

---

[84] Kuyper, *Gemeene Gratie*, II, 215.

"the *entire* change by grace effected in our persons, ending in our dying to sin in death and our being born for heaven."[85] This is how the term was used in early Reformed theology and the Reformed confessions, as in the Belgic Confession, art. 24.[86] Kuyper maintains that both uses of the term are legitimate, but he will be using the word, unless otherwise noted, in its narrower or more limited sense.

Kuyper next makes the broad distinction between first and second grace. *First grace* refers to "God's work in the *sinner*" without his knowledge or volition; the sinner is absolutely passive, while *second grace* denotes "the work wrought in *regenerate* man with his full knowledge and consent."[87] This *first grace*, then, has to do with "the *first implanting of life*." Kuyper unfolds this idea:

> [It is] evident that God did not begin by leading the sinner to repentance, for repentance must be preceded by conviction of sin; nor by bringing him under the hearing of the Word, for this requires an opened ear. Hence the first *conscious* and comparatively cooperative act of man is always *preceded* by the original act of God, planting in him the first principle of a new life, under which act man is wholly *passive* and *unconscious*.[88]

This, in short form, is what Kuyper means by *immediate* or *unmediated* regeneration, for the work of regeneration *in this sense* is directly infused into the soul of the fallen sinner by the Holy Spirit without any use of means.[89]

Kuyper distinguishes eight successive stages in God's gracious work in the life of the sinner: (1) the implanting of the new life-principle ; (2) the keeping of the implanted principle of life; (3) the call by the Word and Spirit, internal and external; (4) the call of God producing the conviction of sin and justification, two acts of the same exercise of faith; (5) the exercise of faith resulting in conversion (here the child of God becomes clearly conscious of the implanted life); (6) conversion merging itself with sanctification; (7) sanctification finished and closed in complete redemption at the time of death; and (8) glorification in the last day, when the inward bliss is manifest in outward glory, and the soul is

---

[85] Kuyper, *Het Werk van den Heiligen Geest*, 378–79 [293]; idem, *E Voto Dordraceno*, III, 407–09.

[86] Kuyper, *Het Werk van den Heiligen Geest*, 378–79 [293]; idem, *E Voto Dordraceno*, III, 402–03; and also, III, 410–11, where Kuyper shows how the Canons of Dort sometimes use the word in the more limited sense.

[87] Kuyper, *Het Werk van den Heiligen Geest*, 382, 429 [295, 339].

[88] Kuyper, *Het Werk van den Heiligen Geest*, 381 [294]; idem, *E Voto Dordraceno*, III, 409.

[89] Kuyper, *E Voto Dordraceno*, III, 412.

reunited with its glorified body, and the enjoyment of the state of perfect happiness.[90]

For Kuyper, the salvation of deceased covenant infants is of principal concern.[91] The practical and theological concern is that covenant infants are the objects of God's salvific activity, which means that infant salvation must needs look different than the salvation of adults. In the case of infants God saves them by implanting a new life-principle in them. Kuyper borrows the language of older Reformed writers who called this the *faith-faculty* (*fides potentialis*), which is followed by the *faith-exercise* (*fides actualis*), and the *faith-power* (*fides habitualis*). The *faith-faculty* means that salvation does not begin with faith itself or the act of repentance; rather, God first plants life where none exists, giving "power to the powerless, hearing to the deaf, and life to the dead."[92]

Kuyper argues that this new principle of life (which is regeneration), can remain "dormant" (like being asleep) for quite some time before the Holy Spirit makes it sprout into manifest and conscious life. Until this happens, however, the Holy Spirit preserves it—"like seed-grain in the ground in winter; like the spark glowing under the ashes, but not kindling the wood; like a subterranean stream coming at last to the surface."[93] Indeed, this sprouting forth to manifest life is the work of the Spirit in the divine call of the gospel through the Word. This is where "means"—as in *means* of grace—come into play. The sprouting-to-life takes place in the person in whom the Holy Spirit, without the use of means, has already wrought the seed of life and the faith-*faculty* (*fides potentialis*), but now the Spirit uses means, namely the Word of God, to produce faith in their hearts, i.e., faith as *the exercise of faith* (*fides actualis*). "Hence the preaching of the Word and the inward working of the Holy Spirit are divine, correspondent operations." Concretely stated: "Under the preaching of the Word the Spirit energizes the faith-*faculty*, and thus the call becomes effectual, for the sleeper arises."[94]

When a capacity for faith, as one who has the new principle of life implanted in them, gives way to an exercise of faith (or what we would call actual faith), repentance and justification are the result of this inward and effectual divine call of the gospel. We could also say that *the acts of*

---

[90] Kuyper, *Het Werk van den Heiligen Geest*, 382–85 [295–297]. Cf. idem, *E Voto Dordraceno*, III, 446–52, where Kuyper treats conversion and sanctification.

[91] This pastoral concern drives his discussion in *E Voto Dordraceno*, III, 5–12; also see his *Het Werk van den Heiligen Geest*, 382, 386, 396, 409 [295, 298, 308, 320].

[92] Kuyper, *Het Werk van den Heiligen Geest*, 382 [295]; cf. Heinrich Heppe, *Reformed Dogmatics: Set Out and Illustrated from the Sources*, rev. edition, ed. Ernst Bizer., trans. G. T. Thomson (London: George Allen & Unwin, 1950; repr., Grand Rapids: Baker Book House, 1978), 540–42.

[93] Kuyper, *Het Werk van den Heiligen Geest*, 383, 403 [295, 313].

[94] Kuyper, *Het Werk van den Heiligen Geest*, 383 [296].

faith[95] are the result, and then this exercise of faith, actually believing and trusting in the Lord, results in conversion, i.e., the children of God actually become conscious that they are reborn and have new life in Christ. Thus "the implanting of the new life *precedes* the first act of faith, but conversion *follows* it."[96]

Of course, in speaking of regeneration Kuyper, like any Reformed theologian, views the unregenerate person as not only "deaf and blind," but worse, for "neither stock nor block is corrupt or ruined, but an unregenerate person is wholly dead and a prey to the most fearful dissolution."[97] A fallen human being may be likened to a corpse: though he seems intact and whole, he is altogether corrupt and befouled with death. The unregenerate are "utterly unprofitable." This is why "every operation of saving grace must be preceded by a quickening of the sinner, by an opening of blind eyes, an unstopping of deaf ears—in short, by the implanting of potential faith [*fides potentialis*]."[98]

Having made this point, Kuyper is concerned to show how the "act of regeneration" in this narrow, technical definition plays out differently with respect to covenant infants than in the case of adult converts. With respect to adults, there is little disagreement regarding how this comes to manifestation, for all agree that regeneration is not an act of moral suasion; fallen persons are neither workers nor coworkers in regeneration; rather, in bringing adults to faith and repentance, God acts *irresistibly* in their hearts, bringing them to new life, etc., making the unwilling willing; and this coincides with conversion. In the case of infants, however, regeneration and conversion do not coincide; nonetheless God makes little children the objects of his saving operations without this coincidence.[99]

Against the Ethical theologians who advocated a doctrine of baptismal regeneration, or at least a kind of sacramental regeneration, which relieved sinners of "inability" and afforded them "the opportunity to choose for or against God," Kuyper argues that regeneration is not tied to the baptismal rite—that is, baptism does not regenerate infants or any other recipient of the sacrament. Baptismal regeneration, then, is emphatically and explicitly denied by Kuyper. As for regeneration itself, Kuyper is careful to state that it is not a tack-on or an additional component of man, as if a regenerate person is part old man and part new man. On the contrary, says Kuyper, the regenerate person is "one man—viz., the old man *before* regeneration, and the new man *after* it—who is

---

95 On the "acts of faith," see Richard A. Muller, *Dictionary of Latin and Greek Theological Terms: Drawn Principally from Protestant Scholastic Sources* [Grand Rapids: Baker, 1985], 22.

96 Kuyper, *Het Werk van den Heiligen Geest*, 384 [296]; idem, *E Voto Dordraceno*, III, 415.

97 Kuyper, *Het Werk van den Heiligen Geest*, 392 [304].

98 Kuyper, *Het Werk van den Heiligen Geest*, 393 [305]; idem, *E Voto Dordraceno*, III, 415.

99 See Kuyper, *Het Werk van den Heiligen Geest*, 393–98 [305–309]; idem, *E Voto Dordraceno*, III, 414, 416–18.

created after God in perfect righteousness and holiness." The regenerate person is in principle changed and has a new nature; his ego or self is renewed, though he must still battle an old nature. As a new creature he is redeemed; he is not two things.[100]

This elicits the question "whether this regenerating act *precedes*, *accompanies*, or *follows* the hearing of the Word." Kuyper believes that his answer to this question constitutes "the solution" to what some view as a controversy. "The Holy Spirit may perform this work in the sinner's heart *before*, *during*, or *after* the preaching of the Word."[101] Kuyper's elaboration on this statement is not to be missed:

> The inward call may be associated with the outward call, or it may follow it. But that which precedes the inward call, viz., the opening of the *deaf ear*, so that it may be heard, is not dependent upon the preaching of the Word; and therefore may *precede* the preaching.
>
> Correct discrimination in this respect is of the greatest importance.[102]

Kuyper thus defines *three* distinct and successive stages when speaking of regeneration in the wider sense:

1st. Regeneration in its *first stage*, when the Lord plants the new life in the dead heart.

2d Regeneration in its *second stage*, when the new-born man comes to conversion.

3d. Regeneration in its *third stage*, when conversion merges into sanctification.[103]

In the first stage, which is quickening, God works *without means*. In the second stage, which is conversion, God *employs means*, namely the preaching of the Word. In the third stage, which is sanctification, God "uses means in addition to ourselves, whom He uses as means."[104] Kuyper is more than willing to speak of regeneration, as Scripture sometimes does and as the confessions sometimes do, in the most comprehensive sense of the restoration and renewal of corrupt man, involving the full scope of God's redemptive work.[105] And speaking of regeneration in this comprehensive sense then allows the distinctions between quickening, conversion, and sanctification.

It is interesting to note that Kuyper does not think that all the minute distinctions he has employed in order to come to clarity on this topic ought to be proclaimed from the pulpit. Only conversion and sanctifica-

---

[100] Kuyper, *Het Werk van den Heiligen Geest*, 401–03 [312-13]; idem, *E Voto Dordraceno*, III, 405, 421.

[101] Kuyper, *Het Werk van den Heiligen Geest*, 407 [317].

[102] Kuyper, *Het Werk van den Heiligen Geest*, 407 [317–18].

[103] Kuyper, *Het Werk van den Heiligen Geest*, 407 [318].

[104] Kuyper, *Het Werk van den Heiligen Geest*, 407–08 [318–19].

[105] Kuyper, *Het Werk van den Heiligen Geest*, 408 [319].

tion ought to be the focus in preaching, since the preaching of the Word is "the appointed means to effect them." But the work of theology can rightly have a broader aim than preaching—an aim that includes the refutation of error. Kuyper was facing opposition from the Ethicals, the Rationalists, and the Supernaturalists.[106]

In any case, to speak of regeneration as *quickening* is especially important concerning the salvation of little children, who cannot manifest the marks of conversion and sanctification. Without regeneration as *quickening* we face a "real danger" of branding covenant children as unsaved, concluding that "our deceased infants must be lost, for they can not hear the Word."[107]

For Kuyper, then, quickening and conversion must be kept distinct, for conversion or the inward call is preceded by quickening, wherein the sinner receives hearing ears; and now being able to hear the Word, the Holy Spirit uses the Word as a means of grace. The passivity that characterized the sinner in quickening passes over into activity and a certain degree of cooperation on the sinner's part. This latter aspect is what Kuyper calls "second grace."[108]

> The elect but unregenerate sinner can do nothing, and the work that is to be wrought in him must be wrought by another. This is the first grace. But after this is accomplished he is no longer passive, for something was brought into him which in the second work of grace will cooperate with God.[109]

Kuyper thus takes up the divine work of calling—a term that he is using in the narrow or limited sense of the call to repentance, i.e., the sinner being called out of darkness into light. This call issues forth primarily and officially from the preaching of the Word—though the Holy Spirit remains the real agent in this work, and both the preacher and the sermon are his instruments. That said, God is free to convey his Word in other ways as well. For Kuyper, the work of calling is the Holy Spirit's work, and it "proceeds in and though the preaching of the Word, and calls upon the *regenerated* sinner to arise from death, and to let Christ give him light."[110] As Kuyper speaks of it here, as the inward call, he is not talking about the outward call addressed to the unregenerate person, for the unregenerate do not have ears to hear.

In considering the operation of the inward call, Kuyper's primary focus is upon already baptized persons—i.e., persons baptized as infants, whose regeneration is assumed and who need to come to conversion.

---

[106] Kuyper, *Het Werk van den Heiligen Geest*, 408–09 [319].
[107] Kuyper, *Het Werk van den Heiligen Geest*, 409 [320].
[108] Kuyper, *Het Werk van den Heiligen Geest*, 428–29 [339].
[109] Kuyper, *Het Werk van den Heiligen Geest*, 429 [339].
[110] Kuyper, *Het Werk van den Heiligen Geest*, 432–34 [340–42]; idem, *E Voto Dordraceno*, III, 432–33.

Moreover, this inward or effectual call is addressed to the elect, whereas the ordinary or outward call addresses the non-elect. The inward call is God's call and requires God's action, even where quickening has preceded it, for the regenerate—or quickened sinners—will not come of themselves.[111]

Kuyper views inward calling as a twofold work: (1) the first work is God coming with the Word, and the Holy Spirit performs an inward operation, making the seed of faith sprout to life in the work of preaching and hearing the Word; and (2) the second work follows wherein the preached Word effectively enters the very center of the sinner's heart and life, bringing with it an illumination of the understanding, such that he comes under the conviction of his sin, and conversion takes full effect.[112] Thus the Holy Spirit operates upon the converted person's will, in the words of the Canons of Dort: God powerfully enlightens the minds of his chosen ones "by the Holy Spirit so that they may rightly understand and discern the things of the Spirit of God" and "he also penetrates into the inmost being of man, opens the closed heart, softens the hard heart, and circumcises the heart that is uncircumcised," besides infusing "new qualities into the will, making the dead will alive, the evil one good, the unwilling one willing. . ." (Canons of Dort, III–IV, art. 11). God does not treat us as blocks and stones or ignore our will and understanding; rather, he "spiritually revives, heals, reforms, and ... bends it back" (Canons of Dort, III–IV, art. 16). None of this "rules out or cancels the use of the gospel. . ." (Canons of Dort, III–IV, art. 17). Hence our wills yield to God, and love enters our souls.

The difference between regeneration and calling comes to this: "*regeneration* takes place independently of the *will* and *understanding;* that it is wrought in us without our aid or cooperation; while in *calling*, the will and understanding begin to act, so that we *hear* with both the outward and inward ear, and with the inclined will are *willing* to go out to the light."[113] Thus far Kuyper's view.

Bavinck's perspective on this question is set forth in the present volume. Since we offer a brief synopsis of the contents of Bavinck's book below, we will not explore his views, as presented in this volume, at this point. It is interesting to note, however, how Bavinck examines immediate regeneration in his *Reformed Dogmatics*.

In a chapter entitled "Calling and Regeneration," Bavinck, in ways similar to Kuyper, maintains that Scripture allows us to speak of regeneration in three distinct ways:

---

[111] Kuyper, *E Voto Dordraceno*, III, 428–31.

[112] Kuyper, *Het Werk van den Heiligen Geest*, 431–33 [345–47]. Kuyper elaborates upon and explains the meaning of the sinner's cooperation in conversion in the chapter that follows this discussion, 434–40 [349–53]; also idem, *E Voto Dordraceno*, III, 424–26, 438.

[113] Kuyper, *Het Werk van den Heiligen Geest*, 434 [348]. Cf. idem, *E Voto Dordraceno*, III, 426–28.

(1) as the principle of the new life planted by the Spirit of God in humans before they believe, (2) as the moral renewal of humans manifesting itself in a holy walk of life, and finally (3) as the restoration of the whole world to its original completeness. Thus rebirth encompasses the entire scope of re-creation from its very first beginning in the heart of people to its ultimate completion in the new heaven and new earth.[114]

For Bavinck, the first, restricted use of regeneration is not to be identified with external calling. External calling, which being distinguished as "a real call" (*vocatio realis*) refers to God's call "through nature, history, environment, various leadings, and experiences," and has as its medium the law as expressed in "the family, society, and state, in religion and morality, in heart and conscience," obliges all humans to live according to God's goodness and truth.[115] This call, however, is insufficient for salvation since it is absent Christ and the gospel. But when external calling is distinguished as "the verbal call" (*vocatio verbalis*), a call that comes to humans in the form of the revealed law and especially in the form of the revealed gospel, this is calling that summons persons to faith in Christ and to dependency upon God's grace.[116] This is a universal offer of grace that is "seriously and sincerely meant" inasmuch as the gospel is preached to persons "not as elect or reprobate but as sinners, all of whom need redemption." The universal offer, however, is "not to all people individually." For Christ's atonement is not a mere offer that has a universal scope; rather, it is effectual and secures "full, real, and total salvation," according to the will and purpose of God. Therefore the call of gospel-preaching reaches its goal in the salvation of the elect, but the external call also reaches its goal for those who reject it. Moreover, this external call, though not a preparatory grace in an Arminian sense, is a "preparatory grace" if understood in the right way. God is the God of nature and grace, of creation and re-creation, and he uses both "the real call" and "the verbal call" to prepare his elect for redemption, though the implantation of spiritual life in regeneration remains God's own immediate "creative work."[117]

It is clear that not all persons to whom God addresses his operations in the external call respond in faith. The reason for this diverse response, Bavinck argues, may not be grounded in the human will, nor may it be founded upon some sort of doctrine of "congruism" or a merely morally suasive operation of divine grace. Instead, the diverse response is rooted

---

[114] Bavinck, *Reformed Dogmatics*, IV, 53.

[115] Bavinck, *Reformed Dogmatics*, IV, 33–34; 76–77; also see Bavinck's comments in *Our Reasonable Faith*, 407–09, where he identifies this sort of call with common grace and argues that by means of this proclamation of the law God curbs sin, represses human passions, and restrains the flow of iniquities. "A human society and a civic righteousness [are] made possible by it, and these in turn open up the way for a higher civilization, a richer culture, and a flowering of arts and sciences."

[116] Bavinck, *Reformed Dogmatics*, IV, 34–35.

[117] Bavinck, *Reformed Dogmatics*, IV, 36–39; idem, *Our Reasonable Faith*, 415–17.

in "the nature of the calling itself"—that is, for the Reformed, it is rooted in the difference between external and internal calling or other such nomenclature.[118]

Bavinck argues for the biblical propriety of this distinction under five points. (1) All humans share the same spiritual and moral incapacity of original sin, and none are worthy of God's kindness or saving operations. "Hence the difference that occurs among people after the calling is inexplicable in terms of human capacities." Divine grace alone accounts for this difference. (2) The proclaimed Word of the gospel is insufficient in itself to change the fallen human heart. Without the secret operation of the Holy Spirit to effect regeneration in us, none would come to faith and salvation. (3) This means that the salvation is a divine work from first to last, "both subjectively and objectively." "The calling is the implementation of divine election," for God alone draws people unto himself. He makes us to will and to do according to his good pleasure. (4) This is why the Scripture calls this "rebirth," and this is also why some notion of "moral suasion" does not capture the biblical portrait of God giving a person a new heart. (5) Last, "Scripture itself speaks of calling in a dual sense." The Bible can speak of calling that is inefficacious and calling that is always efficacious as the realization of election.[119]

In addition, Bavinck pointedly asserts that the difference between the general call through creation and history and the special call through the preaching of the gospel differ not merely in degree "but in essence and kind."[120]

In contrast to the Anabaptists who made regeneration reliant upon "an active faith and repentance," and the Lutherans who took Titus 3:5 as supporting a doctrine of baptismal regeneration—but an "amissible" or losable regeneration— the Reformed carved out their own path. Rather than undervalue the church's ministry and the means of grace, as the Anabaptists did, or overvalue the church and the means of grace, as the Lutherans did, the Reformed initially spoke of regeneration by faith.[121] That language of course was ambiguous, and inasmuch as small children and infants were incapable of such faith, the question arose whether they should be thought of as candidates for baptism and, even more, for salvation itself.[122] The Reformed, notes Bavinck, came to various answers in attempting to provide an affirmative answer to that query.

> They grounded the baptism of the children of the church in the faith of the parents or of the church, in the faith children would exercise in the

---

[118] Bavinck, *Reformed Dogmatics*, IV, 41–42; idem, *Our Reasonable Faith*, 413–15.

[119] Bavinck, *Reformed Dogmatics*, IV, 43–44. The reader is urged to consult these pages for Bavinck's citation of Scripture, etc.; also see pages 46–53 for more of his presentation of the scriptural materials on regeneration.

[120] Bavinck, *Our Reasonable Faith*, 411.

[121] Bavinck, *Reformed Dogmatics*, IV, 55–56.

[122] Bavinck, *Reformed Dogmatics*, IV, 56.

future, or in a largely undefined covenant of grace in which children were included with their parents.[123]

Then, too, others appealed to those scriptural texts which indicate that the Holy Spirit is able to begin his sanctifying operations in the womb.[124] Coupled with this view,

> Others based it on the reality, assumed to exist by faith in the promise of the covenant of grace, that the Holy Spirit had wrought in their hearts [i.e., in the hearts of covenant children] an established disposition of faith and hence of rebirth (in the narrow sense, as the very first life principle).[125]

Here Bavinck is speaking of Kuyper's stated position. But as Bavinck observes, "In the works of [Reformed] theologians, Calvin among them, several of these lines of argument occur side by side, and not one of them is made dominant."[126]

Bavinck proceeds to examine the doctrine of presupposed regeneration, a topic that we have already considered above. At this point we simply note Bavinck's acknowledgement that this doctrine rightly reckons with the fact that faith and repentance have to be understood in light of radical human depravity, and that the blessings of faith and repentance are produced by "a secret internal operation of the Holy Spirit." Regeneration, therefore, has to precede faith and repentance. But the weakness of this doctrine is manifest in light of divine election and practical experience, for not all covenant children who have been baptized, upon reaching maturity, reveal themselves to be regenerate. Therefore a restriction was forced upon this view in terms of divine election, such that "only elect children" may be said to be "as a rule regenerated before their baptism."[127]

Like Kuyper and many Reformed theologians before him, Bavinck affirms immediate regeneration in this first and formative sense, and so he affirms the distinction between "faith as capacity" and "faith as act." He likewise therefore affirms the distinction between "conversion in a passive and an active sense—in other words, between regeneration and repentance (faith), and in the order of redemption ... the former precede[s] the latter."[128]

Indeed, the Reformed were forced to clarify and refine their position on the Holy Spirit's operations in regeneration given that all forms of Pelagianism locate regeneration *after* faith and repentance. All Augustinians, on the other hand, place regeneration *before* faith and repentance.

---

[123] Bavinck, *Reformed Dogmatics*, IV, 56.
[124] Bavinck, *Reformed Dogmatics*, IV, 56.
[125] Bavinck, *Reformed Dogmatics*, IV, 56.
[126] Bavinck, *Reformed Dogmatics*, IV, 56.
[127] Bavinck, *Reformed Dogmatics*, IV, 57.
[128] Bavinck, *Reformed Dogmatics*, IV, 65, 68.

This is a fundamental theological divide wherein human decision is finally determinative for the former view and divine decision is finally determinative for the latter view. Moreover, if original sin is true and if the children of believers are to be regarded as candidates for salvation, and if, being children not yet of the age of discretion (so that they are incapable of faith and repentance by means of the ministry of the Word), then regeneration must run ahead of faith and repentance. In short, faith as capacity must be granted before faith as act, and so sinners are first passive as recipients of the Holy Spirit's work of regeneration in order that they may subsequently be active as those experiencing rebirth and new life.[129]

Bavinck also notes that the word regeneration, in terms of theological formulation, has been understood in at least three senses: (1) as descriptive of "the transformation that begins in the human consciousness as a result of the believing acceptance of the gospel ..." (which he views as defective and prone to foster misunderstanding); (2) as descriptive, broadly conceived, of "the total renewal of a person," brought about by and coinciding with faith (this view, too, was prone to misinterpretation); and (3) as descriptive, narrowly or strictly conceived, of an infusion of new life prior to faith and repentance. Understood in this last sense, regeneration was distinguished from "the progress of regeneration," the latter reality being given such titles as repentance, renewal, and sanctification.[130]

Regeneration, then, conceived in the restricted sense, "does not include the growth and development of the new life but suggests the genesis or origin of that life."[131] Of course, in terms of theological formulation, this definition is more refined than the way Scripture usually speaks. But Reformed writers have always been aware of this, and in speaking of regeneration in this restricted sense they have distinguished between "the activity of God by which he regenerates, and the fruit of that activity in the person who is being regenerated; in other words, between active and passive regeneration."[132] The former is nothing else than "the efficacious call of God." The latter is our active engagement and response to that call, whereby we learn as God teaches, we follow as he draws, we accept as he endows, we blossom and flourish as he plants and waters and grants the increase.[133] But the former always precedes the latter, for this is simply to affirm that the grace of God in Christ is "grace that is full, abundant, free, omnipotent, and insuperable," which is "the heart of the gospel."[134]

It is important to observe that, for Bavinck, the blessings of regeneration are not divorced from Christ and the covenant of grace. Indeed, he

---

[129] Bavinck, *Reformed Dogmatics*, IV, 66–68; idem, *Our Reasonable Faith*, 419–23.
[130] Bavinck, *Reformed Dogmatics*, IV, 76.
[131] Bavinck, *Reformed Dogmatics*, IV, 76.
[132] Bavinck, *Reformed Dogmatics*, IV, 77. For Bavinck's exposition of active regeneration, see IV, 87–95.
[133] Bavinck, *Reformed Dogmatics*, IV, 77.
[134] Bavinck, *Reformed Dogmatics*, IV, 87.

argues that the benefits of the covenant of grace are "applied and distributed only in the internal calling," which from the human side of things means that these are "passively accepted" in regeneration. And so whether this regeneration "takes place in childhood, youth, or later, before or during the hearing of the Word, *logically it always precedes the act of really believing.*"[135] To press this point, Bavinck cites Maccovius who said that to hear the Word "salvifically" requires that one is regenerate.[136] As noted above, Bavinck readily grants that regeneration in the restricted sense, as the infusion of the principle of the new life, may ... precede faith." Indeed, it can "occur in infancy before the awakening of consciousness, in or before baptism, even before birth."[137] No door stands bolted and locked before God that would prevent him from effectuating his saving mercy, for there is "no heart inaccessible" to him.[138]

> With his Spirit he can enter the innermost being of every human, with or without the Word, by way of or apart from all consciousness, in old age or from the moment of conception. Christ's own conception by the Holy Spirit in Mary's womb is proof that the Holy Spirit can, from that moment on and continually, be active in a human being with his sanctifying presence.[139]

Like Kuyper, Bavinck draws comfort from this doctrine. He appeals to the language of the Canons of Dort, I, art. 17, which bids godly parents not to doubt the election and salvation of their children whom God calls from this life at a tender age. Thus Bavinck explicitly affirms the doctrine of immediate regeneration, where regeneration is understood in the restricted sense, for this is simply to affirm that such a regeneration encompasses "in principle the whole person, initially renewing all of one's capacities and powers, and later manifesting and confirming itself in all directions, in faith and repentance, in sanctification and good works."[140]

Moreover, we would be derelict in presenting Bavinck's views if we failed to observe that, for Bavinck, all the blessings of salvation are tied to the covenant of grace and are only bestowed upon a person unto salvation *in union with Christ*. This is not a small point for Bavinck; it ought to be "in the foreground of our consciousness," for "all the benefits of salvation are secured by Christ and present in him...." In fact, Christ distributes all the blessings of the covenant of grace at his pleasure, which include regeneration or new birth, faith and repentance, reconciliation and forgiveness, renewal and sanctification.[141] All these saving gifts and blessings are received only "in communion with Christ," for they never

---

135 Bavinck, *Reformed Dogmatics*, IV, 123; *italics* added.
136 Bavinck, *Reformed Dogmatics*, IV, 123.
137 Bavinck, *Reformed Dogmatics*, IV, 123.
138 Bavinck, *Reformed Dogmatics*, IV, 123.
139 Bavinck, *Reformed Dogmatics*, IV, 123.
140 Bavinck, *Reformed Dogmatics*, IV, 124.
141 Bavinck, *Reformed Dogmatics*, IV, 122.

exist independent of him and he himself secured them for his people. And all of these benefits are applied and distributed individually to persons "only in the internal calling," "passively accepted on the human side in regeneration"; and in logical order "always precedes the act of really believing."[142]

The Synod of Utrecht 1905 addressed this question in a manner that clearly mirrors Bavinck's views. The Conclusions assert that the language of immediate regeneration can be used in a proper sense in order to distinguish the Reformed view from Roman Catholic and Lutheran errors, for the Word and sacraments do not themselves *effect* regeneration; that privilege and work is reserved to the almighty operations of the Holy Spirit. Nonetheless, "this regenerating operation of the Holy Spirit ... should not be in such a way divorced from the preaching of the Word as if these two were separate from each other." As for covenant infants who die at a tender age, Scripture and confession teach us not to doubt their salvation; however, the case of infants ought not to compromise the clear biblical affirmation that "the Gospel is the power of God unto salvation to everyone that believeth, and that in the case of adults the regenerating operation of the Holy Spirit accompanies the preaching of the Gospel."[143]

Synopsis of Bavinck's Treatment

With this broad background in place, we are in a better position to appreciate Bavinck's careful treatment of this last topic in the present volume. As Bavinck tells his readers, his book is intended to bring "greater clarity concerning the doctrine of immediate regeneration," with the aim of facilitating peace in the churches, such that "difference of insight" need not devolve into a disunity of confession. For, indeed, serious disunity was manifesting itself among the churches at that time.

In blazing a trail through this debate, Bavinck's book is a four part project. PART ONE is introductory and provides an orientation to the issues to be examined. Bavinck briefly sketches the concern of the opponents to the doctrine of immediate regeneration. First, according to the critics, this doctrine, coupled with the doctrine of presupposed regeneration, is said to undercut the call to repentance and the call to a life of faithful obedience. If one is presumed saved, then preaching no longer lays claim upon the human heart. The pulpit is emasculated. Meanwhile, and second, inasmuch as the followers of Kuyper followed him also in embracing supralapsarianism, this tended to turn the gospel into bad news for sinners—a message that is as much a sentence of death as it is an announcement of life. Third, when immediate regeneration is conjoined to the doctrine of eternal justification, the practical effect is to make salvation simply a matter of believers *becoming aware* of a grace

---

[142] Bavinck, *Reformed Dogmatics*, IV, 122–23.
[143] In critique of Kuyper's view, see Berkhof, *Systematic Theology*, 468–79, especially 470–72.

that long ago was bestowed upon and effected in them—that over against salvation as a living encounter with God in the call of the gospel. Finally, since immediate regeneration brought with it the notion of a seed of life implanted within the regenerated, a seed that can remain dormant for very many years without germinating and showing signs of life, the interval between regeneration and conversion—the latter being the actual coming of the sinner to faith and repentance—could likewise be very long, with the consequence that those with new life in them can live for many years as though completely dead in sin. This does not encourage a life of piety.

In order to evaluate these charges, Bavinck sets forth three principal questions, which in turn form the focus of Bavinck's study. The first question concerns the manner in which the Holy Spirit works within the human heart. Is this from a distance and through ordinary means or does the Holy Spirit draw close and directly impart the blessing of regeneration? The answer to this question distinguishes defenders of sovereign grace from defenders of free will. The second question inquires into the use of means, for if it is the case that the Holy Spirit directly effectuates spiritual rebirth in the hearts of fallen people, are all means to be excluded or regarded as redundant? The answer to this query sets proponents of the effectual use of means apart from Enthusiasts and Anabaptists who regard means as empty signs. The third question (assuming that the use of means is not detrimental to a proper view of the Spirit's work of regeneration in the human heart) concerns the connection between the immediate operation of the Holy Spirit and the role of means in this operation. In answering this question the Reformed distinguish themselves from Roman Catholics and Lutherans alike, both of which tie grace too exclusively and mechanically to the use of means.

In PART TWO Bavinck sketches what the immediate (or unmediated) operation of the Holy Spirit means. To begin, Bavinck introduces the dispute between Augustine and Pelagius on this first question. Bavinck shows how the immediate operation of the Holy Spirit, understood in the proper sense, is a trait common to all anti-Pelagian theology. While Augustine's doctrine of irresistible grace was never condemned in the Roman Catholic Church, it was weakened over the course of time with the increasing preference for semi-Pelagianism. The Reformed, of course, dispute all forms of Pelagianism. While they altogether agreed on the substance of regenerative grace and the sovereign work of God in awakening dead sinners unto life and faith, the Reformed were not completely united in how to describe the initial moment of the application of salvation, especially the relation between the external call of the gospel and the elect coming to rebirth and life. Clearly, this first coming to life had to be at God's initiative and completely his work. Fallen humans do not distinguish themselves from one another, for in salvation, initially, they are altogether "receptive and passive." An internal, hidden, effectual grace is acknowledged and confessed by all the Reformed—indeed, the internal call is what this is. The nomenclature of "immediate regeneration" was, however, not yet common. But that does not mean this terminology is impermissible, for God does act immediately and directly upon a person to infuse him or her with new life. It is noteworthy that at this point Bavinck quotes Kuyper favorably inasmuch as Kuyper rightly champions Calvinism as the safeguard of the gospel of grace.

Bavinck next reminds his readers that the gospel of grace was once under attack through the teachings of the Remonstrants. He succinctly outlines some of the principal teachings of the Canons of Dort, especially under heads III–IV, wherein human depravity and irresistible grace are carefully treated. In doing so, Bavinck arrives at the answer to the first key question—namely, In what manner does the Holy Spirit work within the human heart?—that is, is this a direct and irresistible operation or does he make use of means? The answer is not in dispute: the Word of God in and by itself is insufficient for regenerating and bringing the sinner to faith and conversion, but must be accompanied by an internal grace, by the Holy Spirit's work, which is internal, spiritual, supernatural, effectual, invincible, and irresistible.

PART THREE, which makes up the bulk of this volume, treats the immediate operation of the Holy Spirit and the means of grace. Bavinck first shows how Augustine and the Reformed understood the means of grace; then he demonstrates how the language of calling and regeneration was understood at the Synod of Dort, and how various Reformed writers used these terms and that the terms had to be refined in order to refute Remonstrant views. Next Bavinck considers the Reformed conception of the covenant of grace and the church, setting the Reformed position in contrast to both Romish and Anabaptist notions. This leads to an examination of the moment of regeneration. Romish and Anabaptist errors are once more noted; the work of divine grace in covenant children is the focus of discussion, including covenant children who die in infancy. Here Bavinck carefully explores the views of Gisbertus Voetius on the regeneration of covenant infants, i.e., presupposed regeneration. Voetius was a very influential theologian of the seventeenth century, from whom Kuy-per derived some of his own accents. Over against Voetius, Bavinck next introduces his readers to Jessaias Hellenius, a prominent eighteenth-century Reformed minister, who opposed Voetius's advocacy of the regeneration of covenant infants. Bavinck appeals to Hellenius, in part, in order to show that the Reformed, though not reaching unanimity on this topic, still allowed distinct views. But more, Bavinck wants to expose the weaknesses of the presupposed regeneration view, for he argues that the doctrine of presupposed regeneration is not without serious theological and practical obstacles.

Specifically, Bavinck asserts that this view is speculative, "traversing a terrain of guesses." It tries to know more than God has revealed in his Word; we simply cannot know when God ordinarily regenerates elect infants. Besides, the problem of undetected hypocrites within the fellowship of the church cannot be eradicated, which means that unregenerate persons abide within the bosom of the church. Clearly, then, regeneration does not always precede baptism. The doctrine of presupposed regeneration, moreover, has no practical benefit and can produce genuine practical harm, for the preaching of the gospel is still indispensable for nurturing elect infants in the way of faith. Meanwhile, presupposed regeneration is vulnerable to promoting false assurance inasmuch as one is tempted to focus upon regeneration instead of faith; and this in turn encourages a nominal Christianity that is spiritually superficial. Likewise, presupposed regeneration might encourage the minister to confine the overtures of the gospel only to persons assumed to be regenerate, which, in effect, constitutes a premature reckoning, as if a person's destiny was decided at birth rather than at death. Preaching is thereby robbed of its seriousness. Finally, a doctrine of presupposed regeneration could be construed in a manner that forms an obstacle to the free and well-meant offer of the gospel.

Bavinck, however, is aware that a potent counter-argument can be set forth in favor of immediate regeneration, namely, that calling cannot precede regeneration because deaf people cannot hear and dead people cannot come alive. Thus, God must first grant the new life of regeneration to the sinner if he or she is to have ears to hear and eyes to see and a heart capable of receiving the gospel in faith. Without regeneration preceding calling, calling is in vain. Bavinck, of course, concedes this point but demonstrates that it is not strictly *apropos*. While Bavinck readily grants that God can work regeneration in the hearts of elect infants apart from their hearing and understanding the Word, uncertainty as to the actual moment of regeneration cannot be overcome. Bavinck carefully sorts out the Reformed opinion on this topic, showing why the Reformed in their dogmatics have always treated calling as first in the order of salvation. It is again important to note that the Reformed forged their position on the anvil of controversy, for they ever had to present their views over against Anabaptist errors.

The Anabaptists, of course, operated with the notion of assuming the non-regeneration of infants and small children, and therefore did not permit the baptism of infants. They denied *means* of grace altogether. The Reformed, however, tied regeneration to the Word of the gospel as a genuine means of grace. The Reformed also had a much more nuanced understanding of the spiritual state of covenant infants, a topic that Scripture addresses rather meagerly. To be sure, Scripture informs us that God is the God of believers and their children, that such children are included in the covenant of grace, and that therefore they have the right to the sign and seal of that covenant, and that they must also be nurtured in the ways of the Lord. But many questions remain unanswered. Do passages like Jeremiah 1:5 and Luke 1:15 teach that children are regenerated in the womb? Bavinck argues that such texts are not conclusive, and God is free in his operations toward his elect. Similarly, does 1 Corinthians

7:14 teach regeneration from infancy? Bavinck maintains that this text does not refer to a "subjective, spiritual renewal" but to "an objective covenant relationship." Again, Bavinck does not deny that many covenant children are indeed regenerated in their youth and even prior to being baptized, nor does Bavinck wish to subvert in any way the comfort that believing parents ought to have regarding the election and salvation of their children who die at a tender age. Early regeneration is possible, but Scripture does not allow us to know beyond what it teaches; and we must resist being overly curious about such matters.

Bavinck also takes up a discussion of covenant adults and their spiritual state, and here Bavinck specifically takes up the work of preaching—both preaching unto the lost afar off and preaching to covenant members of the church. Whereas it is wrongheaded to treat covenant people as unbelievers, it is likewise wrongheaded to fail to call them to faith and repentance after the pattern of the Old Testament prophets, as well as John the Baptist and Jesus. Similarly, the apostolic letters refer to the covenant people as God's elect and members of Christ, yet the churches could be infected with hypocrites not yet detected and with various forms of error and unrighteousness that require continual calls to faith and repentance. Scripture teaches us to regard one another as God's people, but also to be aware that false brothers and sisters slip in as fakes, and they do not constitute the essence of the church.

This discussion clears the way for Bavinck to take up calling and regeneration in relation to the preaching of the gospel. Here Bavinck contrasts a Reformed understanding with a Methodistic approach. He also contrasts it with an approach which assumes that all in the church are saved and therefore they should only hear preaching that edifies—that over against a preaching that also exposes sin, hypocrisy, and, consequently, calls to faith and conversion. The ethical method of preaching inevitably leads to dead orthodoxy, says Bavinck. He believes both forms of proclamation are necessary in the church; otherwise one-sidedness is the result—the one-sidedness of presupposed regeneration and the one-sidedness of presupposed non-regeneration.

This is the answer to the second key question—does the direct operation of the Holy Spirit exclude the use of means? Bavinck maintains that though the Spirit's work is internal and irresistible, the Reformed never called regeneration "immediate" in contrast with and to the exclusion of the Word as a means of grace, to which the Holy Spirit joins himself and makes effectual.

Finally, in PART FOUR of his book, Bavinck presents his discussion of the connection between the immediate operation of the Holy Spirit and the means of grace. Here he treats the means of grace, with special attention given to the Word of God as the means of grace. It is under this part that Bavinck answers the third key question of his study, namely, what is the relation between the Spirit's immediate operation and the use of means?

Bavinck regards this question as weighty and difficult. Dort reminds us that the supernatural operation of the Holy Spirit upon the human heart in regeneration is marvelous, hidden, and inexpressible. This does not, however, exclude the use of means in every respect, nor does it deny the power of means. This is not unrelated to the doctrine of divine providence, wherein the Creator/creature distinction is carefully preserved. The divine decree, too, is important since it shows us that God's ways with humans are integrated, involving means and ends, pathways and outcomes. The means that God uses for the sinner's redemption is not something we are capable of describing in fixed and clear formulations. Various formulations were attempted in the Middle Ages, including the physical operation view and the moral operation view. Rome adopted the former and rejected the latter view, while the Reformed endorsed the latter view and rebuffed the former.

Inasmuch as the Reformed regarded the Word as the principal means of grace, and inasmuch as they viewed the means of grace as possessing a moral operation, this entails that the Word as a means of grace, as a moral operation, refers to the external call of the Word, in both law and gospel. The divine Logos, of course, possesses more than a moral working power, but also a creating and re-creating power, which includes the speaking-power of God in creation and providence. However, when Scripture refers to the Word as the message contained in the Bible in the form of law and of gospel, then that Word, in itself, has power only as a moral operation—appealing, admonishing, persuading. In itself, and as such, it is not an agent. Without the agency of the Holy Spirit it functions as an external call; only with the agency of the Holy Spirit does it function as the internal call and therefore in a saving way.

The consequences of this observation are obvious: regeneration precedes the saving hearing of the Word, at least in sequence. Thus a distinction is required between how the Word operates in regeneration and how it operates in faith and conversion. In the case of adults, regeneration and conversion generally coincide; as for covenant infants, the Holy Spirit is free to regenerate them at a tender age before they are capable of manifesting the signs of new life in the acts of faith and repentance.

In any case, Bavinck shows that the Word has a role in regeneration, for external calling and internal calling are of one fabric. Although they are not always united with one another, such is more an exception than a rule; and the Reformed have always been concerned to keep them connected to each other. Indeed, regeneration is a fruit of the Holy Spirit and is usually connected to the instrumentality of the gospel proclaimed. This is not to deny that a distinction may be made between how the Word functions in regeneration and how it functions in faith and conversion. The Word is indispensable in the act of faith, for the Holy Spirit uses the Word as the means whereby a person proceeds from the capacity for faith to the act of faith. This is not to turn the Word into an agent—the Holy Spirit remains the agent who moves us to faith and trust in Christ—but it is to affirm that the Word is a moral instrument in the Spirit's hands, supplying the believer with the language and the content of the message of the gospel and engaging the faculties of the believer in the way of faith and repentance. Meanwhile, with respect to regeneration, every Reformed person must acknowledge that the Spirit runs ahead and gives us ears to hear and eyes to see. The Spirit must first prepare the soil to make it good in order that the Word may be sown in good soil. To deny this is to succumb to the Remonstrant position. Nonetheless, the moral suasiveness of the Word can still work simultaneously with the regenerating action of the Holy Spirit in the heart of the sinner. In short, regeneration may ordinarily occur under, by, and with the Word, but never through the Word, for the Spirit can and does regenerate apart from the Word, and the Word has no infused power in itself that can effect regeneration.

Rather than render preaching superfluous, preaching is shown to be God's chosen instrument for the work of salvation. The church is not only commanded to preach the gospel, but the parable of the sower powerfully exhibits its saving fruit. God attaches his promise to the proclaimed gospel; believers find assurance through the proclaimed gospel and are warned to examine themselves. God extends his promises to us in the proclaimed gospel, and also to our children. It is God's chosen instrument, his power to save those who believe; yet even in speaking of the power of the Word, we must remember that God, not the Word, is the agent of salvation.

Finally, the solution to the issue in controversy requires that we carefully appreciate the different ways that Scripture uses the term "regeneration." We must distinguish regeneration in the metaphysical sense from regeneration in the ethical sense, but we may not divorce them from one another, for the former is manifest in the latter. Little children, not yet reaching the age of discretion, are certainly the objects of God's saving operations, but as a rule and ordinarily God delights to make use of His own ordained means to bring us into a saving and fruitful relation to Him.

In closing out this summary of Bavinck's presentation, I put forward R. H. Bremmer's synopsis of Bavinck's position:

1.   The calling of the gospel is of the greatest importance and may not, because of divine election, be a message restricted only to the elect.

2.   Scripture speaks of regeneration in a threefold sense: (a) as the principle (*beginsel*) of new life that is implanted in man prior to faith; (b) as moral renewal; and (c) as the restoration of all things.

3.   Calvin and other Reformers, as well as the Belgic Confession, present faith as preceding regeneration. However, the order was later reversed especially for two reasons: (a) the struggle against the Anabaptists, such that it became necessary in regard to little children to speak of the implanting of a first principle of life; and (b) the struggle against the Remonstrants, such that it became necessary to accent the total depravity

of humans, which in turn required that God implant a first principle of life, wherein a person remains wholly passive.

4. Yet all of this may not lead to the conclusion that regeneration always precedes baptism with respect to elect children.

5. Baptized children are to be viewed and treated as elect and re-generated children, until the contrary is decidedly evident from their confession or life.

6. Bavinck distinguishes between the idea of regeneration in the broader sense (that of Calvin and the Reformers) and in a narrower sense (the giving of the faith-capacity or capacity of faith in the implanting [*in-storting*] of the new life).

7. Regarding the latter, he again distinguishes between active re-generation (*regeneratio activa*) and passive regeneration (*regeneratio passiva*). Passive regeneration is the fruit of God's activity in man; active regeneration is identical to the internal call (*vocatio interna*).

8. Immediate regeneration is to be understood as the direct opera-tion of God's Spirit in a person effecting regeneration, wherein neither man's understanding or will cooperates. It is an additional operation that accompanies the Word and gives the capacity of faith.

9. Since Dort, it is common for the Reformed to speak of regenera-tion as preceding faith.

10. In connection with the awakening of faith flowing from the ca-pacity for faith bestowed in regeneration, the Word is described for the first time as means of grace "in the proper sense."

11. The first regeneration takes place under and with the Word, but not through the Word; as for children, the objective presence of the Word must be acknowledged.

12. The disposition (*habitus*) and nature (*qualitates*) given to man by regeneration owe their stability and durability to the Holy Spirit, who elevates the life implanted with regeneration above sin, destruction, and death.[144]

* * * * *

Finally, a few words concerning the editing of this volume. The origi-nal Dutch version of this book consists of four chapters, the third chapter running for some 142 pages. With the goal of clarifying Bavinck's discus-sion for the modern English reader, I have used Bavinck's original chap-ters and their titles to break the present volume into four parts. This means that the sixteen chapter divisions as found in the current work, along with the titles of chapters, as well as all the headings, sub-headings, etc. within each chapter, are my fabrications and have been inserted into

---

144 Bremmer, *Herman Bavinck als Dogmaticus*, 271-72. For Bremmer's whole discus-sion of Bavinck on regeneration, 261–72; cf. Smilde, *Een Eeuw van Strijd over Verbond en Doop*, 185–94. Bavinck treats this entire topic of calling and regeneration, as well as faith and conversion, in his *Reformed Dogmatics*, IV, 33–175.

Bavinck's text for the reader's benefit. In editing this work I have occasionally identified some Scripture references that Bavinck left unidentified; I have done the same with confessional references. In all such cases I have indicated this with the use of square brackets [ ]. Throughout this volume, I have sought to discover and expand on, or cite in full, his rather cryptic or abbreviated references to sources. As for the editor's notes, these are intended to orient the reader to names and ideas that Bavinck mentions which may be a bit obscure, with the goal that his argument and presentation will be rendered more accessible.

May God use Bavinck's book to bless a new generation of believers, and, for the first time, English readers. To His glory!

J. Mark Beach

PART I

INTRODUCTION

1

The Occasion and Rise of the Controversy

1.1 The Purpose of This Study

AMONG REFORMED churches nowadays there is a difference of opinion of no small consequence concerning the order in which the benefits of the covenant of grace relate to one another and follow each other, in the mind of God as well as in their application to humanity.[1]

It is generally well known that in place of the ancient and usual representation of the order of salvation, another perspective has been proposed in recent years, one that at various points diverges from, and even conflicts with, the earlier view most generally prevalent.

Indeed, this newer representation of the order of salvation-benefits has found rather sudden and complete acceptance among many people. Despite this, because of weighty objections, others have been unable to agree with this newer view, and have seen it as conflicting with Scripture and Confession.[2]

---

[1] Ed. note: See the Editor's "Introductory Essay" for the background to this debate, pages ix–lvi; also see Bavinck's thorough discussion of the order (or way) of salvation (*ordo salutis*) in his *Reformed Dogmatics*, ed. John Bolt, trans. John Vriend, 4 vols. (Grand Rapids: Baker Academic, 2002–2008), III, 484–595, where he sets forth the Reformed approach to this question and its concern to champion salvation as wholly a gift of divine grace, the church itself empowered by the Holy Spirit to bring the gospel to the nations. Over against the errors of Pelagianism and semi-Pelagianism, as well as mysticism, pietism, and rationalism, Bavinck demonstrates how the Reformed emphasized the centrality of communion with Christ as the presupposition of the order of salvation, and how the work of salvation and its application to the elect in history is grounded in the eternal intratrinitarian *pactum salutis* or counsel of peace between the Father and Son, with the Holy Spirit being the agent sent forth to administer this grace to sinners. By the turn of the century the diversity of viewpoints on the relationship between calling and regeneration had provoked discord within the Reformed Churches in the Netherlands, as reflected in Bavinck's citation of various incidents of opposition. See footnote 2 below.

[2] Trans. note: We have moved to this footnote the following material from the body of Bavinck's original text as not having immediate interest to a North American audience;

One can even say that this difference of opinion about the order of
salvation-benefits was the basis for the ongoing brotherly quarrel about
Maccovius and his theology.3 People opposed the dry scholastic method
of the Franeker professor, but far more than that—for no one objects to a
genuinely scientific treatment in dogmatic theology—they resisted the
substantive presentation of the truth as set forth by Maccovius in his
teaching. Especially his teachings regarding supralapsarianism, justification from eternity, immediate regeneration, and the like, met with objec-
tion.4 Moreover, it seems that, though on the one hand these views
seemed well protected by the armor of Maccovius, these views were
nonetheless also opposed and rejected for the very reason of being associated with him.

All these points of dispute regarding the order of salvation seem to be
under discussion even more vigorously throughout the churches, and
they occasion difference of sentiment. When one visits a church, or receives letters from some church members, where the atmosphere is
heavy with legitimate conscientious objection and serious concern, then
the reality cannot be camouflaged that in all these doctrinal differences
hardly any agreement has been reached at all.

---

however, this material does show the nature of the disharmony that was in evidence during
this period: "Rev. ten Hoor developed several of these objections already when he wrote in
the *Vrije Kerk* [*Free Church*] an evaluation of the Encyclopaedie [Arrangement and Explanation of Theological Subjects] of Dr. Kuyper. The Consistory in Bedum thought these objections were so weighty that they submitted an appeal to the deputies for relations with the
Theological Faculty of the Free University, which appeal was then discussed at the Synod of
Middelburg in 1896, but was dismissed on the basis of formal and material considerations.

The appellants, however, were not convinced that they were mistaken, as became evident
when Rev. T. Bos devoted several articles in the *Vrije Kerk* to the issues in question—
articles that were published separately by Mr. Donner of Leiden under the title, 'Nine Doctrinal Subjects, Simply Explained and Defended for Reformed People.'

Following him, came Mr. Huisman of Appingedam with a volume of 337 pages, in which
he compared several fundamental truths of the Christian religion—examined in terms of
God's Word, the Confessions, Calvin and others of our Reformed fathers—with the views of
Dr. Kuyper.

"Recently the pen was taken up yet again by Mr. J. H. Wessels of Utrecht, in order to investigate and evaluate on the basis of God's Word the existing difference of opinion regarding the doctrine of the covenant.

"At the same time, articles were placed in the magazine of Prof. Lindeboom, entitled
'What Does Scripture Say?,' by Mr. J. of M., articles which attempted to adduce proofs from
Reformed theology for the claim that calling precedes regeneration.

"At the ministers' conference held last year in Zwolle, the question of immediate regeneration was also discussed, and provided occasion for a lively debate."

3 Ed. note: Johannes Maccovius (1578–1644) studied at Franeker and became professor of theology at that institution in 1615. He is remembered for his extreme and polemical
advocacy of supralapsarianism against Sibrandus Lubbertus and for the censure he received
at the Synod of Dort for his speculative and philosophical approach to theology. He was also
censured while a professor for his dubious lifestyle and morals. His chief works are *Collegia
theologica* (1623) and *Loci communes theologici* (1650).

4 Ed. note: These would be the very topics treated synodically in the Conclusions of
Utrecht 1905. See the appendix, at the end of this work.

On the one side, people doubt whether anyone in our churches is teaching that, generally speaking, the regeneration of elect infants occurs before baptism, and they believe that surely such a view cannot be defended with certainty on the basis of Holy Scripture. At the same time, on the other side, many complain that much contemporary preaching of the Word seems almost to suggest that there are no unregenerate in the church any longer. It seems as though even when a person has continued living for years in an unconverted state, he must still be considered to be regenerated.

It seems that especially the objections being registered by the latter group are increasing in weight and in number. Ministers are no longer preaching discriminatingly—so goes the complaint of many nowadays. The godless are no longer being warned that they will fare badly. Sermons are no longer being preached with an urgency that communicates the message that anyone who is not regenerated by water and the Spirit will not see the kingdom of God. Preaching no longer lays it upon the listener's heart that it will profit nothing, though we have the name of Christian and are physically alive, if we are still dead in sins and trespasses. Many are convinced that to teach that baptism presupposes regeneration and that all who are baptized are to be considered regenerated inevitably robs the ministry of the Word of its essence and its power. Their overwhelming fear is that this teaching will lead many to build their houses on sand and to deceive themselves all the way into eternity.

Whether or not these objecting brothers and sisters are right, it cannot be denied that their reservations are very serious and arise among many believers from a pious conscience.

For that reason, all those complaints deserve to be heard with meekness. They are not coming strictly from the old "A" groups only, but just as frequently from the churches that since 1886 became reformed and are known mostly as "B" churches.[5] Moreover, these complaints involve truths of very deep significance for theology and church, for the administration of the Word and Sacrament, for doctrine and life, for theory and practice.

Of all those truths, the doctrine of immediate regeneration occupies a central place, especially in Reformed theology.[6] In the closest possible connection to this teaching lies the relationship between Word and Spirit, between Scripture and church, between doctrine and life, between mind and heart. This teaching involves the most important question, namely, in which way and in which order the Holy Spirit applies the benefits obtained through the suffering and dying of Christ.

---

[5] Ed. note: See the Editor's "Introductory Essay" regarding "A" churches and "B" churches, page xiv, footnote 14.

[6] Ed. note: See the Editor's "Introductory Essay," pages xxxiii–xlvi, for a definition and brief explanation of the meaning of the terms "immediate" and "mediate" regeneration. Cf. Bavinck, *Reformed Dogmatics*, IV, 80–84.

We intend to shed light on this doctrine in the following chapters, in a manner as objective, non-partisan, and straightforward as possible. We do so in the quiet hope that the historic Reformed presentation of this doctrine, not the particular view of one or another group, may receive the endorsement of all the brothers and sisters in our churches, and will help bring an end to our differences, or at least help reduce them.

1.2 The Supralapsarian Position

The order of the benefits of divine salvation, as formulated recently by many speakers and writers, which is now encountering objection, can be summarized briefly as follows.

God has from eternity purposed and determined, so it is formulated by advocates of the one side, to glorify His attributes of mercy and justice by means of the eternal salvation of a portion of His rational creatures, and by means of the eternal condemnation of another portion.

In order to reach this goal that had been established from before all things, God decided first to create such rational creatures, then to permit them together to fall into sin, and finally to bring to redemption the elect portion of humanity through Christ, and to prepare for eternal condemnation the other reprobate portion that was on the path of sin.

According to this view, supralapsarianism—which corresponds with the order required by this line of thinking, namely, that the establishment of the goal precedes the establishment of the means—deserves preference over infralapsarianism. It is indeed a harsh truth; but even if it might not be confessional, it is quite certainly scriptural.

As people occasionally formulate the matter, supralapsarianism is comparable to a physician who must inform the patient with a fatal disease of that fact, which in this case refers to the non-elect needing to be told the truth of their reprobation. It is like the judge who must inform the criminal convicted of a capital crime of his death sentence. Such a physician and judge must do this, of course, with tenderness in his heart, filled with sadness and moved by pity. That pertains, however, merely to the form and the manner, but not to the substance itself. Supralapsarianism is the announcement of the truth of reprobation to the reprobate.

Similarly, the announcement of the gospel is nothing else than making known to the elect their eternal salvation, bringing to light that which has existed already from eternity.

1.2.1 *Eternal justification and immediate regeneration*

For, as this view sees it, election and justification occur together.[7] The elect are justified initially not within time, but from eternity. Abra-

---

[7] Ed. note: It should be noted that not all supralapsarians held to "justification from eternity," though Abraham Kuyper and many of his followers embraced this doctrine, following Maccovius and certain eighteenth-century Reformed theologians. This doctrine was

ham, for example, was justified already before the foundation of the world. Within time he was justified only before the court of his own conscience and received personal knowledge of his justification.

This eternal justification, therefore, necessarily includes the Holy Spirit's regeneration within time. Among the elect who live under the administration of the covenant, this regeneration occurs as a rule very early in life, according to some. Most often the first seed of new life is implanted already in the mother's womb or immediately after birth. It is even possible—although this cannot be said with certainty—that someone is regenerated at the very same moment he is born. Just as with circumcision, so baptism is a sign and seal of regeneration.

Therefore this regeneration is possible before birth or immediately at birth, although one must distinguish between an immediate and a mediate operation of the Holy Spirit. According to the judgment of those who advocate this order of salvation, the *immediate* operation consists in the Holy Spirit implanting the seed of new life within the heart of the elect apart from or prior to the Word, whereby they are transferred from death to life. Some argue the claim that this immediate regeneration must precede the Word, since a deaf person cannot hear, a dead person cannot rise, a natural man cannot give ear to the summons of the gospel unto faith and repentance.

But if an elect person is regenerated in this manner, immediately, only by the Holy Spirit, apart from the Word, then God will see to it that sooner or later such a person will become acquainted with the gospel. Because he is regenerated he can now hear the gospel that is coming to him, can obey its summons, and can be rendered capable of faith and repentance. Upon the regenerated person who can hear, the Holy Spirit works *mediately, with and through the Word that is preached.*

1.2.2 *Immediate regeneration without immediate conversion*

But this is not yet to say concerning an elect person who was regenerated before or at the moment of birth, that when such a person becomes aware and hears the gospel, he also instantaneously accepts it in faith and turns to God with a true heart.

No, as this view teaches emphatically, the seed of regeneration can remain hidden in the heart without germinating, until a person is thirty, fifty, or even seventy years old. Many years can pass between regeneration and conversion.[8] Even though in the first moments of their existence

---

controverted among the Reformed and received a "mixed" reception in the late nineteenth century by the revitalized Calvinism that Kuyper helped to form and to consolidate. Kuyper defends this doctrine, for example, in his book *The Work of the Holy Spirit*, trans. Henri De Vries; with explanatory notes by Henri De Vries, with an introduction by Benjamin B. Warfield (New York: Funk & Wagnalls, 1900), 367–371. See the critique of this view by Louis Berkhof, *Systematic Theology*, 4th ed. (Grand Rapids: Eerdmans, 1939, 1941), 517–520.

[8] Trans. note: Throughout this translation the Dutch word "bekeering" has been rendered, depending on the context, as either "repentance" or "conversion."

the elect are regenerated unto eternal life, they can nevertheless continue for a very long time unconverted and unbelieving—yes, they can even live in terrible sin and surrender to various forms of unrighteousness. Nevertheless, in His time the Lord brings to light, by means of the effectual internal calling, that reality which perhaps many years before had been worked by the Holy Spirit in the heart of the elect immediately and apart from the Word.

1.2.3 *Regeneration precedes calling*

Therefore, regeneration precedes calling, often within time, but in any case, in that order. Where there is no life, there is no possibility of faith and repentance in response to the summons of the gospel. For the regenerate who can hear, effectual calling makes the Word of God to be spirit and life.

The Word is not thereby creating anything new, but merely bringing to light what is already there. The Word acquaints the regenerated person with the new life that the Holy Spirit bestows upon him. The Word itself is not a seed of regeneration, as others claim with an appeal to 1 Peter 1:23, but the Word merely makes the seed of regeneration, that first seed of the new life, develop. Under the moistening dew of the Holy Spirit, the Word cultivates new life unto deeds of faith and repentance, makes this new life self-aware, and makes it bear fruit unto the glory of the Lord's name. The Word serves to make manifest those who are regenerated, both unto themselves and unto others.

Among the human race, therefore, the dividing line runs not between believers and unbelievers, since many regenerated persons can live for years in unbelief, but it runs between the regenerate and the unregenerate. Here on earth it is not faith, but regeneration that draws the line properly between the elect and the reprobate portions of humanity.

Both segments exist sharply alongside and over against each other. From regenerated humanity proceed another awareness, another insight, another perspective and evaluation of all things, another art and science.[9] For what has been implanted in the regenerate as a seed gradually surfaces within their consciousness. Even as faith and repentance develop from regeneration, so too the new life manifests itself gradually in its proper character and nature in every domain of human knowledge and activity. The regenerated person feels a different content impinging upon his consciousness. He sees and thinks and acts differently than the unregenerate, because he shares a different life.

---

[9] Ed. note: See, for example, Abraham Kuyper's *Encyclopedia of Sacred Theology*, trans. J. Hendrik De Vries, with an introduction by Benjamin B. Warfield (New York: Charles Scribner's Sons, 1898), § 49, pp. 155–176.

1.2.4 *The church as organism*

Therefore, finally, according to this formulation of the doctrine, the church as organism precedes the church as institution. The church as organism consists of reborn people who manifest their new life throughout the entire broad terrain of creation, in family, state, and society, or in science and art, and the like. Thus the church as institution is absolutely not the *whole* manifestation of the new life of the regenerate; rather, it occupies a very modest place that is limited on every side. It does not stand above family, society, and state, but among and alongside them, with a temporary, transitory, and clearly defined task.

That task consists in this: equipped by God with the means of grace, the church as institute transforms, under the operation of the Holy Spirit, the life of regeneration into deeds of faith and repentance. It presupposes the church as organism, which is regeneration, which is worked by the Holy Spirit apart from the Word before the heart is aware and which is therefore already presupposed at baptism. The church as institute calls the regenerate, who can now hear, unto faith and repentance.

As institute, thus, the church focuses upon only the regenerate. There is indeed an external call to the unregenerate, but this serves only to remove from them any excuse. The internal, effectual calling, which is paired with the external calling, is directed only to the regenerate. To these their calling is made known together with salvation, in which they share already from eternity; to the others, the church as institute merely declares judgment.

1.3 Three Key Questions

To distinguish is to learn. In the discussion of the doctrine of immediate regeneration it is of highest importance to take this seriously to heart. To neglect this entangles one in various difficulties and brings others into confusion, rather than clarifying their insight.

In connection with this doctrine, three questions need to be kept distinct.

First, in what manner does the Holy Spirit work within the human heart? Does He remain outside at a distance, and does He work in the human heart merely along those ordinary pathways to which we are bound in our interaction with other people, along the paths of understanding and volition, by word and example? Or does the Holy Spirit descend into the human heart such that nothing stands between Him and the inner being of the human person, and does He work within a person directly and irresistibly?

From this first question a second is to be distinguished. If the latter is the case, namely, if the Holy Spirit is present within a person immediately and performs His work directly, does not this direct operation exclude the use of means? If the operation of the Holy Spirit within the heart is immediate, does that not entail the claim that the use of means is superfluous, unprofitable, yes, even mistaken and detrimental?

Finally, a third question arises: If the immediate operation of the Holy Spirit in the human heart does not make the use of means superfluous or detrimental, how must we conceive of the connection that exists between the immediate operation of the Spirit and the function of the means?

The answer to the first question draws the boundary between those who confess sovereign grace and those who defend free will. The answer to the second question distinguishes those who maintain the power of the means of grace, from all so-called enthusiasts who consider the means of grace superfluous or denigrate them to empty signs. And the answer to the third question distinguishes between the Reformed on the one hand, and on the other hand the Roman Catholics, Lutherans, and others who restrict grace to, and confine it within, the means of Word or sacrament. The combination of the threefold answer assures the confessors of the Reformed religion a unique, distinct place among the churches of Christendom.[10]

---

[10] Ed. note: Bavinck takes up and answers the first question in chapters 2 and 3 (pages 13–29); the second question in chapters 4–12 (pages 33–128); and the last question in chapters 13–16 (pages 131–167).

PART II

THE IMMEDIATE OPERATION
OF THE HOLY SPIRIT

2

Differing Conceptions of Divine Grace

THE FIRST question mentioned at the end of the last chapter arose within the Christian church during the conflict between Augustine and Pelagius.

2.1 Augustine versus Pelagius

The latter taught that Adam's transgression had no consequences for his posterity other than simply providing a bad example. All people were subjected to guilt and pollution not by nature but by their own sinful action. They were not dead and not even weakened by sins and trespasses, but could, if they willed, furnish themselves unto virtue and keep the law. Since, however, the sinful environment in which people lived had such a great influence upon them that it darkened their understanding and weakened their will, there was need of an external grace from the outside, which would assist them in keeping the law. That external grace consisted in the preaching of the natural law among pagans, of the moral law among Israel, and of the gospel among Christians. So this grace was and remained entirely objective; it was not absolutely necessary, nor did it consist in a recreation or renewal of the person, but it was merely an external and incidental means of assistance coming from the outside in order to make it easier for the person to fulfill the law and obtain salvation. There was thus no place in the system of Pelagius for an internal, regenerating, recreating grace.

Before Pelagius appeared with his teaching, however, Augustine had already come to an entirely different opinion regarding grace, through his study of Holy Scripture and in connection with his own life experience. Especially Paul's question in 1 Corinthians 4:7—"For who sees anything different in you? What do you have that you did not receive?"—showed him the way with regard to this doctrine of grace.

According to Augustine, as a consequence of Adam's transgression, man was dead in sins and trespasses; and therefore an external, helping grace was not adequate for his salvation. Augustine did indeed refer to the external benefits, such as the proclamation of the Word and the administration of the sacraments, with the term "grace." But this grace is not sufficient. Another, internal grace, a grace of the Holy Spirit, must also come along to regenerate a person and move a person to faith.

This grace does not consist, then, in that it comes to us only externally, didactically, and admonishingly, offering us help and support for believing in Christ and fulfilling His commands. But it is an internal grace, a secret in-breathing (inspiration) of God, a bestowing of faith and love through the Holy Spirit, a communication of power that enlightens the understanding, bends the will, and creates within us all good. It is distributed not according to any merit, but purely according to God's mercy, out of pure grace, and it works irrefutably, invincibly, irresistibly. This grace precedes every good work, prepares and accomplishes every good work in us, and creates in us first of all the capacity, the willing, in order only then as cooperating grace to bring about in us the doing itself. It supplies us the capacity to believe and to love, but then also makes us actually believe and love. Through grace, the intellect loses its blindness and the will its weakness. In this way human capacities are not suppressed or destroyed through grace, but rather restored to their original power and purity.

Now Augustine frequently calls this grace an internal, secret, effectual, creating grace, but never, as far as I know, an immediate grace. Nevertheless, there is no doubt about whether he conceived of this operation of grace in the sinner's heart as working immediately—but then always when the meaning of this expression is properly understood. Augustine absolutely did not mean that this grace works apart from the institution of the church, outside of the administration of Word and sacrament. On the contrary, he connected the operation of grace as closely as possible to the one, holy, catholic church. For Augustine, however, the operation of grace is immediate in the sense that grace, paired unmixed with the means of grace, nonetheless works immediately within the human heart apart from anything coming to stand between the operation of the Holy Spirit and the fruit of that operation, namely, the renewing of the human heart.

That appears in general already from his doctrine of God's omnipresence. For this was not understood by Augustine in such a way that God with His being is confined to heaven, from there to behold and direct all things at a distance. Rather, as one who is infinitely exalted above every creature, God is nonetheless with His being immediately present in every creature. He is entirely in heaven and entirely on earth and entirely in both and in everything that exists. He is neither confined by nor excluded from anything. He Himself is everywhere entirely. There is an essential difference between the being of God and the being of His creatures. Nevertheless, He is immediately present in all things, with His entire being. In Him we live and move and have our being. He Himself supports all things directly by the word of His power.

Corresponding to this, Augustine taught with respect to the realm of spiritual life, that God with His Spirit is immediately present and works in the hearts of His elect, whom He calls to life. For the grace through which life is poured into the dead sinner may be paired with external means; grace itself penetrates the heart, and is dependent upon no human rational insight or human act of free will, but works irrefutably and irresistibly. It advises in such a way that it persuades. Grace comes to man, who does not will, in such a way that he does will. It works apart from us, apart from our consent, apart from our will, so that we will. When it has worked such that we will, it continues to work along with us, and turns capacity into activity, and turns willing into doing.

Understood in this sense, the doctrine of immediately-working grace is the characteristic feature of all anti-Pelagian theology.

Augustine's teaching on internal, irresistible grace was never condemned in the Roman Catholic Church, but it was nevertheless gradually weakened and altered.

2.2 Semi-Pelagianism

In contrast to Pelagianism, which ascribed the beginning and continuation of faith to human will, Rome taught the need of a prior and prevenient grace. It is hardly clear, however, what must be understood by prevenient grace. The church's confessions speak in vague terms, capable of various interpretations; and Roman Catholic theologians diverge significantly in describing this prevenient grace.

Some identify it with the external call that comes to all people in the gospel. Others think of an internal operation of the Holy Spirit upon the human understanding and will. There are even those who definitely view it as a gracious assistance, as an internal, supernatural gift whereby God enlightens the understanding and, as some expressly say, moves the human will *immediately* unto believing.

In any case the official doctrine of Rome firmly teaches that such prevenient grace can be not only accepted but also refused and rejected by a person. So even though prevenient grace may bestow the capacity to believe, it does not bestow faith itself. It does not work both the willing and the doing according to God's good pleasure. Between its working and genuine believing such grace inserts the free will of man who accepts it and cooperates with it, but can also refuse and reject it. Prevenient grace is not creating, irresistible grace that works alone, and in this sense it is not immediate grace. In its operation, it is dependent on human will.

2.3 The Reformed versus Semi-Pelagianism

The Reformation opposed this semi-Pelagianism. Originally there were no differences among the Reformers in this opposition. Later, however, the Lutherans retraced their steps and once again made the works of grace dependent upon human will. For they claimed in general that covenant children in baptism, or adults under the administration of the Word, received sufficient power in order not to resist God's grace in Christ and thereby, if they willed, to believe. If they are willing, they are brought to repentance through the preaching of the law and to regeneration through the preaching of the gospel. Here, then, regeneration was conceived as being dependent on human will, on a person's accepting prevenient grace. Grace is not immediate and not irresistible.

The Reformed, however, judged differently. They returned to the teaching of Paul and of Augustine, and persevered in that understanding despite all argument and opposition. With respect to the order of the benefits of salvation, they proceeded from the straightforward idea that there is no fellowship in the benefits of Christ apart from prior fellowship in the person of Christ. All the benefits of the covenant of grace come to the elect from Christ, even the preparatory benefits of repentance and faith, which lead further to the forgiveness of sins, to sanctification, to salvation, and to glorification.[1]

If this was so, then the bestowing of Christ to the elect and the mystical union of Christ and the elect must have preceded the gift of all other benefits. This was taught by all the Reformed since Calvin. The granting of the elect to Christ and their union with Him occurred already from eternity, in the decree. It is confirmed in the promises of the gospel from Genesis 3:15 on, and has been realized objectively in history as before our eyes, in the incarnation, crucifixion, and resurrection of Christ. For at that time Christ took our nature, crucified us with Himself, and raised and glorified His entire church along with Himself. But this objective union with Christ is not enough; it must also be brought about subjectively. Acquiring salvation comes first, but it ought still to be followed by its application. So the question arose: How does this subjective application of the benefits of the covenant begin? When does the union between Christ and the elect come into existence subjectively, from the human side and within a person?

At first there was a very significant difference of opinion on this question among the Reformed, to the extent that the initial moment in the application of salvation was identified by quite different terms. Everyone saw the external call through the gospel as the beginning point. But this comes to elect and reprobate alike, and does not decide the question as to when and whereby the application of salvation has its beginning in the elect. So people saw this application of the benefits of the covenant as beginning with the internal call, with repentance, with faith, with conversion, with regeneration, with effectual grace, etc.

---

[1] Ed. note: This is a significant passage in Bavinck's work, confirmed also in his *Reformed Dogmatics*, III, 228–32, 469–70, 494, 510, 580, and shows how he safeguards sovereign grace and divine election in connection with a standard Reformed doctrine of the covenant of grace.

Wide diversity obtained, thus, in the use of words whereby the initial beginning of the application of the benefits of salvation was identified. In terms of *substance*, there was nevertheless complete agreement. All of the Reformed confessed that the beginning could not rest with the human person, but only with God. For the person was by nature incapable of any good and inclined toward all evil. Discrimination among the human race could not possibly be explained from the person, discrimination which in the light of Scripture and experience repeatedly came to be observed in the fruit and outworking of the call. People cannot discriminate themselves, for they were all alike dead in sins and trespasses. But God discriminated among them, according to His eternal good pleasure and by the power of His grace.

In this way God was and remained the initiator in the entire work of salvation—not only for the acquiring, but also for the applying—and the human person was receptive and passive. He could function actively, that is, believe and be converted, only at the point where, by God's recreating, effectual, irresistible grace, he had received the power for, and was made capable of, faith and repentance.

2.4 The Proper Sense of Immediate Regeneration

The Reformed agreed with the confession of Augustine regarding the internal, hidden, effectual grace—though they did not all follow the same line of reasoning. Among the elect of the Lord this grace is paired in the Lord's time with the external call, penetrates the heart, and there plants the principle of the new life, where it works faith and repentance.

Although in the gospel, grace is coupled with the external call, such grace is not confined to the word of the gospel, but penetrates the human heart, affects as it were the human person immediately in his most hidden essence, and renews him in principle according to the image of God apart from his knowing and willing. It is absolutely independent of any consent of one's intellect or of any act of one's free will. Between this operation of grace and the human person who is reborn, there is nothing, no word, no sacrament, no church or priest, no act of cognition or will. Within the heart of the elect the Holy Spirit works the grace of regeneration (faith, repentance, or whatever one might call this first moment) directly and immediately, as well as irresistibly.

It may be considered superfluous to adduce proofs for this from Reformed theology. Anyone can find such proofs regarding the internal call among every Reformed writer and in every Reformed symbol. Of course, the internal call or regeneration or the gift of faith are seldom termed immediate. Almost without exception people are of a mind to describe it as effectual, irresistible, and rather gentle. Nevertheless there is not the least doubt, however, that this grace, which implants the very first principle of the new life within the sinner's heart, may *in this sense* be termed immediate, to the extent that whether or not coupled

with the Word, it works within the person directly, without an interme-
diary and without being dependent upon a person's intellectual agreement or act of free will.

Calvin puts it so correctly and beautifully this way: God does not (as
has been long taught and believed for many centuries) move our will in
such a way that it would remain a matter of our choice to obey or to resist
this impulse, but in such a way that He effectually moves and bends our
will. He works the willing within us, which is to say nothing else than that
through His Spirit the Lord guides, bends, and directs our heart, and
therein exercises lordship as if it were His own domain. The intermediate
motion (*motus medius*), whereby it would supposedly be up to us
whether or not to obey, is thus excluded by the effectual establishment of
perseverance (*Institutes* II.iii.10).

Therefore Dr. Kuyper defined the principle and essence of Calvinism
with this formulation: Calvinism seeks God not *within* the creature, as
with paganism; Calvinism does not isolate God *from* the creature, as with
Islam; Calvinism posits *between* God and the creature no mediated fellowship, as with Rome; rather, Calvinism proclaims the exalted idea that
God who stands high in majesty above every creature, nevertheless,
through His Holy Spirit exercises *immediate* fellowship with that creature. This also belongs to the heart and core of the Calvinist confession of
predestination: fellowship with God, unto eternity—which is to say, thoroughly imbued with His counsel of decree. There is no other kind of grace
than that which comes to us directly from God. And every moment of life,
our entire spiritual existence, is borne by God Himself. Every child of
God experiences direct fellowship with Him, and serves Him in his entire
existence.

3

The Reformed Defense of Divine Grace against the Remonstrants

3.1 The Reformed versus the Remonstrants

THIS DOCTRINE of the immediate operation of the Holy Spirit in the heart of the sinner who is made capable of being regenerated and accepting Christ and all His benefits in faith, was forcefully maintained and developed more broadly by the Reformed in the Netherlands in their conflict with the Remonstrants.[1]

3.1.1 *The revival of the semi-Pelagian error*

Arminius and his followers fell back into the error of semi-Pelagianism and made the operation of grace dependent upon the human will. Already in his claims regarding predestination, published on February 7, 1604, Arminius taught that God, who is not only a righteous Judge but also a loving Father, had from eternity made this distinction within the fallen human race, namely, that God would pardon the sins of, and bestow eternal life upon, those who turn away from their sins and place their trust in Christ, but He would punish the hardhearted; and further,

---

[1] Ed. note: Naturally, Bavinck is here referring to the controversy that raged in the Netherlands which gave rise to the National Synod of Dordrecht (1618–19), wherein the five doctrinal grievances of the Remonstrants were adjudicated, namely, conditional election, non-penal substitutionary atonement, mitigated human depravity, resistible grace, and cooperative perseverance. As such, "Remonstrants" is a name given to the adherents of the theological views of Arminius after his death, from the "Remonstrance" or grievance which was composed in 1610 as an exposition and vindication of their views. Most likely written by Jan Uytenbogaert, the remonstrance was addressed to the States of Holland. For their part, besides the five points under dispute, the Remonstrants pleaded academic freedom and a free investigation of the Bible unhampered by tight subscription to confessional symbols.

that it was pleasing to God that all people be converted and, having come to a knowledge of the truth, continue therein, but He compelled no one.

At the 1611 conference in The Hague, the Remonstrants did say that a person does not acquire saving faith on his own nor by virtue of his free will, but that it is necessary that he be reborn and renewed in understanding, disposition, and will by God in Christ through His Holy Spirit, such that the grace of God constitutes the principle, the progress, and the perfection of all good.

But they turned all of this upside down by adding that the way this grace works is not irresistible, and they were compelled to explain how it was that the human will does not work alongside grace but nevertheless, enabled by grace, renders itself capable of faith and repentance or of refusing and rejecting the grace received.

In this very trajectory they then also explained at the Synod of Dort that the effectual grace whereby a person is converted is not irresistible; and although God does move the will by means of the Word and the internal operation of His Spirit, He both supplies the power to believe or requisite supernatural powers, and also indeed causes a person to believe; nevertheless, a person on his own can despise this grace and not believe, and in this way can, as a consequence, be lost through his own fault.

They clarified their opinions still further with this explanation: Although, according to the entirely free will of God, the inequity of divine grace may be very great, nevertheless, the Holy Spirit gives or is prepared to give as much grace to one and all alike, to whom God's Word is preached, as is sufficient for advancing the conversion of people in various stages. In that regard, not only do those whom God had declared, according to His decree of absolute election, to be willing to save, receive grace sufficient unto faith and repentance, but also those who are not actually converted receive sufficient grace.

This explanation leaves nothing unclear. According to the sentiment of the Remonstrants, all who live under the gospel receive or can receive grace sufficient unto faith and repentance. But whether they eventually believe and are converted depends upon human will. The grace of the Holy Spirit is thus dependent upon the person; his consent, his free decision of the will, stands between grace and its operation. Thereby the Remonstrants denied the internal, effectual, irresistible grace of the Holy Spirit that works alone—in other words, the immediate and directly working grace of the Holy Spirit, and they accepted only a moral, advisory grace.

This may be confirmed abundantly with a citation from Episcopius, since here he employs the word *immediately*.[2] In his forty-sixth theologi-

---

[2] Ed. note: Simon Episcopius (1583–1643) was a very influential Arminian or Remonstrant theologian, who, among others, represented the Arminian cause at the Synod of

cal disputation he concludes with the question: Whether any *immediate* activity of the Holy Spirit upon the human intellect or will is required, or whether it is promised in Scripture that someone can believe simply on the basis of the externally preached Word?

To this question he provides a *negative* answer. Even if such activity might be present, it is nevertheless not required; in any case, a person remains free to resist such activity.

3.1.2 *Dort's rejection of Remonstrant errors*

This Remonstrant sentiment was rejected at the Synod of Dort. Over against that claim, Reformed Christians in those days argued that, since by nature man is dead in sins and trespasses, in applying the benefits of the covenant God must be the primary Agent who by His grace operating within a person brings about not only the capacity to believe, but also the believing itself.

The decisions of the Synod which record the Reformed teaching on this important point are familiar, and for our purpose need to be recalled merely with a few words.

First, the fathers of Dort declare in this regard that faith and repentance are not to be ascribed to the person, as if by an exercise of one's free will a person can distinguish himself from others who with equal or like sufficient grace were supplied unto faith and repentance. Rather, faith and repentance are to be ascribed to God who, even as He has chosen His own in Christ from eternity, so also these same persons He calls effectually within time, bestowing upon them faith and repentance and, having plucked them from the power of darkness, transfers them into the kingdom of His Son [Canons of Dort, II, art. 7].

Secondly, the fathers of Dort confess that when God executes this His good pleasure within the elect, He not only causes the gospel to be preached externally to them, such that the Holy Spirit effectually enlightens their understanding, but through the external power of the same regenerating Spirit He also penetrates the innermost recesses of a person, opens their closed hearts, renders what is hard to be soft, circumcises the uncircumcised, infuses new capacities into the human will, and makes those who were dead to be alive, those who were evil to be good, those who were unwilling to be compliant, and those who were stubborn to be submissive [Canons of Dort, III–IV, art. 10, 11].

Furthermore, they describe this operation of God's Spirit further with the terms *regeneration, renewal, new creation, resurrection from the dead*, and *making alive*. They also declare that apart from us, God works all of these within us. For this does not occur by means of moral advice, whereby it would remain within human power whether or not to

Dordrecht (1618-19). He wrote a thorough exposition of Arminian theology in four volumes, *Institutiones theologicae* (1650–51).

be regenerated, whether or not to be converted. Rather, it is an entirely supernatural, omnipotent, and at the same time fully intimate, wonderful, and inexpressible operation; in its excellence it is to be esteemed neither less nor lower than the creation of the world or the resurrection of the dead [Canons of Dort, III–IV, art. 12].

Finally, from all of this they formulated the decision that everyone in whose heart God works in such a miraculous manner, is certainly, infallibly, and effectually regenerated and actually believes. To that extent faith is a gift of God, not in the sense that it is offered by God to man's free will, but it is actually bestowed, breathed in, and infused within a person. In addition, faith is a gift of God not in the sense that God grants merely the capacity to believe, whereas the consent or act of believing would subsequently accord with the person's free will; but it is a gift of God in this way, that God actualizes within a person both the will to believe and believing itself. It is God alone who works both the willing and the doing, and is thus all in all [Canons of Dort, III–IV, art. 14].

This is the judgment that the Synod of Dort rendered against the sentiments of the Remonstrants. A prevenient, moral, advisory grace is inadequate for bringing a person to faith and repentance. By means of the power that the Word exercises, an other, internal, secret operation of the Holy Spirit must come alongside, which in the first place bestows the capacity for faith and repentance and thereafter in the second place causes that capacity to be realized with infallible certainty in the act of faith and repentance.

This operation of the Holy Spirit is described by the Synod of Dort, just as by the various foreign and national delegates in their judgments, in assorted ways. It is called an internal, hidden, secret, powerful, effectual, supernatural, almighty, insurmountable, irresistible, gracious, lovely grace [Canons of Dort, III–IV, art. 12].

But the phrase *immediate grace* or *immediate regeneration* is not used. It was described this way, as we shall see later, by several Reformed theologians. When properly understood, this description is not to be rejected. But it was perhaps intentionally avoided by the Synod of Dort and by many theologians because it easily occasions misunderstanding and could be thought to support a Remonstrant objection that we will identify later.

Nevertheless, it is certain that according to Reformed teaching, the Holy Spirit brings about regeneration and faith not in such a way that He remains limited to working through the means of grace [Canons of Dort, III–IV, art. 17]. On the contrary, He penetrates to the innermost recesses of the human heart; He opens the closed heart; apart from us He works within us to make us alive; with His divine power He even dwells within a person and infuses new dispositions of intellect, will, and inclinations, such that the darkness, the obduracy and dissoluteness disappear, replaced by illumination, willingness, and righteousness [Canons of Dort, III–IV, art. 11].

3.2 The Internal and Invincible Grace of the Holy Spirit as the Way of Salvation

Different answers may be given to the question whether one can, without being misunderstood, call this operation of the Spirit an immediate operation. Concerning the matter itself, there is no difference of sentiment. This touches upon the heart of Reformed theology, the very core of Holy Scripture in its teaching concerning the application of salvation.

Although the matter itself is clear, we may nevertheless devote a few words to indicate the deep significance involved in the Reformed teaching concerning the internal and invincible grace of the Holy Spirit.

In the first place, this involves *a soteriological interest*. This means that the entire work of salvation, both in its acquisition and application, is intimately involved in this doctrine of grace. For everyone can see immediately that if a moral, advisory grace is adequate for human regeneration, then the entire biblical teaching concerning sin is affected, and along with it the entire doctrine of salvation as this, according to Scripture, has been acquired by Christ and is applied.

At first the Remonstrants presented a friendly enough face. The third and fourth articles that they submitted at the conference in The Hague and at the Synod of Dort appeared rather innocent. They declared that a person does not possess saving faith in himself or by virtue of his free will; that he must be regenerated and renewed by God in Christ through His Holy Spirit in understanding, inclinations, will, and in all his powers; and that the grace of God is the principle, progress, and perfection of everything good.

The poison, however, appeared to have been hidden within their starting point. At the end of the fourth article they said that the operation of this grace was not irresistible. Thereby the Remonstrants made it appear as if their objection applied merely to the term *irresistible*. But this was all the more dishonest because that term was not at all genuinely desired by the Reformed, and occasionally even rejected and preferably replaced with the term *invincible*. Moreover, it was particularly the Remonstrants who imposed this term—borrowed from the Jesuits—upon the Reformed.

Nevertheless, their sentiments gradually became more evident. According to them divine grace was certainly necessary. That grace consisted, however, merely in a moral advice supplied by the Word of God. At the conference in The Hague they expressed it this way: we believe on the basis of God's Word that God's Spirit performs no other power in repentance than through the Word (*per verbum*), because the Word is the only seed of regeneration.

With this the entire biblical doctrine of sin was jeopardized. For if an advisory grace is adequate, if a person is not dead in sins and trespasses, if his understanding may be in some sense darkened and his will in some sense weakened, then his freedom and power to accept the gospel cannot be denied. The Remonstrants did agree to the former, as though that power was offered and bestowed by the Holy Spirit to all who live under the gospel. But that power appeared in fact to be nothing more than the preaching of the gospel itself. Thus they later declared straightforwardly that each person, as long as he employed his reason, apart from any special, immediate, or inward illumination, can easily understand the meaning of the Holy Spirit which is required for salvation, for believing, and for acting.

But if a person is not dead in sins and trespasses, then the character of the work of salvation is entirely changed. Christ may then have acquired the possibility of salvation, but salvation itself is not His work. All of His priestly office becomes superfluous and falls away; there is no longer any place for His sacrifice. It is sufficient that He was a prophet who proclaimed the truth and, by means of that preaching, arouses a person to faith and repentance, so that along this route a person himself acquires salvation.

For many, this Remonstrant pathway seems to create the possibility of heavenly redemption. In fact, however, it removes this possibility for thousands and for millions. For if, as was said at the conference in The Hague, the Word of God is the only seed of regeneration, then every infant dying in infancy, everyone who is mentally impaired, and everyone suffering from mental incapacity is excluded from salvation. Even worse, one is compelled to contradict Scripture in its simple declaration that Christ is the way, the truth, and the life, that no one can come to the Father except through Him, and that no other name is given under heaven whereby men are to be saved than the name of Jesus alone.

3.3 The Internal Grace of the Holy Spirit and God's Relationship to the Creation

In this way the Remonstrant denial of internal grace cuts deeply into the entire confession of Christian truth. But it also involves a second theological concern, namely, that *the relationship between God and His creature* in general is entirely altered. For if God's Spirit cannot dwell within a person, but must remain outside of him and can work upon him only from the outside through the Word, then such a teaching accepts in principle a manner of God relating to the world that is directly contradicted by Holy Scripture.

For certainly our God dwells in heaven and does all that pleases Him. Unlike the teaching of pantheism, God is not confined within the world nor is He identical to its substance. An infinite distance exists between God and His creation. That distance is infinite, however, not in quantity but in quality, not in terms of space but in terms of nature and essence. For even though God dwells in heaven in the sense that He reveals Himself there in an entirely special manner, nevertheless with His being He is everywhere present, upon earth and in hell, in man and beast, in matter and spirit. The heaven of heavens cannot contain Him. He supports everything by the word of His power. In Him we live, we move, and have our being. He is not far removed from any of us. His providence is an almighty and everywhere present power whereby He maintains and governs all things.

The providence of God in this biblical, Reformed sense cannot be maintained from the standpoint of those who oppose internal grace. Their God is a God at a distance. He lives at an immeasurable, endless distance from the world. There is always something standing between Him and the innermost being of His creatures. Although He is acknowledged as the creator, this idea is construed in such a way that once the world had been created, God left the creation to itself. He equipped the creation with power sufficient for its own development, power that is not only natural but also intellectual and moral, religious and spiritual. At best He needs to intervene from the outside only now and then in order to put things right and tidy things up again whenever the world is in danger of falling apart in one way or another. For the rest, the world runs like a machine, like a clock. In this view, revelation, prophecy, and miracle are altogether foreign elements, which for that reason are restricted as much as possible and ultimately rejected, since they are entirely superfluous or even detrimental and unworthy of God. Deism leads to rationalism and moralism.

3.4 The Internal Grace of the Holy Spirit as a Religious-Covenantal Issue

Finally, there is also *a deep religious interest* at stake in this denial of internal grace. For according to its essence, religion is nothing less than fellowship with God, the most deep, inward, and tender fellowship that can be imagined and understood second only to the fellowship between the three persons of the Godhead and the fellowship between the two natures of Christ. That is what Scripture expresses in its beautiful doctrine of the covenant. For the covenant refers to that act of God whereby God places man as His image in relationship to Himself and causes him to dwell continually in His fellowship. That fellowship is more intimate and tender than the fellowship between husband and wife, between the vine and its branches, between a foundation and its superstructure. Scripture can hardly find words or metaphors sufficiently powerful and clear to make us understand something of that fellowship.

The view that teaches that grace is merely moral, however, knows nothing of that kind of religion. It has no place for a covenant, but only for a contract, such as that between a master and his servant. God is the master who gives commands and precepts, and man is His slave who relates to Him in terms of wages, who lays claim upon God for a wage in proportion to the work he renders. This is the religion of the Pharisee, especially suited for the self-righteous and for salvation by works, without comfort and compassion for tax collectors and sinners, for the penitent Mary Magdalenes and for the weeping Peters of the world.

History has placed its seal upon the decisions of the Synod of Dort. The doctrine of the Remonstrants, at first glance so moderate and sweet, paved the way for rationalism and deism, for the disappearance and dying away of all religion.[3]

Consequently, all genuine religion everywhere and always, in every land and every church, has returned to Calvin, to Augustine, to Paul and John, to Holy Scripture.

The human heart has been created for God and does not rest until it finds rest in His Father-heart. A God who dwells at a distance is no God who satisfies the needs of our heart. In Him we must live, move, and have our being.

That is maintained in the doctrine of internal, invincible grace. For therein we confess that God Himself with His Spirit comes to make His dwelling in us, and places us within a covenant fellowship which knows no abandonment or alteration.

Just as Jesus says: in order that they all may be one, even as you, Father, in me and I in you, that they also may be in us, so that the world may believe that you have sent me [John 17:21–23].

3.5 Divine Sovereignty and Human Responsibility

Although there were weighty, religious interests involved in the doctrine of internal grace, nevertheless, the Reformed did not confess and defend such grace in the first place for those reasons and on the basis of such considerations. Rather, they were firmly convinced that the doctrine of the invincible grace of the Holy Spirit was revealed by God in His Word and was based upon Holy Scripture. Not a human line of reasoning and reflection, but the Word of God was the firm basis upon which they rested their confession, the staff upon which they leaned, and the light whereby they walked.

For investigating Scripture and for deepening the knowledge of the truth, the conflict with the Remonstrants was beneficial to no small degree. Already in an earlier era a more or less clear distinction had been

---

[3] Ed. note: Bavinck is referring to the subsequent deformation and degeneration of the Remonstrant position, or at least a large wing of it, wherein it became latitudinarian, succumbing to rationalism and liberalism. Initially, from 1618 till 1632 Remonstrants were forbidden to hold church services in Holland, so that many preachers were deposed from office and others were also exiled. Organizing into their own fellowship of churches, in 1619 they formed the Remonstrant Reformed Brotherhood, with Uytenbogaert and Episcopius assuming the leadership, and later changed the name to the Remonstrant Reformed Church. They founded a seminary at Amsterdam in 1634, after the period of exile. From 1634 till 1795, after the revolution, when the relations between Church and State were revised, the Remonstrants were tolerated in Holland but not officially recognized or supported by the State.

made, in terms of covenant children and in opposition to the Anabaptists, between the capacity for faith and the act of faith, between conversion in a passive sense and in an active sense, or in several instances even between regeneration and conversion.

But at that point in history, this distinction had not yet generally penetrated the Reformed consciousness, nor had it been taken up widely within the Reformed confessions and dogmatics. Concerning this distinction the Belgic Confession and the Heidelberg Catechism provide merely faint pointers. Often the description of the application of the benefits of salvation was begun with the doctrine of faith or of conversion.

Change came to this situation, however, in connection with the religious quarrels that occurred at the beginning of the seventeenth century. The Remonstrants realized this very clearly at the conference in The Hague, for example, when they pressured the Reformed to agree with their position. The Remonstrants themselves taught that, since no one believes without beforehand wanting to believe, therefore a person has the power either to come or not to come to faith, because he either still possesses that power by nature or receives such power through the preaching of the gospel. In one way or another, the will had to have been free in order (as they specifically put it) for a person to receive or not to receive the offered Spirit of regeneration. So the regeneration or renewal of the person begins with, and depends on, the consent of the person's will. Faith is not first infused as a capacity, but begins as a work and as a deed. The disposition of faith does not precede the actual believing, but is the fruit thereof and is acquired through continual exercise.

To support this opinion of theirs, the Remonstrants appealed to all those places where Scripture speaks of the general offer of grace and where a person is called unto faith and repentance. From His side, God had done everything there was to do for the salvation of the individual. He had designed and dug around His vineyard, cleared it of stones, and planted choice vines; and He now asks: What more shall I do for my vineyard that I have left undone (Isa. 5:1–4)?

So according to this portrayal, it depends entirely on the person, as to whether or not he wants to come to Christ (John 5:40), wants to listen to His Word (Jer. 7:26; Ezek. 12:2; Zech. 7:11; Matt. 13:14; Acts 28:26), wants to keep His commands (Ps. 78:56), and wants to resist the Holy Spirit (Isa. 63:10; Acts 7:51). The decision about faith and unbelief rests with the person and lies in his hand.

Moreover, there is no doubt that Scripture lays the responsibility for unbelief not with God but with the individual person. The Reformed churches that gathered at Dordrecht heartily confessed this teaching in this way: There are many who, having been called by the administration of the gospel, do not come and are not converted, the guilt for which lies neither in the gospel, nor in Christ who is offered in the gospel, nor in God who by the gospel calls and even bestows various gifts upon those whom He calls. Rather, such guilt lies with those who have been called, of whom some, having become careless, do not accept the word of life; others do accept it, but not with their heart of hearts and therefore, after the short-lived rejoicing of temporary faith, return again to their former state; others choke the seed of the Word with the thistles of the cares and desires of the world, and produce no fruit—all of which our Savior teaches in the parable of the seed in Matthew 13 [Canons of Dort, III–IV, art. 9].

So the Reformed position both must and can do full justice to those passages of Holy Scripture to which the Remonstrants appeal. Scripture may not be twisted, in terms of any of its formulations, to fit our system. Scripture places beyond all doubt that in the external call God offers the gospel to sinners without discrimination, and that the person who despises this call has only himself to blame for his unbelief and perdition. In the call of the gospel God comes to us along the moral pathway; He treats us not as stocks and blocks, but deals with us as rational creatures [Canons of Dort, III–IV, art. 16]. In the external call, God maintains His claim on a person. The sinner may well imagine that by sinning he becomes genuinely free and is released from service to God. But that is not true. God's claim upon the person remains inalienable and unimpeachable, no matter how deeply the person may fall. For that reason God calls a person continuously through nature and history, through law and gospel, so that the person may realize that he belongs by right to God and has been created and designed unto His service and honor.

Although Scripture clearly teaches all of this, however, and places the guilt for unbelief on the person, it does not stop there. For the call has quite a varied outcome among people. For some, Christ is the occasion for falling; for others, He is the occasion for rising. For the one, the gospel is an aroma of death unto death; for the other, a fragrance of life unto life. Whence comes this different outcome? How does it happen that whereas many harden themselves, others come to faith in Christ and find their redemption in Him?

The cause of that, according to the teaching of Scripture, cannot lie within the individual. For by nature all people are alike. They are all born in unrighteousness and in sin their mothers conceived them. The imagination of their hearts is evil from their youth, such that out of the heart proceed all manner of wicked thoughts and iniquities. Their understanding is darkened, so that they cannot see the kingdom of God and cannot understand the things of the Spirit of God. The thoughts of their flesh are enmity against God, such that these imaginations are not submissive to the law of God, nor can they be. All of them are bondservants to sin, condemnable before the face of God, and of themselves they can neither think anything good nor do anything good—something as impossible as an Ethiopian changing his skin or a leopard its spots (Jer. 13:23), or a bad tree producing good fruit.

Nevertheless, if the call results in a varied outcome, the cause thereof does not lie within the person. People do not differentiate themselves.

God is the only one who makes distinction according to His good pleasure. He does so in this manner, namely that those whom He has chosen in Christ from eternity He calls effectually within history, enlightens their understanding by the Holy Spirit, penetrates their heart of hearts with the effectual work of the same regenerating Spirit, opens the closed heart, infuses new capacities in the will and changes it from dead to living and from evil to good, so that like a good tree it can produce the fruits of good works.

For thus Scripture tells us that according to His promise the Lord will give His people a new heart of flesh and a new spirit, so that as a consequence they may know the Lord, love Him with their whole heart, be converted unto Him, fear Him, and not depart from Him, walking in His precepts and honoring His claims, as they perform them (Deut. 20:6; Ps. 51:12; Jer. 24:7; 31:33; 32:39–40; Ezek. 11:19; 36:26; etc.).

All of these and similar passages of Scripture were brought forward by the Reformed in order to counter the sentiments of the Remonstrants. Their error compelled the Reformed to search Scripture on this point more deeply than before, and to reflect with still more fervor than before on the truth entrusted to them.

God is the primary actor in the work of redemption. He gives a new heart, apart from any merit or condition having been achieved from our side, merely and only according to His good pleasure. He enlightens the understanding, bends the will, governs the impulses, regenerates, awakens, vivifies, and He does that within us quite apart from our doing. From our side there is nothing between this operation of God's Spirit within our hearts and the fruit thereof, which is termed *regeneration* in a narrow sense, or new creation, resurrection, vivification. No consent of our intellect, no decision of our will, no desire of our heart comes in between. God accomplishes this work within our hearts through His Spirit, and He does this directly, internally, and invincibly.

But when a person is thus renewed in intellect, heart, and will, having been moved by God, he then begins also to work. By the grace he has received, he believes and is converted, loves God, walks according to His precepts and keeps His commandments (Canons of Dort, III–IV, art. 12).

On the basis of Holy Scripture, the Synod of Dort made this distinction between regeneration and conversion (faith) the common property of the Reformed church and of Reformed theology.

PART III

THE IMMEDIATE OPERATION OF THE HOLY SPIRIT AND THE MEANS OF GRACE

4

Augustine and the Reformed on the Means of Grace

4.1 The Reformed versus the Remonstrants

FOR OUR purposes the first question raised earlier has been adequately answered in the preceding chapter.

4.1.1 *The first question answered*

On the basis of God's Word and in line with Augustine, the Reformed taught that the Word alone was insufficient for regenerating the sinner and bringing the sinner to faith and repentance. The Word had to be accompanied by an internal grace, by an operation of the Holy Spirit, in order to make alive once again the person who is dead in sins and transgressions.

That grace was described further in various ways. It was termed an internal, spiritual, supernatural, effectual, invincible, and irresistible grace. It was viewed as a divine power that, according to the word of Paul in Ephesians 1:19–20, was likened to the immense working of that power that God wrought in Christ when He raised Him from the dead and placed Him at His right hand in heaven.

Occasionally Reformed theologians also called this grace an *immediate* grace. But that term was used in opposition to the doctrine of the Pelagians and Remonstrants, who accepted merely a moral operation of the Spirit through the Word, inserted the person's will between this working and regeneration, and made regeneration dependent upon the consent of that will. So with the Remonstrants regeneration was always mediate *in this sense*: that it could occur only when a person gave prior consent.

In contrast, the Reformed occasionally said that the Holy Spirit worked in the human heart *immediately*. The grace of the Holy Spirit was not confined to the Word, nor did it operate merely through the Word, but along with and alongside the Word. With His divine power the Holy Spirit penetrated the innermost recesses of the human heart, and accomplished regeneration *in* the person while still doing so *apart from* the person.

4.1.2 *Consideration of the second question*[1]

With this phrase *immediate grace*, however, they never intended to exclude the means of grace of the Word in connection with regeneration, such that regeneration would come to stand over against repentance and faith, these latter two supposedly occurring mediately through the Word.

This will become clear for us as we turn now to answer the second question raised earlier, namely: If the Holy Spirit is immediately present and accomplishes His work directly within the person whom He desires to regenerate, does this direct operation then not exclude the use of the means of grace?[2] If the operation of the Spirit within the human heart bears an immediate character, does that not entail that the use of means of grace is superfluous, unprofitable, yes, even mistaken and detrimental?

The supposition contained within this question is significant. The answer given to this question determines the relationship between the Reformed teaching and all of those movements, such as, for example, the Baptists, who consider the means of grace superfluous or reduce them to empty signs, at least in connection with bringing a person from being dead in sin to being alive unto God. Moreover, the question has contemporary relevance because many today hold the view that the immediate operation of the Holy Spirit in regeneration constitutes a contrast with the mediate operation of the Holy Spirit in connection with faith and repentance.

---

[1] Ed. note: See pages 9–10, footnote 10.

[2] Ed. note: Regarding the Reformed conception of the means of grace, see among others, Henry Bullinger, *The Decades of Henry Bullinger*, ed. Thomas Harding (1849–52; repr. Grand Rapids: Reformed Heritage Books, 2004), I.2; V.3–10; John Calvin, *Institutes of the Christian Religion*, 2 vols., ed. John C. McNeill, trans. Ford Lewis Battles (Philadelphia: Westminster Press, 1960), vol. 2, book IV, chapters iii, xiv–xvii; Francis Turretin, *Institutes of Elenctic Theology*, ed. James T. Dennison, Jr., trans. George Musgrave Giger (Phillipsburg, New Jersey: P&R Publishing, 1992–1996), vol. 1, topic XIX; Charles Hodge, *Systematic Theology* (New York: Scribner, Armstrong and Co., 1871–72), 3: 466–709; William G. T. Shedd, *Dogmatic Theology,* 3 rd ed., ed. Alan W. Gomes ([1888–89] Phillipsburg, NJ: P&R, 2003), 809–827; Herman Bavinck, *Reformed Dogmatics*, 4: 443–585; W. Heyns, *Manual of Reformed Doctrine* (Grand Rapids: Eerdmans, 1926), 188–234; M. J. Bosma, *Exposition of Reformed Doctrine,* 5th ed. (Grand Rapids: Zondervan, 1927), 248–283; Henry Beets, *The Compendium Explained: A Popular Exposition of the Abridgement of the Heidelberg Catechism.*, 4th ed. (Grand Rapids: Eerdmans, 1941), 225–259; and Louis Berkhof, *Systematic Theology*, 604–658.

4.2 Augustine and the Means of Grace

Earlier we saw that the doctrine of internal, effectual grace was first taught and defended in the Christian church by Augustine. It was this same church father who first sensed the weight of the theological objection mentioned above and brought to light the connection between grace and the means of grace, defending this especially against the Donatists.[3]

4.2.1 *Augustine's doctrine of the church*

The consideration derived from the doctrine of Augustine, and used subsequently against his own position, went like this: If God is the only cause of salvation, who by the grace of the Holy Spirit leads the elect with infallible certainty unto faith and repentance, what room then remains for a church that, with its means of grace (as Rome later taught), is the indispensable mediator of salvation?

For Augustine, who was a member of the Catholic church, this consideration had been more significant than for the Reformers, who later rejected the Catholic notion of the church, since the doctrine of internal grace appeared to conflict directly with the Catholic view of the absolute necessity of the church and its means of grace.

In reality, then, Augustine's doctrine of the church contained elements directly influenced by his doctrine of grace, elements that are therefore quite similar to the Reformational view. Thus he distinguished between the true and pure body of the church that included only the elect, and the church as a mixed society of believers and unbelievers. To the true church belong those who, although they may still lead godless lives or are snared in unbelief and heresy, are nevertheless chosen by God and therefore will be brought to God at some time. On the other hand, there are many within the church who do not belong to the elect and will never share in salvation. There is chaff among the wheat; there are bad fish among the good; there are many sheep outside of the fold and many wolves within the sheepfold of the church of Christ. With regard to the fellowship of the sacraments, many are *with* the church who are nevertheless in reality not *in* the church.

---

[3] Ed. note: The Donatists were a separatist/schismatic movement in North Africa in the fourth century. They objected to the reinstatement of Christians who had surrendered the Scriptures and/or renounced faith in Christ during persecution. Augustine strongly opposed the tenets of Donatism, and argued that the validity of a sacrament does not depend upon the worthiness of the minister, and also that it is God's prerogative to truly know his own, the elect, which is the invisible church, to be distinguished from the visible church which is mixed with undetected hypocrites. See, for example, the Belgic Confession, art. 29, and the Second Helvetic Confession, XVII.16; XIX.3.

4.2.2 *Augustine on grace and the church*

No matter how well and beautifully Augustine has formulated all of this, and notwithstanding that subsequent Protestant theologians have often cited it with agreement, we may not for a moment draw the conclusion that Augustine, with his doctrine of grace, would have arrived at another notion of the church than what prevailed at that time. It would be closer to the truth to say that Augustine did not weaken but rather strengthened and confirmed the Roman Catholic notion of the church that had already begun to develop in his day.

From the time of his conversion, the church with its means of grace and treasures of salvation, with its expansive unity and broad catholicity, had made a deep impression upon Augustine. It was to the instrumentality of the church that Augustine owed his knowledge of the truth and his faith in the gospel. So later when he was compelled to defend the right and the truth of the Catholic Church against a Donatists, he at that point formulated, alongside his doctrine of grace, a doctrine of the church wherein he exalted the church as the dwelling and the domain of the Holy Spirit.

True enough, for Augustine the church could no longer be the dispenser of grace. For it was God who bestowed saving grace inwardly and secretly through the operation of the Holy Spirit. Nevertheless, for Augustine the church could still be, and in fact was, the sphere within which the Holy Spirit, with His grace, exclusively dwelt and worked. Outside of the church there was no salvation. Whoever refused the church as his mother could not have God as his Father.

It is true that Augustine acknowledged that heretics outside the church could still possess a large measure of the truth. They could still believe many truths; they could even participate in baptism and the ordinances. But they were nonetheless isolating these gifts from the church and holding them in a manner that was unlawful and impermissible, not as something to which they had a right but as something they had stolen. The benefits of that truth and of baptism could then also not accrue to them as blessing. Rather, these accrued to them only unto the deepening of their condemnation. Only when they returned in penitence to the one, holy, universal church, could they share that grace which led infallibly unto salvation.

For the church is the temple of the Holy Spirit. There He dwells with His grace; only there does He infuse love within the human heart, a love which supplements faith and binds the believer with God and Jesus Christ. Even though true faith and true love are by no means granted to every one who is in the church, it is nevertheless certain that outside the church no one comes unto salvation. Everyone who is saved is brought in the Lord's time into the church here upon earth and through the church is thus received into heavenly glory. For Augustine, church and priest and means of grace are not infallible guarantees of salvation, but they are nevertheless necessary prerequisite conditions of salvation.

Augustine did not leave the matter here, however. He paved the way especially for the Roman Catholic notion of the church when, in opposition to the Donatists, he retreated more and more to the notion of the church as an *institution*, and took refuge there. The Donatists registered many criticisms of the Catholic Church of those days; they went so far as to break fellowship and establish a church alongside the Catholic Church, which initially enjoyed wide acceptance. In that time the church was in many respects truly defective. Not only was there a widespread division concerning many points of doctrine, but the holiness of church members and especially of priests left much to be desired.

In order at this point to defend the Catholic Church as being nevertheless the one, true, holy, Christian church, Augustine moved away from thinking of the church as the fellowship of believers and focused on the church as the custodian of the means of grace. No matter how many defects and errors might have characterized the members of the church, the church itself in its entirety as an institution of redemption continued to be the bride of Christ without blemish or spot, His only dove, the dwelling of the Holy Spirit, the preserver of the treasures of salvation. Separating from the church was therefore never permissible. Any one who left the church thereby gave evidence of pride and disobedience, and surrendered the salvation of his soul.

When after Augustine the doctrine of internal grace was compromised in a semi-Pelagian sense, at that point the Roman Catholic notion of the church was thereby born, which elevated the church to the position of mediator of salvation, of preserver and dispenser of all grace for all people, the only ark of salvation for the entire human race. For in that church Christ continued through His Spirit to live as Prophet, Priest, and King, and to dispense all the gifts of grace. Those gifts of grace He dispenses exclusively by means of priest and sacrament. There is no fellowship with Christ other than through the mediation of the church as an institution, that is, through the priest who with the sacrament possesses control over grace. For grace descends on the sacrament, with which in one way or another it is inseparably connected. God does not dispense His grace internally and secretly by the operation of the Holy Spirit. But He entrusts grace to the priest, who bestows it in the sacrament. For that reason there is no salvation outside the Church, that is to say, apart from the priest and apart from the sacrament.

4.3 The Reformed on Grace and the Church

Between divine grace and the church with its sacraments, Rome had established such an indissoluble connection that for the person outside of the reach of these instruments there was no salvation to be obtained.

This connection was broken by the Reformation, or at least significantly modified. Indeed, there was no salvation outside the church, but this church did not coincide with the Roman Catholic Church but was equivalent to the catholic church that included every believer from all times and places. Salvation was indeed bound to the Word, but this Word does not work only when it is proclaimed by the minister in the ecclesiastical gatherings, but is also powerful when a person reads and studies the Word with a desire for salvation. The sacraments are indeed instruments for the strengthening of faith, but the thing signified is not confined within the sign and is not dispensed by the minister, but by God. A person is dependent for his salvation only upon God and His grace. For the Reformation, religion once again became direct fellowship with God.

4.4 Are the Means of Grace Needed?

Given this view, however, the question naturally arose once again: If God's grace is the sole direct cause of salvation, why then are the means of grace, the preaching of the Word and the administration of the sacraments, still necessary?

4.4.1 *The Anabaptist answer*

The one appears to exclude the other completely; and the mystical movements of those days, such as the Anabaptists, immediately drew the conclusion that the means of grace, if not detrimental, were nevertheless rather superfluous and useless. They viewed them as nothing other than external signs and symbolic actions, which set before the eyes only that which existed, but they could not bring into existence what was not there. For God alone, whether Christ in us, or the Spirit, or the internal word, or the inward light, or however else they termed the matter of regeneration, brought about new life within a person, the life of faith and repentance. Word and sacrament could do nothing else than provide an indication and symbol of that internal grace. The external, preached Word merely gave expression to what had been written internally upon the heart of the spiritual person; and the sacraments set before people's eyes merely that which Christ through His Spirit had bestowed internally upon believers.

4.4.2 *The Reformed answer*

The Reformed, however, could not agree with this. They were prevented in doing so by Holy Scripture which, although it teaches an internal grace, nevertheless binds as decisively as possible this salvation to faith, and faith to the hearing of the Word of God.

Accordingly, in their confession they declared that genuine faith, being wrought within a person by the hearing of the Word of God by the operation of the Holy Spirit, regenerates him and makes him a new person (Belgic Confession, Art. 24). They also confessed that the faith by which we are made to share in Christ and all His benefits comes from the Holy Spirit, who works it within our hearts through the preaching of the holy gospel and strengthens it through the use of the sacraments (Heidelberg Catechism, Lord's Day 25).

One could reply that both of these explanations from our confessions are in no way decisive with regard to the issue before us. For no one among us denies that Word and sacrament are means of grace for faith and conversion in a so-called "active" sense, or also for regeneration in the broader meaning of renewal and sanctification. There is no doubt that Article 24 of the Belgic Confession is dealing only with regeneration in a broader sense, and that in Lord's Day 25 the Heidelberg Catechism is thinking only of active, conscious faith, not of the capacity or disposition of faith. The question under discussion, however, is whether regeneration as the infusion of the first principle of the new life, and faith as capacity or disposition, are not accomplished by the Holy Spirit without and apart from the Word.

This consideration, however, takes nothing away from the powerful validity of the expressions cited above. For the distinction between regeneration and conversion, as that arose later, was still unknown in the days when the Belgic Confession and the Heidelberg Catechism were composed. This distinction existed then already in its preliminary form, but it was not clearly formulated by anyone. The confessions and the writings of theologians saw new life as beginning with repentance, faith, and conversion. No one posited a clear contrast between the beginning of new life as something accomplished only by the Holy Spirit *apart from* the Word, and the progress of the new life as something accomplished by the Holy Spirit *with* the Word.

When the Belgic Confession (Art. 24) and the Heidelberg Catechism (LD 25) say, therefore, that true faith is wrought in a person through the hearing of the Word of God and the operation of the Holy Spirit, at that point it is unmistakably clear that not only are they thinking of the development of spiritual life in deeds of faith and repentance, but they are including the new life in its entirety, from the point of its first beginning all the way to its highest development here on earth. The general, common understanding is that the very first beginning of spiritual life is accomplished by the Holy Spirit with the use of the word of the gospel.

Article 35 of the Belgic Confession puts the matter beyond all doubt. There we confess that our Savior Jesus Christ has ordained and instituted the sacrament of the Lord's Supper in order to nurture and to strengthen those whom He has already regenerated and has engrafted into His family, which is His church. Those who are regenerated have within themselves a twofold life, the one physical and temporal, which they received at their first birth and which is common to all people; the other spiritual and heavenly, which is given them in the second birth, which occurs through the Word of the gospel in the fellowship of the body of Christ, and this life is not common except only to those who are the elect of God.

From these words we see clearly that when it speaks of regeneration, the Belgic Confession at that point has in mind not only the progress and development, but also the beginning and the origin of spiritual life. For it declares that such spiritual life is *given* in the second birth, and that from the second birth this new life not only receives its development but also its beginning. Concerning this beginning of the new life in the second birth, the Belgic Confession acknowledges that this new life comes into existence *through the word of the gospel*. According to our confession the gospel is the means of grace in the hand of the Holy Spirit, not only in relation to faith and conversion in their active sense, but also in relation to regeneration in its narrower sense, in relation to the infusion of the very first principle of the new life.

This same idea is expressed in the Heidelberg Catechism. In Lord's Day 3 it is said only that we are entirely unable to do any good and inclined toward all evil unless we are regenerated by the Spirit of God. Whether or not the Holy Spirit uses the Word in that context is not mentioned. In Lord's Day 21, however, we read explicitly that the Son of God gathers, protects, and preserves a church for Himself *through His Spirit and Word*. The fact that here the Spirit is mentioned first is not to be understood as though the gathering of the church occurs only through the Spirit and without the Word, while the protecting and preserving of the church occurs through the Spirit in connection with the Word. For all three—the gathering as well as the protecting and preserving of the church—occur through Spirit and Word together. The Spirit occupies the first place here because He is the person acting as He makes use of the Word as His instrument and with that Word stands in service to the Son of God.

For this reason, when Lord's Day 25 says that faith makes us share in Christ and all His benefits, or when Lord's Day 7 describes faith as that instrument whereby we are engrafted into Christ and receive all His benefits, then the cause of this faith in its entirety, both in its passive and active senses, lies in the Holy Spirit who works it in our hearts through the proclamation of the holy gospel.

For these reasons the claim is incapable of contradiction that each of our earliest confessions place calling before regeneration within the order of salvation, and they understand the Word of God to be a means of grace not only for the maturing of spiritual life but also for the beginning of spiritual life.

5

Calling and Regeneration at the Synod of Dort

5.1 The Central Place of the Word

THE PRECEDING sketch might lead some to conclude that a later generation of Reformed theologians came to think differently about the relationship between calling and regeneration than the earlier Reformers who had formulated, for example, the Belgic Confession and the Heidelberg Catechism.

One might even be inclined to expect such a change in their position when one takes into account that at first virtually no distinction was made between regeneration (in the narrow sense) and conversion.

One might even suppose that when this distinction was eventually made and became part of Reformed theology, then it would be natural to portray the difference between regeneration and conversion in such a way that the former occurred through the Holy Spirit alone, immediately, and the latter was accomplished by the Holy Spirit mediately, that is, with and through the Word.

Anyone harboring this expectation, however, will be disappointed upon careful investigation of later Reformed theology. At no point did any Reformed theologian distinguish between and contrast regeneration and conversion in such a way that, in the Spirit's working, regeneration always occurred *apart from* the Word, whereas conversion always occurred *through* the Word.

This is all the more significant because when the Reformed confessed and maintained the doctrine of internal, effectual, and irresistible grace, they were accused by their opponents that this doctrine robbed the means of grace of all their power and rendered them superfluous. So the Reformed were compelled to reflect intentionally upon the connection between the Word as a means of grace and the gracious operations known as regeneration and conversion, and also to give a clear account of their position.

5.2 The Remonstrant Objection[1]

For the Remonstrants registered many serious objections against the doctrine of effectual and invincible grace. In opposition to that teaching they not only appealed to numerous passages in Holy Scripture, but they also attempted to argue that such a doctrine made people careless, took away from them all freedom and responsibility, introduced physical compulsion and pagan fatalism, and—to mention no more criticisms—it also made the preaching of the gospel superfluous and robbed the Word as a means of grace of all its power.

This last consideration especially occupies our attention here. It was formulated by the Remonstrants this way: if the Word is not sufficient unto conversion and is not the only seed of regeneration, but rather if a special, supernatural, almighty, irresistible power of the Holy Spirit must accompany the Word, then the Word becomes entirely superfluous and can well be omitted. The moral operation of the Word is then placed entirely in the shadow, yes, wholly suppressed, through the supernatural operation of the Spirit. Given that view, it is no longer even possible to maintain in any way whatsoever the preaching of the Word as a means of grace. For the moral operation of the Word is obviously of an entirely different nature than the supernatural operation of the Holy Spirit, and for that reason it cannot even function as means or instrument.

After all, the Remonstrants claimed, both of these claims contradict each other—on the one hand, that through a supernatural, irresistible power (and thus immediately), God accomplishes regeneration within the human heart; and on the other hand, that God nevertheless employs means in connection with regeneration. For in the nature of the case, an immediate operation excludes all means (*Immediata enim action medium excludit*).

5.3 The Reformed Response

It is of the highest importance, then, to apprehend how the Reformed responded to this Remonstrant objection. If the doctrine of immediate regeneration in that sense were conceded, namely, that it always occurs apart from and without the Word, simply and only through the Holy Spirit, then the Reformed could have sufficed by giving a simple answer. Then they could have said that the Remonstrants were right in their position; that indeed regeneration occurs as an immediate fruit of the operation of the Holy Spirit apart from and without the Word; that the Word does indeed function as the means unto faith and conversion, but not as the means for the infusion of the original principle of the new life.

---

[1] Ed. note: Concerning the Remonstrants, see page 19, footnote 1.

But the Reformed did *not* respond to the objection of the Remonstrants with this answer. On the contrary, they exerted great effort to maintain the Word also as the means of grace for the beginning of spiritual life, as the seed of regeneration.

Preeminent proof of this is the official formulation of the Synod of Dort. In various sections the Canons of Dort proceed without fanfare from the supposition that calling precedes regeneration, and that the Word is the means not only for maintaining and nurturing, but also for the begetting and the beginning of spiritual life (e.g., I, art. 16; III–IV, art. 6, 9, 10, 12). But in III–IV, art. 17 the Canons formulate the matter decisively and clearly. With language that leaves no doubt whatsoever concerning its convictions, the Synod there said:

> As the almighty operation of God whereby He brings forth and supports this our natural life does not exclude but require the use of means by which God, of His infinite mercy and goodness, has chosen to exert His influence, *so also the aforementioned supernatural operation of God by which we are regenerated in no wise excludes or subverts the use of the gospel, which the most wise God has ordained to be the seed of regeneration and food of the soul.*

With these words the Synod of Dort decisively rejected the Remonstrant objection that the supernatural operation of the Holy Spirit excluded the Word as a means of grace. Moreover, the Synod declared as the doctrine of the Reformed churches in the Netherlands and in other lands, that the most-wise God has appointed the gospel not only to be the food of the soul but also to be the seed of regeneration.

This conviction was adopted at the Synod of Dort by no small majority. It was not the peculiar opinion of the infralapsarian delegates; rather, it was the joint judgment of all the members of the Synod—on this point there was absolutely no difference. According to the judgment of all the delegates, *as a rule* the Word precedes the Spirit, calling precedes regeneration. Anyone still in doubt should read carefully the judgments registered by the various delegates concerning the third and fourth heads of doctrine.

By way of illustration several sentences can be cited here from those judgments. The Dutch professors said that the primary cause of the operation of faith is the grace of God, who is mightier than everyone, who has supplied the indwelling capacity or the virtue of faith, and *He awakens the same through the proclamation of the gospel and through the effectual operation of the Holy Spirit.*

The delegates from Gelderland believed that God calls unto salvation all those whom it pleases Him to call, *ordinarily through the external preaching of the Word* and through the internal operation of the Holy Spirit.

The delegates from South Holland confessed that a twofold grace was required for the regeneration of people, *external* (which is the divine call through nature and Scripture) and internal (which consists in the effectual and invincible grace of the Holy Spirit).

This was how all of the Dutch delegates spoke, without distinction and without exception. In opposition to the teaching of the Remonstrants which claimed that the Word is the only and the sufficient seed of regeneration, all of the Dutch delegates sought to bring to light the truth that without doubt the Word is a means and a seed of regeneration, but that the Word alone and in itself is inadequate, such that it must be accompanied by a powerful, invincible, internal grace of the Holy Spirit.

With this position the judgments of the foreign delegates agreed entirely. The English delegates even posited a preparatory grace prior to regeneration, and said that God regenerates through the Spirit, *using the means of the divine Word*, for which reason we are said to be regenerated by the imperishable seed of the Word (1 Pet. 1:23).

The delegates from the Palatinate called the gospel an *ordinary means* of the grace of regeneration. The delegates from Hesse said that through the Word, as through an *ordinary means*, God illumines internally with the grace of the Holy Spirit the understanding of those whom He wills. The Swiss theologians confessed their belief that faith is wrought in the *ordinary manner through God's Word*, while the Holy Spirit internally illumines the understanding and renews the will. The same view was expressed by the foreign delegates from Nassau and Wetterau, from Geneva, Bremen, and Emden.

According to all of them, the Word is the means or tool that the Holy Spirit employs for regenerating and renewing a person. Without exception they all viewed calling as preceding regeneration.

5.4 Refutation of the Remonstrants by Reformed Theologians

With a few short, powerful sentences, the Synod of Dort expressed its confession concerning the Word as the means of regeneration in the hand of the Holy Spirit. But at the same time, the Synod was not in a position to submit a fulsome argument in refutation of the Remonstrant objection that the immediate operation of the Holy Spirit in the sinner's heart made the use of the means of grace, especially of the Word, superfluous and unprofitable.

5.4.1 Franciscus Gomarus

Such a refutation, however, was formulated by various Reformed theologians. One of them, Gomarus,[2] devoted a short treatise to refuting

---

[2] Ed. note: Franciscus Gomarus (1563–1641) was the chief opponent of Arminius. He studied at Strasbourg, Neustadt, Oxford, Cambridge, and Heidelberg. In 1594 he was appointed professor of theology at Leiden. Gomarus resigned from the faculty at Leiden when, after the death of Arminius in 1609, Conrad Vorstius was appointed to the theological faculty, a champion of Arminius's views. Gomarus eventually went to Groningen in 1618,

this Remonstrant objection, an essay that sets forth the state of this difference very clearly, which because of its importance deserves to be included here in broad outline.[3]

When the Remonstrants argue, so Gomarus reasoned, that the immediate operation of God excludes the use of means, then the nature of the difference must be stated clearly.

Faith can be distinguished as the disposition and as the act. Concerning the disposition of faith, we confess on the basis of Scripture (e.g., Eph. 1:18–19; Ezek. 36:26; John 6:44–45; etc.) that this is brought about by God's almighty power rather than mediately by us, through our power. But when the word *immediately* is used in opposition to the preaching of the gospel as an essential prerequisite instrument whereby the Holy Spirit and He alone implants faith, then it is inaccurate to insist that we are claiming that God works immediately.

By contrast, as far as the act of faith is concerned, this arises not immediately, through almighty power, but mediately through a person who is gifted with the power of faith and is awakened through the Word of God and the help of the Spirit as the proximate and immediate cause. For we are not saying that it is God who believes, but rather it is the person who believes, that is, the person who has been given the disposition of faith. Therefore through His Word God externally commands a person to perform the act of faith, while through His Spirit He internally confers this disposition upon that person and thus equips him for believing, and through the hearing of the Word and with His help God awakens the person in reality to believe.

So when we are dealing with the power or the disposition of faith, it is not at all invalid to say that God requires that disposition in relation to the elect and at the same time brings it about immediately within them. For the requirement or command to believe indicates their debt toward God, but not what they can perform; and the promise indicates the source from which that faith flows forth unto them. It was this way with Lazarus when he had died; Christ had promised his resurrection (John 11:23). And although from his own strength he could not hear Christ and rise up, because he was dead, nevertheless Christ commanded him externally to come out of the tomb (v. 43) while simultaneously internally imparting to him life and power, so that he could hear, could come out of the tomb, and in this way could obey Jesus' command (v. 44). In the same way Christ commanded the lame man (Matt. 9:6)—who at that point was absolutely powerless in himself—to take up his bed and go home, while at the same time through His divine power He internally bestowed the health and the resources that enabled him to obey the Lord's command.

---

where he stayed until his death in 1641. He was a delegate to the Synod of Dort. Gomarus's chief theological work is the *Disputationes theologicae* (1644).

[3] See Gomarus, *Opera theologica omnia* (Amsterdam, J. Jansson, 1644), 1: 104–106.

5.4.2 *Gomarus's answer to an additional objection*

These thoughts were developed yet further by Gomarus when he answered the objection of the Remonstrants that had been expressed in a somewhat different form. For the Remonstrants said that if before receiving irresistible grace a person cannot be converted, and if when receiving this grace he is certainly and infallibly converted, then it is both unnecessary and unprofitable to be concerned about the means of grace.

To this Gomarus responded as follows: At the very outset the equivocation in the argument must be eliminated, and to do that it is again necessary to distinguish between conversion as disposition and as act. The former consists in the fact that a person is regenerated by the power of the Holy Spirit. The latter refers to the already regenerated person through the Word of God and the assistance of the Spirit putting into practice the powers received by actually believing and loving.

The preaching of the gospel is ordinarily required for conversion in both senses. It is required for conversion in the former sense (which is regeneration), because, although God alone regenerates in the proper sense, the preaching of the Word is nevertheless ordinarily required for such regeneration, as a preceding effectual instrument for correctly understanding the sense of the gospel, and as a preceding necessary supplement whereby the Holy Spirit, in desiring to convert a person, connects the power of regeneration in the elect.

For this reason the gospel is also called a ministry of the Spirit (2 Cor. 3:8), for when the elect hear the gospel and understand its meaning and the Holy Spirit intends to convert them, at that point in agreement with the promises of the New Covenant (Jer. 31:33, etc.) He creates in their hearts the disposition of faith in that gospel.

This, then, is what we read in 1 Peter 1:23 as well: You have been born again not of perishable but of imperishable seed, through the Word of the living God. Here, as verse 25 indicates, the Word of God is the gospel, which is identified here as the means or the route unto regeneration. The seed is the power of the Holy Spirit whereby He regenerates, as we read also in 1 John 3:9: one who is born of God does not sin, for God's seed remains in him.

For it may well be true, Gomarus said, that many well-known interpreters understand this seed that Peter speaks about to refer to the gospel, but this does not seem to agree with the manner of expression he uses. For he does not say: *out of* the seed and *out of* the Word, but rather he distinguishes them this way: being born *out of* the seed and *through* the Word. If, however, it were to refer to the gospel, the expression would have to be understood figuratively, just as when in 1 Corinthians 4:15 Paul says: through the gospel I have become your father. For this means that I have proclaimed the gospel to you and when you heard it, you were regenerated by the power of the Holy Spirit.

In that sense, according to Gomarus, we are to understand our theologians when they call the preaching of the gospel the instrument of regeneration. The gospel is that, however, not in the proper sense, for an instrument in the proper sense is a second cause subordinated to a first cause. But the gospel is an instrument in an improper sense, even as Scriptural usage entails a figurative manner of speaking whereby the Bible often ascribes to a sign that is administered the activity of the thing signified, on account of the correspondence existing between both the sign and the thing signified.

So although the dispositional conversion—which is regeneration—is brought about by the almighty grace of God's Spirit, nevertheless the preaching and hearing of God's Word are not unprofitable thereunto but rather are necessary as a preceding supplement, which by virtue of God's appointment are required for the grace of the regenerating Spirit.

With regard to actual conversion, the proclaiming and hearing of God's Word are necessary for that as well, so that the disposition of faith among the regenerated may progress to the activities of faith. In this instance the hearing of the preached gospel is not simply a preceding necessary supplement, as with regeneration, but an effectual instrument for awakening the activities of faith and love (Rom. 10:14–15; 1 Cor. 3:5).

5.4.3 Gomarus's further explanation

When, in the face of this clear response, Gomarus's opponents nevertheless continued to persist in seeing this immediately working grace to be in conflict with using means, Gomarus explains himself further, saying that while such grace working irresistibly or immediately excludes interposing anything between this grace and the regeneration this grace accomplishes—such as any human freedom of the will to choose—it does not exclude the use of means as preceding the operation of grace within the sinner's heart. God makes use of the Word in order that thereby the almighty power of the Holy Spirit might work simultaneously in the human heart, bearing immediately the fruit of regeneration. So the Word as an instrument does not stand between the almighty power of the Holy Spirit and the regeneration worked immediately by that power, but the Word serves as instrument for God in order to make that power of the Holy Spirit to dwell and to work within a person.

Our opponents wrongly burden us, Gomarus said in conclusion, with the complaint that we teach that faith either as disposition or as act is implanted by the Holy Spirit before the proclamation of the gospel; for we expressly teach the very opposite, on the basis of Scripture.

But we do confess that when bringing faith into existence, the Holy Spirit does not cooperate with the human person as with a partner; for God alone is the working cause of faith. Nevertheless He works this faith after the God-appointed instrument of the preaching of the gospel has preceded; whereas thereafter He cooperates with the human person who has received the disposition of faith, in order to make that capacity of faith progress further into actions of faith.

5.5 The Right Conception of Immediate Regeneration

In his aforementioned treatment, Gomarus set forth clearly the difference concerning immediate regeneration and responded with the Reformed understanding.

5.5.1 *The Remonstrant view*

Regeneration may be called immediate in opposition to the Remonstrants who inserted the free consent of the intellect and the free act of the will between the advisory moral operation of the Holy Spirit that comes to a person in the preaching of the Word, and regeneration as the fruit of that operation within the human heart. With the Remonstrants, regeneration, faith, and conversion thus became dependent upon and tied to a condition that had to be fulfilled by the person. They denied, therefore, that *along with* the Word a special effectual operation of the Holy Spirit had to occur within the sinner's heart; they denied any operation of the Holy Spirit *alongside* the Word; and they insisted that the moral operation of the Spirit *in* and *by* the Word was sufficient to convert and renew a person who wanted to be converted and renewed. So for them the Word was the solitary and sufficient cause of regeneration, the sole seed of regeneration, always as long as the person from his side only removed the impediments and permitted that Word to perform its moral operation upon and within him.

5.5.2 *The English delegation at Dort*

In opposition to this Remonstrant error, the Reformed occasionally called regeneration *immediate.*

Thus, for example, the phrase appears not only with Gomarus, but also with the English theologians at the Synod of Dort, who surely could not be accused of excluding the Word in connection with regeneration, since they spoke about a number of preparations unto regeneration, such as going to church, hearing God's Word, etc. If with the term *immediate* one wanted to exclude this operation of the Word, these theologians correctly and emphatically rejected such a view. For they insisted that in order to regenerate people, God uses the ministry of men and the instrument of the Word (1 Cor. 4:15). If God had wanted to regenerate and justify a person *immediately*, then that would not have required a person to have become ready through any knowledge, any sorrow, any desire, any hope of forgiveness.[4]

---

[4] *Acta of Handelingen der Nationale Synode*, ed. J. H. Donner and S. A. Van den Hoorn (Leiden: J. H. Donner, n.d.), 470.

Nevertheless, a few pages later they did not hesitate to use the very same term if it could be serviceable in arguing against the Remonstrant position. For there they declare emphatically that in connection with this work of regeneration, the person stands by passively, and it does not lie within the strength of the human will to resist God when He thus regenerates *immediately*.[5]

At this point sufficient light has been shed on the extent to which the Reformed were indeed willing to speak of regeneration as an immediate operation of the Holy Spirit—and where they drew the line.

When one consults various writings of the Reformed theologians, however, one soon discovers that they also called regeneration immediate, with a view and in opposition to a movement different than that of the Remonstrants. In the interests of both completeness and avoiding any misunderstanding, this disagreement also deserves to be explained briefly.

5.5.3 *John Cameron's peculiar view*

Once the courageous generation of Reformers had passed from the scene, a dominant fear began to undermine the courage of many in the Reformed churches that the firm confession of God's sovereignty would make people careless and godless. For that reason, various steps were undertaken to maintain over against the *all*-accomplishing work of God, the *self*-accomplishing work of man, and to place in the foreground more prominently than before man's moral nature.

Such an attempt was made by John Cameron,[6] who had been born in Scotland but in his youth had moved to France, where in 1624 he was appointed as professor of theology in Montauban. Even though already in the following year he died at the age of forty-eight, his person and work had great influence on French theology. Amyraut, Placaeus, Cappell, and Pajon traveled further down the path he had paved.[7]

---

[5] *Acta of Handelingen der Nationale Synode,* 473.

[6] Ed. note: John Cameron (c. 1579/80–1625) was one of the most influential Reformed theologians of France in the seventeenth century, and founder of the "moderate" school of Calvinism (known as "Amyraldianism"). Cameron was born in Glasgow and lived in Scotland until 1600, when he went to France. In 1602 he was made professor of philosophy at Sedan, and studied theology for four years at Paris, Geneva, and Heidelberg. In 1608 he became pastor at Bordeaux, where he preached with great success until 1618, when he became professor of theology at Saumur, but with the dispersion of the University in 1621 by the civil wars he returned to Glasgow, where he taught a short time, and in 1624 was chosen professor of theology at Montauban, France, where he was killed in a political tumult in 1625. Cameron's theology was modified Calvinism. He opposed the imputation of the active righteousness of Christ, and the non-concurrence of the human will with the grace of God in man's conversion. He adopted from Arminius the doctrine of universal redemption, though modified in significant ways.

[7] Ed. note: These writers were all Amyraldians, and taught at the French Academy of Saumur. Moïse Amyraut (1596–1664), was a French Reformed theologian who studied Reformed theology under the distinguished Scottish theologian John Cameron at the Acad-

This Cameron taught, among other things, that the will always follows the final conclusion of the practical reason. For example, a drunkard knows very well with his *theoretical* reason that it is wrong to misuse alcohol. But various practical considerations relating to the delight that he will enjoy in drinking presents alcohol to his *practical* reason as something desirable. When now this practical reason has spoken its final word in the choice to drink, thereupon follows the human will inevitably and necessarily.

Cameron came to this doctrine because he wanted to maintain the moral nature of man. Man is a moral being. That comes to expression especially in his will, which deserves to be called the moral, the ethical principle within a person. Therefore that will can be moved, and can be directed to perform one thing or another, in no other way than in a moral, ethical manner. This direction, thus, is preceded by a conclusion drawn by practical reason. When this conclusion exists, then the will moves in the direction stipulated by the understanding, by itself, freely and necessarily.

From this pastoral doctrine Cameron deduced with regard to regeneration that regeneration did not need to consist of the infusing of new powers or dispositions within the will. If God merely illumines the understanding effectually through His Spirit, then the will followed of its own accord, such that it would be unnecessary to furnish the will as it functions on its own, with new powers. According to this teaching,

---

emy of Saumur and was ordained thereafter. In 1633 Amyraut was installed as professor of theology at Saumur, succeeding Jean Daillé. Under the leadership of Amyraut and his colleagues Louis Cappel and Joshua de la Place, the Saumur Academy became one of the leading theological schools in France. Amyraut's name in its Latinized form was Amyraldus, and "Amyraldianism" refers to the peculiar and distinct tenets of the theology developed under Cameron and the School of Saumur. Amyraut sought union with the Lutherans, though they were staunchly opposed to the Canons of Dort (1618–19), particularly its doctrine of the scope and intent of Christ's atoning work, and its teaching on election and reprobation. Amyraut propounded a view of hypothetical universalism or a hypothetical universal predestination whereby God was said to will the salvation of all people on the condition that they believe. Thus, ideally Christ's atonement was sufficient for all and intended for all conditionally, but because of universal human depravity, in practice it was efficient only for the elect. Amyraut distinguished between an objective grace (offering salvation to all men on condition of repentance and faith) and a subjective grace (operating morally in the conversion of the soul, which is particular and given only to the elect). What functions as key for Amyraut is that, unlike the Canons of Dort, his view places divine election *after* the redeeming work of Christ. Hence it is "post-redemptionist" in its view of the particularism of salvation in the order of the divine decrees. Amyraut's views, and the distinct views of his colleagues on other important topics, were strongly opposed by many other Reformed writers, both in France and beyond. Amyraut was tried for heresy at three national synods (1637, 1644, and 1659) but was acquitted in each case. The *Formula Consensus Helvetica* (1675) was prepared by the Swiss Reformed churches in part to counter the Saumurian theology of Amyraut and his colleagues. Notwithstanding such protests, Amyraut and the School of Saumur exercised considerable influence until the Reformed cause was crushed in France with the revocation of the Edit of Nantes (1598) by Louis XIV on 18 October, 1685.

then, regeneration consists in principle strictly in the illumination of the intellect.

Cameron did not lack disciples. Under his influence the famous School of Saumur came into existence in France. Here in our country his convictions were adopted by several theologians, among whom was one who has been mentioned among us several times of late, Johannes Maccovius, professor in Franeker.

The majority of Reformed theologians, however, resisted this teaching of the French professor, and continued to insist that regeneration consisted not merely in the illumination of the intellect, but also in the renewing of the will. In fact, the Synod of Dort had explicitly declared in chapter III–IV, art. 11, that by the Holy Spirit God not only effectually enlightens the understanding of the elect, but also by the effectual power of the same regenerating Spirit penetrates the inmost being of man, opens the closed heart, softens the hard heart, circumcises the uncircumcised heart, *infuses new qualities into the will*, and makes alive the dead will, makes good the evil will, makes compliant the stubborn will, and makes submissive the rebellious will. The conviction of Cameron could hardly be reconciled with this teaching.

5.5.4 *The views of other Reformed writers*

In contrast to this one-sided intellectualist line of Cameron, Maccovius, and others, Reformed theologians occasionally expressed themselves in such a way that the regeneration of a person occurred *directly* and *immediately* not only within the intellect but also within the will—that is, not exclusively under the instrumentality and as a consequence of the illumination of the intellect.

This is what we read in the well-known *Synopsis purioris theologiae*, which states that the preeminent effectual cause of faith is God the Father in the Son by the Holy Spirit, who illumines the intellect and moves and bends the will that has turned away from God. God does this not simply in a figurative way and with a so-called *moral* action by illuminating the intellect and presenting the judgment of practical reason to the will, which would then necessarily act according to that judgment. Rather, He does this also through an operation that *immediately* affects the will and enters into its movement and action.[8]

In his *Theoretical-Practical Theology*, Mastricht says that some Reformed theologians do accept a supernatural operation of the Holy Spirit

---

[8] Andreas Rivetus, "De Fide et Perseverantia Sanctorum," in *Synopsis purioris theologiae, disputationibus quinquaginta duabus comprehensa ac conscripta per Johannem Polyandrum, Andream Rivetum, Antonium Walaeum, Antonium Thysium* (Leiden, 1625), XXXI.9. Ed. note: This work, co-authored by Johannes Polyander, Andreas Rivetus, Antonius Walaeus, and Antonius Thysius, all of whom were members of the theological faculty at Leiden, was highly honored and was one of the most popular short dogmatics of that period. Herman Bavinck edited the modernized Dutch edition, translated by Dirk van Dijk, first issued in 1881 and reissued in 1964, 1966, in two volumes.

upon the will, but through the instrumentality of the intellect, which God illumines and convicts in regeneration so powerfully that the will can do nothing else than follow. But the Synod of Dort and other Reformed theologians, he continues, extend the supernatural operation in regeneration also to include the will, and this in an *immediate* sense, so that God infuses a new inclination within the will.[9] This conviction Mastricht considered the most acceptable.

In contrast, Turretin was focusing more on the conflict with the Remonstrants when, in his *Elenctic Theology* he deals extensively with the subject of *immediate* grace. As he states the matter, although the Holy Spirit does not, in the effectual calling, work *apart from* the Word, nevertheless, He does not work merely mediately *through* the Word, but He works also *with* the Word *immediately* within the soul, so that the working necessarily engenders its effect. The Holy Spirit does not work apart from the Word, for God desires to treat us in a manner that corresponds to our rational nature; however, no matter what the power of the Word may be, it is inadequate apart from the *immediate* operation of the Holy Spirit.[10]

Alexander Comrie expresses himself along the same line. He repeatedly speaks of regeneration as an immediate work of the Holy Spirit. He does so in opposition to all full Pelagians and semi-Pelagians, who all held to an objective grace and a moral persuasion and refused to acknowledge an almighty *immediate* power of the Holy Spirit with the Word.[11]

---

[9] Ed. note: See Petrus van Mastricht, *Theoretico-practica theologia* (Utrecht, 1714), VI.3.26. Petrus van Mastricht (1630–1706) was a Reformed theologian who studied at Duisburg and Utrecht. He served as a pastor in Cleves and Gluckstadt before being called in 1662 to be professor of oriental languages and practical theology at Frankfurt-on-the-Oder. In 1669 he was appointed professor of theology at Duisburg and in 1677 succeeded Voetius as professor of theology at Utrecht. His chief theological work was *Theoretico-practica theologia* (1714, new edition, 1724).

[10] Ed. note: See Francis Turretin, *Institutes of Elenctic Theology*, XV.4.23–24. Francis Turretin (Turrettini) (1623–1687) was a highly regarded Reformed theologian from Geneva, being the son of Benedict and the father of Jean Alphonse Turrettini. He studied at Geneva, Leiden, Utrecht, Paris, Saumur, Montauban, and Nimes. He was called to be pastor of the Italian congregation in Geneva in 1648 and was appointed professor of theology at the academy in 1653. He was one of the originators of the *Formula Consensus Helvetica* (1675), which opposed Amyraldianism. His major theological work is the *Institutio theologiae elencticae* (1679–1685). During his life he also published two volumes of sermons (in French) and several important theological treatises.

[11] Ed. note: See Alexander Comrie, *Stellige en praktikale verklaring van den Heidelbergschen Katechismus, volgens de leer en gronden der Hervorming: waarin de waarheden van onzen godsdienst op eene klare en bevindelijke wijze voorgesteld en betoogd worden; de natuurlingen ontdekt; de zoekenden bestuurd; de zwakken vertroost en de sterken tot hunnen pligt, volgens eene evangelische leiding* (Nijkerk, 1856), 145–146; 365–366. Alexander Comrie (1706–1774) was a Scot who was catechized by Ebenezer and Ralph Erskine, and who adhered to the writings of Thomas Boston. He studied at Groningen and Leiden, and was awarded a doctorate in philosophy at the latter school in 1734. He pastored at Woubrugge, the Netherlands, for thirty-eight years until 1773. Like Voetius,

Finally—to mention no others—à Brakel was in complete agreement on this point. In the chapter on Calling, he raises the question whether the internal call, even though it occurs by means of the Word, is an *immediate* and effectual divine operation, affecting and altering a person's intellect, will, and inclinations. He gives this answer: Even though a person cannot comprehend the manner of God's supernatural operation, how He *immediately* touches the soul with and through the Word, nonetheless the Word teaches us that God does this. What is more, He uses the Word as an means, but joined to this means is an *immediate*, effectual operation that touches the soul, and with respect to a person's intellect, will, and dispositional state, effectually changes the soul.[12]

Comrie labored to unite classic Reformed doctrine, scholastic methodology, and biblical piety. His best known work, *A.B.C. des geloofs*, was written in 1739 (translated in 1978 as *The ABC of Faith*). He also wrote a major work on the biblical properties of faith entitled *Verhandeling van eenige eigenschappen des zaligmakende geloofs*, and a commentary on the first seven Lord's Days of the Heidelberg Catechism (1753) (which is the work that Bavinck cites here), besides other theological and polemical works.

[12] Ed. note: See Wilhelmus à Brakel, *The Christian's Reasonable Service in which the Divine Truths concerning the Covenant of Grace are expounded, defended against Opposing parties, and their practice advocated as well as the Administration of this Covenant in the Old and New Testaments*, trans. Bartel Elshout, with a biographical sketch by W. Fieret and an essay on the "Dutch Second Reformation" by Joel Beeke. 4 vols. (Ligonier, PA: Soli Deo Gloria Publications, 1992–95), II: 225–26. Wilhelmus à Brakel (1635–1711) studied at Franeker and was admitted into the ministry in 1659, but pursued further study under Voetius and Andreas Essenius at Utrecht. He served five congregations during a ministry that spanned fifty years. He became well-known for his book *De Trappen des Geestelycken Levens* [*The Steps of the Spiritual Life*]. In the latter years of his life he labored on his most important work, *ΛΟΓΙΚΗ ΛΑΤΡΕΙΑ, dat is De Redelijke Godsdienst* [*The Christian's Reasonable Service*], 1700 (3 vols.), with an expanded edition produced in 1707. This dogmatic work was aimed more at a lay audience and combined traditional Reformed dogmatic theology with an accent on piety and Christian living.

6

Calling and Regeneration in Other Reformed Theologians

WE TRUST that all of this sets forth clearly in what sense the early Reformed spoke of regeneration as an *immediate* operation of the Holy Spirit.

By expressing themselves this way, they had a twofold purpose. First, with this description of regeneration they wanted to cut off the Pelagian and Remonstrant error, which claimed that regeneration was dependent upon an intermediating decision of the human will. Second, they were seeking to avoid the position of Cameron and others, which taught that the renewal of the human will occurs merely in a mediate way, namely, through the instrumentality of the intellect.

The expression *immediate regeneration*, however, was never employed by the Reformed in earlier days to exclude the means of grace of the Word from the operation of regeneration by the Holy Spirit. In their treatments of the order of salvation, everyone of them placed calling before regeneration. On this point they all agreed. Whether or not they were correct is a matter we will consider later. But the fact is beyond doubt that all of the Reformed confessions and likewise all Reformed theologians begin their explanation of the order of salvation with calling, and only then move on to regeneration (also in its narrower sense).

Numerous and lengthy citations are not needed to illustrate this. Anyone can be easily persuaded if he but opens the confessions or the writings of the Reformed theologians. We would make an exception for only a couple of writers who to this day are viewed by many as outstanding exponents of Reformed principles and in that sense are often contrasted with others.

6.1 John Calvin on Calling and Regeneration

Calvin is the first to occupy our attention. As was said earlier, in the early days after the Reformation the beginning point of the application of the benefits of salvation was identified with various terms. What was fixed, however, is that God was the initiator in the work of salvation. But whether the very first benefit bestowed upon a person should be called repentance or faith, conversion or regeneration, was a matter of differing opinion. Many began their treatment of the application of the benefits of salvation with a discussion of faith. This was Calvin's approach in his *Institutes* (III.ii.); at that point it is obvious that the Word as means of grace is not excluded at the beginning of spiritual life, that is, at the point where faith begins. For faith is itself knowledge and includes knowledge, knowledge of God and of Christ (III.ii.2). Such faith embraces Christ clothed in the garment of Holy Scripture and reaches out to Christ when the gospel has opened the way. Faith is inseparably bound to the Word, and can no more be detached from the Word than the sunbeams from the sun. Take the Word away, and there would be no more faith. It is the mirror in which faith beholds God. To those whom God desires to draw to Himself God presents Himself through His Word (III.ii.6). Faith rests upon the promise of the gospel and needs the Word, just as the fruit needs the root of the tree (III.ii.29, 31).

Since Calvin saw the spiritual life as beginning with faith, he had as yet no place for regeneration in the narrower sense. He did mention regeneration, but he understood regeneration not as an infusion of the very first new life principle that precedes faith, but rather as the entire spiritual renewal of a person as that comes into existence through faith and is itself the fruit of faith. After treating faith in III.ii., Calvin proceeded in III.iii. to explain *that we are regenerated by faith.*

6.2 Calvin Anticipates the Distinction between Dispositional and Active Regeneration

Various circumstances compelled the Reformed, however, to get back behind the act of faith in connection with the operation known as conversion. The infant children of believers certainly could not yet believe but nevertheless had a right to baptism. When a child died in infancy, Scripture teaches that they are not lost but saved, just as much as adult believers. This last phenomenon appeared frequently in circumstances where they did not exercise active faith while they nevertheless possessed the principle of faith, unless one wished to fall into the unscriptural doctrine of the apostasy of the saints. Finally, a person is unable to come, on his own, to faith and conversion; faith and conversion are the fruit of an almighty operation of the Holy Spirit. So it was obvious that gradually a distinction would emerge between the operation of the Holy Spirit and the fruit of that operation, or to say it differently: between the disposition and the act of faith, between conversion in the sense of disposition and in the active sense, or between regeneration in its narrow sense and faith (with conversion).

We do not find this distinction expressed clearly or developed extensively in Calvin. But it is nevertheless present in Calvin in principle and in seed form. In the *Institutes*, his chapter on faith (III.ii.) was preceded by a chapter on the secret operation of the Holy Spirit (III.i.). Because each day showed that many do not accept the gospel, we must, says Calvin, ascend higher and consider the operation of the Holy Spirit. He is the One who binds us to Christ, who brings about faith within us, who through the gospel illumines our understanding. The Holy Spirit is actually *the root and the seed of the heavenly life within us* (III.i.2). He vouchsafes unto the elect *the living root of faith*, so that they may persevere unto the end (III.ii.11).

By means of this distinction Calvin secures the possibility for accepting a saving operation of the Holy Spirit to be at work within infants as well, and for defending the legitimacy of infant baptism. With an appeal to the example of John the Baptist, Calvin can now show that the Holy Spirit is not limited by the conscious awareness of the person, and can also regenerate a person unto eternal life apart from the acts of faith and repentance. It would be superfluous for our purposes, however, to explain this any further.

Although Calvin acknowledged in principle the distinction between the seed of faith and the act of faith and, with a view to the children of believers, permitted both of these to be temporarily separated, nevertheless, this did not for a moment change the order in which he treated the benefits of salvation. His position was always that as a rule, in the ordinary economy of salvation, the Word precedes, and the Holy Spirit with His work supplements the Word; this calling is first and is followed by the illumination of the understanding and the renewal of the will.

Thus he says, to mention but one illustration, that teachers would cry aloud to no purpose, did not Christ, by means of His Spirit, the internal Teacher, draw to Himself those who are given Him of the Father (III.i.4). The Word cannot penetrate our hearts unless the Spirit, that internal Teacher, fashions an entrance for it by His enlightening power (III.ii.34). The proclamation of the gospel is not in itself a convincing proof of election. But God teaches His elect effectually, so that He brings them to faith (III.xxiv.1). Calling consists not only in the proclamation of the Word, but also in the illumination by the Spirit (III.xxiv.2). With this special call God vouchsafes usually only the elect, when through the internal illumination of His Spirit He causes the preached Word to take up occupancy within their hearts. It accompanies the Spirit of regeneration (III.xxiv.8). Through God's calling, the elect are not gathered into the sheepfold of Christ from their mother's womb instantly or all at the same time, but in such a way as it pleases God to impart His grace unto them (III.xxiv.10). Although Calvin acknowledges that for young children regeneration can occur apart from the Word and thus faith does not come from hearing for them, he nonetheless holds fast to the rule that the Word is the only seed of spiritual regeneration for adults (IV.xvi.18). When the Apostle calls hearing a means unto faith, he has in view the ordinary economy and dispensation that the Lord is accustomed to follow in calling His own (IV.xvi.10).

From these and other places it is clear, and quite certain, that with respect to many children of believers Calvin accepts a form of regeneration apart from the preaching of the gospel. But when he formulates the general rule and indicates the order of the benefits of salvation, then he always places calling before regeneration, the preaching of the Word before the operation of the Spirit. Or better still, he seeks to keep both intimately connected with each other.

This is expressed very clearly in his treatise against Pighius regarding free will.[1] Calvin distinguished a twofold divine operation within the elect, namely, an external operation through the Word and an internal operation through the Spirit. Pighius[2] registered this objection to such a view: the preaching of the Word precedes the operation of the Spirit, or it follows. The latter is impossible, since then believers would be exhorted in vain to seek that which they had already received, namely, regeneration. The former is also impossible, because according to Calvin the unregenerate person can neither desire nor seek the good.

In refuting this objection, Calvin appeals to Paul who says, on the one hand, that faith comes by hearing and, on the other hand, that faith is a gift of God, and both then are reconciled in the fact that the ministry of the Spirit was entrusted to him. What the Apostle meant by this, as Calvin puts it literally, he explains this way: that by His Spirit God effectually implants within the hearts of people that which He speaks to their ears not earlier or later but simultaneously. By the Word people are thus awakened to seek their regeneration. When? At that point when the Spirit of God makes this His effectual means to arouse within them just such a desire. It does not suit us to prescribe for God a schedule for His works. Nevertheless we must hold firmly to the connection Paul supplies

---

[1] Ed. note: Bavinck's reference is to *Ioanni Calvini noviodunensis Opera omnia, in novem tomos digesta*, 9 vols. (Amsterdam: Johann Jacob Schipper, 1667–71), VIII, 156. See also John Calvin, *Defensio sanae et orthodoxae doctrinae de servitute et liberatione humani artitrii adversus calumnias Alberti Pighii Campensis* (1543), translated into English as *The Bondage and Liberation of the Will: A Defense of the Orthodox Doctrine of Human Choice against Pighius*, ed. A. N. S. Lane, trans. G. I. Davies. Texts and Studies in Reformation and Post-Reformation Thought, ed. Richard A. Muller (Grand Rapids: Baker Academic, 1996), 163–66.

[2] Ed. note: Albert Pighius (c. 1490–1542) was a Dutch humanist and Roman Catholic theologian, a native of Kampen in the Netherlands. He studied at Louvain and Paris and in 1523 was called to Rome by Hadrian VI. Here he took a prominent part in writing on the main issues of his time. His principal work, *Hierarchiae Ecclesiasticae Assertio* (1538), was an elaborate defense of both tradition, as a source of Christian truth coordinate with Scripture, and of church hierarchy. In his opposition to Martin Luther and John Calvin he emphasized human free will to such an extent as to imperil belief in original sin. His views on papal infallibility also had great influence.

us between the secret operation of the Spirit and the external preaching of men; for then we will be freed from every difficulty.

6.3 Seventeenth-Century Reformed Theologians on Calling and Regeneration

6.3.1 *Johannes Maccovius*

Having indicated Calvin's views about the connection between calling and regeneration, we turn now to consider those of the Franeker professor Johannes Maccovius.[3]

One should not infer, however, that no other Reformed theologians lived between Calvin and Maccovius who could not have been identified as belonging to the same line as these two.

Whatever accomplishments the Franeker professor may have rendered on behalf of Reformed theology, in recent times he is certainly being lauded beyond measure in our land. Some portray him as the father of scientific Reformed theology, as the man who has brought the long-dominant Biblical Theology within the fold of scientific theology, who as a faithful, strict, valiant Calvinist, by introducing the scholastic method, pioneered the path that we in our day should follow in the practice of sacred theology.

All of this is quite an exaggeration, as anyone can surmise after a bit of reflection. For it seems quite evident that the earliest divines who arose at the time of the Reformation stayed as closely as possible to Holy Scripture as they set forth the truth. The liabilities of the scholastic theology of the Middle Ages were clear to everyone. The errors that had crept into the doctrine and life of the church appeared to be a result of, or at least closely related to, the subtle manner of dealing with the truths of the faith that was common during the Middle Ages. The earliest theologians of the Reformation, therefore, were to a greater or lesser degree motivated by a reaction against the philosophy of Aristotle, against the razor thin and foreign distinctions of scholasticism, against the entire spirit and method of the Middle Ages. People wanted to recover the uncompromised, pure truth as that had been revealed by God, and they therefore returned to Scripture. Melanchthon's dogmatics was actually an exposition of Paul's epistle to the Romans, and Calvin's *Institutes* was originally an exposition of the Apostles' Creed.

It was just as plain, however, that they would not be able to remain at this point. First of all, within their own circles the need arose to develop further the truth that they confessed, to clarify its inner connectedness, and to relate it to the entirety of knowledge that people had acquired in other areas. Secondly, people were compelled by their conflicts with the Roman Catholics, the Anabaptists, the Socinians, etc., to give ever more

---

[3] Ed. note: See page 4, footnote 3.

clear explanations of the doctrines they confessed, and to polish and perfect these doctrines from all sides. Once they began this undertaking, they needed the contributions of logic, psychology, and philosophy; they had to investigate history and harvest the gains of what had been done by others in former times in response to various errors and heresies. Aristotle was honored once again, and the works of the church fathers and of the medieval theologians were consulted zealously by the men of the Reformation.

This new approach did not begin with Maccovius, but appeared already during the earliest period after the Reformation. Melanchthon very quickly retreated from his denigration of Aristotle and of philosophy. In addition to studying Augustine, Calvin had studied Thomas Aquinas as well and was quite temperate in his evaluation of philosophy. When one consults the theologians who came after them, one quickly discovers that acquaintance with philosophy and scholasticism gradually increased. The works, for example, of Martyr, Polanus, Zanchius, Piscator (abroad), and of both Trelcatiusses, Gomarus, and others (here in the Netherlands), are adequate demonstration of this claim.[4]

---

[4] Ed. note: Peter Martyr Vermigli (1500–1562) was a Reformed theologian who studied at Padua and Bologna. In 1542 he openly espoused reform and left Italy for Basel and Strasbourg. In December of 1542 he succeeded Capito as professor of theology in Strasbourg. From 1547 to 1553, Vermigli taught at Oxford. On the accession of Mary he returned to Strasbourg (1553–1556) but ended his career in Zürich (1556–1562). His well-known dogmatic work, the *Loci communes*, was gathered out of his writings and published posthumously by Robert Masson in 1576.

Amandus Polanus von Polansdorf (1561–1610) was a Reformed theologian who was educated at Tübingen, Basel, and Geneva. He was appointed professor of Old Testament at Basel in 1596 and served as dean of the theological faculty from 1598 to 1609. His dogmatic works are *Partitiones theologicae, pars I & II* (1590, 1596), and *Syntagma theologiae christianae* (1609).

Jerome Zanchius (1516–1590) studied at Padua and was a member of the Augustinian order, associated with Peter Martyr Vermigli at Lucca. His evangelical preaching forced him to flee Italy. He was appointed professor of Old Testament at Strasbourg, a post he held until 1563. In 1568 he went to Heidelberg as Ursinus's successor in theology. He left Heidelberg for Neustadt in 1576 on the accession of the Lutheran elector, Ludwig VI, and remained there as professor of theology until his death. His works include the beginning of a vast *Summa* of the Reformed faith: *Praefatiuncula in locos communes*; *De tribus Elohim*; *De natura Dei*; *De operibus Dei*; and *De primi hominis lapsu, de peccato et de lege Dei* (all in *Opera*, 1617). Zanchi also wrote an extended confession of faith, *De religione christiana fides* (1585).

Lucas Trelcatius (the younger) (1573–1607) was a Reformed theologian who received his education at Leiden and became professor of theology there in 1603. He participated in the debate with Arminius over predestination and Christology. His major work is the *Scholastica et methodica locorum communium s. theologiae institutio* (1604).

Lucas Trelcatius (the elder) (1542–1602), father of the earlier mentioned Trelcatius, studied at Paris, where he joined the cause of the Reformation, and at Orleans. He fled to England and taught oriental languages in London. From 1578 to 1585 he was pastor of the Walloon church in Rijssel in the South Netherlands, and then went to Leiden as pastor. In 1587 he became professor at Leiden, where he later died. For Gomarus, see page 44, footnote 2.

So Maccovius was merely traveling the path pioneered by others before him. But his nature and character were such that as he progressed along this path, to some degree he lost sight of wisdom and caution. An example can illustrate this. The Reformed usually distinguished between God's will of decree and God's will of precept. Maccovius objected to this, however, insisting that the will of precept was not a will in the proper sense, but rather that the will of decree was the only, genuine divine will. Consequently, sin was not only included within God's counsel, but had also been decreed by God. Such a position appeared to be very consistent. By these and similar arguments Maccovius acquired for himself the reputation of being a strict Calvinist. Although the position of Maccovius contained some truth, he was nevertheless not one whit more consistent than those theologians whose distinction between God's secret and God's revealed will he was opposing. For when he came to the doctrine of sin, he was compelled to speak of God's permission, against which the same objections could be raised as against the will of precept. The bottom line, here and elsewhere, was that Maccovius was engaging in idle word games and was not advancing the discussion with all his scholastic distinctions. For that reason the Synod of Dort rapped him on the knuckles and ordered him to be more careful.

Maccovius with his way of arguing would not have been so lightly dismissed if he were not discredited by one particular liability, namely, his life. His manner of life left a lot to be desired. It was anything but Christian. People charged him, apparently not without valid cause, of leading a "belluina vita," of living like an animal. Was it any wonder that sober, pious men like Lubbertus, Ames, and others sought a connection between his doctrine and his life, basing their objections against the former especially on the latter? If God *has willed* sin, then why not live according to the desires of the flesh?

Regardless of the outcome of all of this, regarding the issue before us, Maccovius held a position no different from most Reformed theologians of his day.

Within the doctrine of the order of salvation, he distinguished himself, if you will, by positing two special ideas. First, he argued that the application of the benefits of salvation began not with regeneration or faith or conversion, but with justification. Maccovius did not, however, teach a justification from eternity, since he expressly opposed this teaching. But he thought that justification occurred for all the elect with the mother promise of Genesis 3:15, and he tried to prove this with an appeal to Titus 1:2, where the phrase "before times eternal" refers not to eternity but to a time long ago.[5]

---

[5] Johannes Maccovius, *Loci communes theologici; ex omnibus ejus, quae extant, collegiis, thesibus, per locos comm. disputatis, manuscripts antiquis, recentioribus, undiquaque sollicite conquisitis, collecti, digesti, aucti, indice capitum, rerumque locupletati* (Franeker, 1650), 676.

Following justification, then, we have sanctification, beginning with regeneration. At this point Maccovius placed all the emphasis, in direct opposition to the English theologians—and here we have, if you will, the second special feature of his doctrine of the order of salvation—on the fact that there are no preparations prior to regeneration. For one or the other is true: either the so-called preparations do not necessarily lead to regeneration, whereupon they are then not preparations; or they follow upon regeneration and are the marks and fruit of regeneration. A person cannot hear the gospel *savingly* unless he is first regenerated.

Although Maccovius developed this point extensively and returned to it repeatedly, he was not teaching anything really new. That was and still is the Reformed conviction. Each of us acknowledges that the *saving* hearing of the gospel presupposes regeneration.

But that in no way contradicts the claim that Maccovius was describing the connection between calling and regeneration in the same way as all other Reformed theologians were doing. He never described regeneration as immediate, in the sense that every operation of the Word would have been excluded in connection with regeneration. In no way did he deny that God through His Word calls and can call the spiritually dead.

On the contrary, with a view to Ezekiel 37:4 and John 11:43, Maccovius says pointedly that God through His Word genuinely calls also those who are spiritually dead. God does that and can do that, because it is God who calls those things which are not as though they were, and by means of such calling brings them into existence.

For example, God demands, Maccovius continued, that the unregenerate circumcise the foreskins of their hearts (Jer. 4:4; Ezek. 18:31). He does so not because the unregenerate can do this themselves, but because God thereby wants to make them aware of their impotence. God works the willing and the doing, and Paul nonetheless exhorts that we ourselves work out our own salvation with fear and trembling. We are obligated to believe, and yet no one can come to Christ unless the Father draws him.

Even the preaching of the Word is not unprofitable for those who never receive the gift of regeneration and who thus can never hear the Word savingly. For God has definitely willed that the gospel should be proclaimed to them as well, insofar as they live under the dispensation of grace, so that they would be without excuse. Concerning those elect not yet regenerated, the preaching of the gospel is even less futile. For when the Word is preached externally to them, God often opens their heart, as He did with Lydia, and calls them internally by His Spirit.

According to Maccovius, therefore, the Word can be called a seed of regeneration. This seed possessed not a physical but a moral power—as we shall see below—for only by His Spirit is God the author of regeneration; nevertheless, the Word may be called a seed of regeneration for two reasons. First, because the Word of God is regularly joined to the gift of regeneration; what God commands externally through His Word He completes internally through His Spirit. Second, because God makes known to us from and through that Word that we are regenerated, and in this way explains regeneration to us.[6]

So Maccovius also subscribed to the doctrine that calling—as a rule even the external, but in any case the internal calling—precedes regeneration.

6.3.2 *Gisbertus Voetius*

Still more remarkable than the opinion of Maccovius concerning the relation between calling and regeneration was that of Voetius.[7] Maccovius did not specify the time when the elect are regenerated. He said that the children of believers had to be baptized because *some* of them had the Holy Spirit, or also because they all possessed not internal, but certainly external holiness, or covenant holiness. For that reason he could very easily posit as a rule that calling precedes regeneration.

But Voetius was of the opinion that all the elect born to believing parents in the covenant were regenerated in their infancy, before baptism. He did have an objection against accepting this in connection with those elect who for years—well into their twenties, forties, or sixties—live in sin and only then come to conversion. But he accepted the possibility that the seed of regeneration, sown within the heart during those first days of life, remained latent for that long under the soil.

He was deeply inclined to this idea because according to Holy Scripture, the children of believers together with their parents share in the promises of God, because otherwise circumcision and baptism would be denigrated to empty signs, and because only with this reasoning could the arguments against the Anabaptists be sustained. Not only such children as those who show from their infancy that they share in the life of grace, but also others, like Abraham, Manasseh, the sinner in Luke 7, the murderer on the cross, Cornelius, Lydia, Augustine, Luther, who at a later age were converted, were according to Voetius quite probably regenerated already in their youth. According to his opinion, a view that should not be rejected out of hand is the claim that an elect infant is regenerated

---

[6] Maccovius, *Loci communes theologici*, 51–54; 606–715; idem, *Collegia theologica quae extant omnia* (Franeker, 1641), 396–408; idem, *Joannes Maccovius redivivus: seu manuscripta eius tertium iam typis exscripta* (Franeker, 1647; Amsterdam, 1659), 108–110.

[7] Ed. note: Gisbertus Voetius (1589–1676) was a very influential and prolific Dutch Reformed theologian. He studied at the University of Leiden (1604–11) under Gomarus. Between 1611 and 1634, he served several congregations and in 1618 was one of the delegates from South Holland to the Synod of Dort. In 1634 he was called as professor of theology to the newly established University of Utrecht. Voetius was both a bitter polemicist against the Cocceians and Cartesians and a major influence on the development of Reformed piety and practical theology. His major, and highly scholastic, theological treatises are found in the *Selectae disputationes theologicae,* 5 vols. (1648–1669).

at the very moment of conception, although one would do well to abstain from a fixed judgment about this.[8]

All of this notwithstanding, although one would have expected differently from Voetius on the basis of this conviction, he nevertheless believed that in the order of salvation, calling precedes regeneration. He acknowledged that the elect children of believers are regenerated apart from an external call.[9] He even admitted that with adults as well, regeneration can occur apart from the Word either preceding it or being joined to it.[10] But when he set and arranged the benefits of salvation in connection with each other, he nonetheless placed calling before regeneration.

Thus he described regeneration as that act of God within elect sinners who through Christ are saved, justified in an active sense, and *called*, whereby God changes them from the depravity of sin to a new life.[11] Reconciliation, justification, adoption as children in an objective sense all precede. Then follows the calling. Thereafter come regeneration, sanctification, and glorification.[12] Calling is that benefit whereby God presents and offers the goods of the covenant; regeneration makes a person suited to share in them.[13] The cause of regeneration is twofold; the physical cause is the power of God, but the moral cause, so termed because it precedes the first-named cause or is joined to it, is calling.[14] Within the order of salvation, the saving, effectual calling precedes regeneration, but within historical time it coincides or is joined with regeneration.[15]

6.3.3 *Petrus van Mastricht*

Peter van Mastricht had the same view. He called it the usual opinion of the Reformed theologians, which holds that baptism presupposes regeneration as already having occurred with elect infants.[16] He acknowledged further that in special instances God can call a person only internally apart from the Word.[17] But when he discussed the order of salvation, he again placed calling ahead of regeneration.

After Mastricht had discussed in his dogmatics the person and work of Christ, he moved on to the doctrine of the application of the benefits of salvation. In that context he spoke first about the nature of this application and said, among other things, that the instrument of this application

---

8 Gisbertus Voetius, *Selectae disputationes theologicae*, 5 vols. (Utrecht, 1648–1669), II, 402–468.

9 Voetius, *Selectae disputationes theologicae*, II, 434.

10 Voetius, *Selectae disputationes theologicae*, II, 461.

11 Voetius, *Selectae disputationes theologicae*, II, 436.

12 Voetius, *Selectae disputationes theologicae*, II, 433.

13 Voetius, *Selectae disputationes theologicae*, II, 464, 452.

14 Voetius, *Selectae disputationes theologicae*, II, 449.

15 Voetius, *Selectae disputationes theologicae*, II, 452.

16 Mastricht, *Theoretico-practica theologia*, VI 3, 31.

17 Mastricht, *Theoretico-practica theologia*, VI 2, 19.

is the ministry of the Word.[18] He then discussed calling, at which point he remarked that the special calling, which is shared only by the elect, first of all precedes regeneration, at which point it presupposes nothing about them, and secondly, follows regeneration to then awaken the regenerated person unto faith and conversion.[19] In the next chapter he then discussed regeneration, describing it as that act of the Holy Spirit whereby He infuses within persons who are elect, saved, and *called* the initial life principle whereby they can accept the Savior.[20]

6.3.4 *Alexander Comrie*

Finally, there can be no doubt about the order in which Alexander Comrie placed calling and regeneration. In his exposition of the Heidelberg Catechism,[21] he discussed in depth the question whether for the vivifying and infusing of true saving faith that regenerates us and makes us new creatures, any prior capacities, qualities, and accomplishments must proceed from our side, as preparations unto the vivifying and infusing of faith.

Although Comrie rejected as bluntly as possible every actual preparation for regeneration understood in a Pelagian or Remonstrant sense, he nevertheless believed that we may speak of some preparations for regeneration in a good sense, in the sense with which the English theologians spoke of them, because nothing is more clear than that the Spirit first uses the law to slay the sinner, by pressing the same demand and curse upon the conscience, in order to oppress and frighten the sinner, emptying him of any hope of ever coming to grace through something in himself, before and until the Spirit then *uses the gospel to make him alive.*[22]

From this we see Comrie's opinion at its clearest. He then set out to explain it further. It is not the Word itself that regenerates a person, but it is nevertheless God's immediate power in itself that affects and regenerates the soul.[23] The Holy Spirit works the inwrought faith through the Word and awakens it thereafter unto deeds of faith.[24] Naturally this applies, according to Comrie, only to older people. But even with older people he believed that it was God's usual way to use the law upon the conscience of older people and thereafter to make them alive through the gospel.[25]

---

[18] Mastricht, *Theoretico-practica theologia*, VI 1, 18.
[19] Mastricht, *Theoretico-practica theologia*, VI 2, 17.
[20] Mastricht, *Theoretico-practica theologia*, VI 3, 6.
[21] Comrie, *Stellige en praktikale verklaring van den Heidelbergschen Katechismus*, 358–359.
[22] Comrie, *Stellige en praktikale verklaring*, 367.
[23] Comrie, *Stellige en praktikale verklaring*, 165.
[24] Comrie, *Stellige en praktikale verklaring*, 398.
[25] Comrie, *Stellige en praktikale verklaring*, 370–371.

6.4 The Westminster Confession

To cite more writers would be superfluous and is not worth the trouble. Permit us to mention one more confession that was formulated in the Reformed churches after the conflict over infant baptism and after the distinction between regeneration and conversion had been generally accepted in Reformed theology.

We are referring to the Westminster Confession, written in 1645. In chapter X it discusses effectual calling and shows clearly that calling precedes regeneration. It says that all those whom God has predestined unto life, and those only, He is pleased, in His appointed and accepted time, effectually to call, by His Word and Spirit, out of that state of sin and death, in which they are by nature, to grace and salvation, by Jesus Christ. He does this by enlightening their minds spiritually and savingly to understand the things of God, taking away their heart of stone, and giving unto them a heart of flesh, etc.

The effectuality of this calling is due to God's free and special grace alone, and not to any foreseen good within a person, for with this calling the person is entirely passive, until by God's Spirit the person is made alive and renewed, equipped to respond to the calling and to accept the grace offered.

This is, as it were, the rule which the Westminster Confession sets forth with regard to calling. Later in the same chapter, it acknowledges that elect infants who die in infancy are regenerated and saved by Christ through the Spirit (who works when, and where, and how He pleases), as also are all other elect persons who are incapable of being outwardly called by the ministry of the Word.

Without hesitation it may be claimed that at this point the Westminster Confession is reproducing the view that dominated the Reformed church and Reformed theology with regard to the connection between calling and regeneration. Reformed folk readily acknowledged that with children and in a few other special cases, the Holy Spirit can regenerate and has genuinely regenerated apart from the Word. But the order of salvation was not determined by these exceptions. No matter how many they may be, they were nevertheless treated as exceptions. The rule was taken from the pattern of adults who are first called and then regenerated. Thus the doctrinal-theological discussion of calling generally preceded the discussion of regeneration.

7

The Reformed Conception of the Covenant of Grace and the Church

WITHOUT EXCEPTION, all of the confessions and doctrinal manuals that came into use among the Reformed churches placed calling ahead of regeneration. No difference of opinion about this fact is possible. Anyone can clearly see, on the basis of even the most superficial study, that this claim is valid. No change was made to this sequence even after the distinction between regeneration and conversion was clarified and generally accepted. No one had even the slightest inclination to reverse the relationship between calling and regeneration in their doctrinal treatments, although people readily and openly acknowledged that in numerous instances regeneration occurred apart from the Word, simply and only through the effectual operation of the Holy Spirit.

The Reformed must have had good reasons for holding firmly to this ancient, tried, and tested position. We need not look very far for those reasons. We want to mention several of them briefly.

7.1 The Covenant contra Roman Catholicism and Anabaptism

The first reason lies in the deep and glorious concept of the covenant, which occupies such an important place in Reformed doctrine. Other churches know nothing of this concept, or ascribe to it merely a subordinate value. But apart from this doctrine of the covenant, the Reformed confessions and Reformed theology cannot be understood at any point whatsoever.

The Reformed came to this doctrine of the covenant under the illumination of Holy Scripture and under the influence of the opposition they had to render from the very beginning against the Roman Catholics, on the one hand, and the Anabaptists, on the other hand.

7.1.1 *Rome's view*

Roman Catholic teaching has been saturated for a long time with the idea that obtaining salvation was tied, from start to finish, to the sacraments. Even though a child may be born to believing parents, within the circle of the Christian church, God has not yet connected any sanctifying grace to these realities. Viewed apart from this, such an infant is entirely equal to children born to pagan parents except for this advantage: the child born to believing parents has the opportunity to receive baptism from the hand of the priest. Such baptism is what grants the child the first, sanctifying grace, the grace of regeneration.

Thus regeneration does not precede baptism and is not presupposed by baptism. For God bestows this grace not outside of the institution of the church, apart from the priest and the sacrament. Rather, regeneration is bestowed in and through baptism, apart from presupposing anything positive, only by virtue of the act performed (*ex opere operato*). Just like fire through its inner power brings about warmth to anyone who comes into contact with it, so too the sacrament of baptism bestows the grace of regeneration to anyone who receives it without placing any impediment in its way. For the sacrament does not merely portray grace, but contains grace within itself; the sacrament is a container that holds grace, a conduit through which grace flows. One who is baptized is at that very moment regenerated, engrafted into the church (that is, into the body of Christ), transferred from the state of natural life into that of spiritual life. Baptism is therefore also absolutely necessary for salvation. The church as an institution—that is to say, the priest with the sacrament—stands between God and the soul of a person. There is no fellowship with God except through the ministry of the priest.

7.1.2 *The Anabaptist view*

This was Rome's position. In direct opposition to that were the Anabaptists. Dominated wholly and completely in all their thinking by the opposition between nature and grace, they could not concede that external, sensible, material signs—which is what the sacraments are—do in fact communicate internal, spiritual grace. On the contrary, grace in general, and especially regeneration, is worked within the human heart immediately and directly by God's Spirit. Sacraments can merely signify grace bestowed beforehand by God. Therefore the sacraments may be administered only to such persons who can give clear demonstration of their faith. Baptism may only follow upon personal confession and therefore cannot be administered to children. For children cannot confess faith; and thus one cannot speak of children possessing regeneration and faith.

7.1.3 *The Reformed view and its advantages*

Between both of these positions the Reformed take their stance. From Scripture they took the idea of covenant and in so doing, they immediately acquired two important advantages.

First, with their idea of the covenant they were in a strong position against Rome, which claimed that every communication of grace was tied to the institution of the church, to the sacraments, and to the priest. For the covenant supplied the right and freedom to believe that children born to believing parents had received the grace of regeneration through the Spirit of God already before having coming into contact with the institution of the church, with its sacraments and its minister.

This view, of course, did not entail the claim that children received this benefit *because* they had been born to believing parents, as if their birth were something meritorious and would have granted them any right or claim to such a benefit. But according to the revelation in God's Word, God is so good that in His electing and in the dispensing of His grace, He follows the line of generations and receives into His covenant both parents and their seed together. So the children of believers are to be viewed as holy, not by nature but through the benefit of the covenant of grace, in which they together with their parents are included according to God's arrangement.

Given this position, therefore, baptism is not administered to children of the church in order to make them holy, in order to make them partakers of sanctifying grace, but because they are sanctified in Christ and therefore as members of His church ought to be baptized. Baptism is no conduit through which grace flows to the baptized person, but a sign and seal of received grace, of the covenant, in which the child is included together with his parents.

Therefore baptism is not absolutely necessary for salvation. There is no longer any room for the practice of emergency baptism. For baptism does not bestow any special grace that cannot be bestowed beforehand by God's Spirit, apart from baptism. For dispensing His grace God is not bound to any institution of the church, to any sacrament or priest. He is free and powerful to glorify His grace unto little babies who are not yet cognizant, who cannot hear the Word, and who for one valid reason or another are deprived of the sacrament.

It was with some measure of difficulty that the Reformed in those early days arrived at this position and continued to maintain it in the face of the conflict that arose with their opponents. But despite this, the idea of the covenant was from the outset a unique element of the Reformed confession. Zwingli was among the first to derive it from Holy Scripture and to defend it, along with others, against the Anabaptists. Calvin as well opened up this doctrine and unfolded it with greater clarity. On the basis of this doctrine of the covenant, which God revealed in His Word, we may confess with confidence and gratitude that although our children do not understand these things, they may not therefore be excluded from baptism, since they are without their knowledge also partakers in the condemnation of Adam and so again are received unto grace in Christ.[1]

So the Reformed position has room for a regeneration that precedes the external call through the Word, the administration of baptism, and the operation of the institution of the church. That room involves those covenant children whom God calls out of this life in their infancy and concerning whose election and salvation godly parents must not doubt [see Canons of Dort, I, art. 17]. That room involves all those elect who are incapable of receiving the external calling through the ministry of the Word, such as deaf mutes and the like. Finally, that room involves also the elect children of the covenant who are regenerated before they come to conscious awareness. But all of this does not contradict the claim that in their doctrinal discussions, the Reformed always placed regeneration after calling.

The reason for that lay in the doctrine of the covenant, as that was maintained especially against the Anabaptists. To this doctrine they owed the advantage, over against Rome, that they were able to make the dispensing of grace to occur independent of priest and sacrament. But that doctrine also gave them the advantage, over against the Anabaptists, of being able to maintain the connection between Word and Spirit, between calling and regeneration.

7.2 Further Refutation of Anabaptist Errors

The doctrine of the covenant procured for the Reformed an important advantage over against the Roman Catholic view of the church as mediator of salvation. But it was no less important to them in their struggle against the Anabaptists who separated the operation of the Holy Spirit wholly and entirely from the Word of God that comes to us in Holy Scripture.

7.2.1 Anabaptist traits

As we have already observed, in the days of the Reformation this radical party was governed in their entire thought and practice by the sharp contrast which placed nature and grace in opposition to each other. According to their conviction, there exists and there can exist no connection

---

[1] Ed. note: Here Bavinck uses the exact words of "De Formulieren om de Heilige Sacramenten te bedienen" [The Forms for the Administration of the Holy Sacraments], specifically the Form "Om den Heiligen Doop aan de kinderen te bedienen" [The Form for the Administration of Holy Baptism to Children] used in the Reformed churches in the Netherlands at that time. This can be found in English translation in *Psalter Hymnal*, Centennial edition, Doctrinal Standards and Liturgy of the Christian Reformed Church (Grand Rapids: Publication Committee of the Christian Reformed Church, Inc., 1959), appended pages 85–87; and *Book of Praise: Anglo-Genevan Psalter*, revised ed. (Winnipeg, Manitoba: Premier Printing Ltd., 1984), 584–587.

between these two; nature and grace stood over against each other like light and darkness, day and night, heaven and earth, like Creator and creature. For that reason, a radical separation had to emerge eventually between nature and grace, not only in doctrine but also in life, both in theory and in practice.

By virtue of that opposition and separation, the Anabaptists taught that the first man Adam, because he was from the dust of the ground, could not yet have been the true image of God, could not have shared in true knowledge, righteousness, and holiness; the second Man, Christ, could not have received His human nature from the virgin Mary, but He must have brought it with Him from heaven; believers who had been born of God from above and had received a new, heavenly substance in that regeneration, were to be viewed not merely as renewed, but as new heavenly people in origin and essence, people whose position now was against the world, having nothing more to do with the world.

That had to become apparent in various ways in the practice of Christian living. The Anabaptists could not deny that believers still had a body, and still needed food and drink and clothes, and still lived on earth and in the world. But as happens with all super-spiritual people, even though reality was far too powerful, they nevertheless prohibited believers from holding any office in civil government, from taking any oath, from rendering any military service. They required, through any number of minutiae, that believers distinguish themselves from the world by the way they wore their hair, by the color and style of their clothes, by their forms of etiquette and interaction, even by the demeanor and manner of facial expressions. The church had to consist of a separated group of pious people, a state within a state, an island in the ocean, a drop of oil on the waters. They had to attempt, in a revolutionary manner, to realize the Kingdom of God here on earth on their own plot of ground; or if that did not work, as happened in Munster, they had to await in quiet passivity the return of Christ, looking in hope to the future.

7.2.2 *Grace against nature and Spirit against Word*

Obviously this position has no room for the means of grace. For these instruments, such as, for example, the human language of the Word, and the water, together with the bread and the wine, of the sacraments—these are all instruments taken from nature, even though they are made serviceable, according to our doctrine, to divine grace. But given the position of the Anabaptists, how could anything from nature, any element from God's creation, ever be made serviceable to grace? Here grace requires not the renewal but the banishment of nature. Nature is entirely incapable of being a bearer or conveyor of grace. That applied not only to the sacraments, which according to the Anabaptists were merely external, sensible, representational signs. That applied to the entire institution of the church with all of its offices and ministries. That applied as well to the Word of God, which was deposited in Holy Scripture.

It is true that, taught by bitter experience, the Anabaptists later moderated their radical principles. But the principle that animated and guided their entire movement is nonetheless clearly discernible. Not only the sacrament, but also the Word was placed over against grace, as an external, sensible sign that can never function as a means of grace. There is no possibility either for any subjective but also for any objective, historical mediating of salvation. Regeneration cannot occur through the Word. It is immediate, not only in the sense gladly confessed by the Reformed, that the Word must be accompanied by a direct, effectual, irresistible operation of the Holy Spirit within the human heart; but for the Anabaptists it is immediate also in this other sense, that in no way whatsoever can the Word serve as an instrument of grace. In Scripture the Word is called seed of regeneration, but that is merely a figurative way of speaking. The only seed of regeneration is God, through His Holy Spirit. But when a person is regenerated, only then, at a subsequent point, does the Word come to make known to him that he has been regenerated so that the person recognizes himself as regenerated. So the Word possesses a subordinate significance; it comes afterward. It merely makes manifest what is already present internally. It merely brings to expression what, through God's Spirit, has been accomplished within the person. It merely expresses what has already been written upon the human heart.

Therefore pride of place belongs not to the Word, but to the Spirit, who ignites the inner light within our hearts before and outside and apart from the Word, thereby to lead us through to the external light of the Word. The internal Word is what saves us, whereas the external Word merely makes that more clear to us. So both of them, the internal and the external Word, are related to one another as soul and body, life and death, heaven and earth, spirit and flesh, kernel and husk, silver and dross, truth and symbol, sword and sheath, light and lantern, Christ and the manger, God and nature, Creator and creature.

Knowledge of the external Word supplies nothing by itself, leaving us cold and dead. In order truly to understand, the internal Word is the prerequisite. Just as words can teach us something only when we know their subject matter, so too Scripture can teach us only when Christ already dwells in our hearts and has taught us through His Spirit. The external Word is but a sign, a shadow, a figure, a symbol of spiritual life and spiritual knowledge. In itself that Word has no value whatsoever. Apart from and outside of the Spirit, it is a dead letter, a paper pope, a closed book, full of contradictions, from whose verses every heretic draws his heresy, from which a person can prove anything and nothing with a few isolated verses torn from their contexts.

But the internal Word is spirit and life, truth and power. This internal Word was identified with quite varied terms by the Anabaptists and movements associated with them. They spoke of an internal Word, but also of an internal light, a spiritual light, of regeneration, the creation of God within us, of Christ within us, of the Holy Spirit, etc. From those inclined toward mysticism, one need not expect crisp and clear distinctions that are so necessary especially here. Nevertheless, whatever term was used, it was understood to refer to that new heavenly life coming directly from above, infused by God's Spirit suddenly and immediately, apart from the Word, within the human heart—often even in a pantheistic manner that identified it with Christ or with God, or with the divine nature.

7.2.3 The way of mysticism

This in brief was the doctrine of the Anabaptists concerning the internal Word and its relationship to Scripture. In the time of the Reformation this was not something altogether new, and was not promulgated initially at that time. It had been expressed already by many sects and groups during the Middle Ages, and during the early centuries of the Christian church. Its fundamental idea, although modified in a Christian way within Christian circles, is essential to all mysticism, wherever and whenever it has appeared—whether in India or Greece, in Persia or Egypt. Simply stated, it is this: in order to find truth or life or salvation—in a word, to find God—a person need not go outside of himself but need only descend within himself. God dwells within a person, making His abode within the person either through nature or through a special, supernatural descent into the person. After all, religion does not involve doctrine or activity, thinking or doing, but religion involves living in God, union and communion with God, which can be enjoyed only in the depths of one's psyche, in the immediacy of one's consciousness.

When we express this fundamental concept in such a general way and strip it of the particular forms in which it appears with its various tendencies, anyone can easily recall seeing this idea in various philosophical and religious systems of earlier and later times. Nowadays one finds it resurfacing in the philosophy of Hegel, in the theology of Schleiermacher, in the modern tendency of Scholten, in the ethical theology of De la Saussaye, Sr.[2] One discovers it even in Plato's doctrine of

---

[2] Ed. note: Here Bavinck refers to a variety of philosophical and theological movements and approaches that reflected the diversified theological climate in which he labored. In short form, Hegel (1770–1831) attempted to define Christianity as the pinnacle of historical achievement. This great synthesis, however, eventually had to become, with advancing history, just another thesis, and God became a redundancy. Thus Hegel's thought led to pantheism and relativism in theology, and in the hands of his left-wing followers, it ushered in atheism. Meanwhile, Schleiermacher (1768–1834) argued that theology should proceed from below, starting with humans and their sense of the divine in the feeling of absolute dependence. His thought tended toward mysticism and subjectivism, but was driven to deliver the intellectual culture of his day from agnosticism and from the ascendency of the intellect that leads to rationalism and atheism. Schleiermacher's views were adopted in the Netherlands particularly by what became known as Groninger theology, which may be characterized as a form of Christian humanism, being Arian in Christology, Pelagian in anthropology, and rationalistic and critical in its approach to the Bible. J. H. Scholten (1811–1885)

innate ideas, according to which a person draws the knowledge of the truth not from the world around him but from within himself.

Moreover, one can easily see where the implications of this notion lead. When this notion has been expressed at any time in history by a person of deep seriousness and firm conviction, finding warm and enthusiastic agreement within any circle small or large, it frequently gives birth to exuberance, courage, enthusiasm, and deep and glorious mysticism. This was the case at first with the Anabaptists as well. At that time there were many upright believers among them, many genuine children of God. Whatever one might say about the Anabaptists, one must never forget that in large numbers and with remarkable courage of faith, they sacrificed their goods and their blood for the cause of the Lord.

But the principle soon manifested its mistaken implications. First, people came to be satisfied with the internal Word alone, despising Scripture and church, office and sacrament, appealing to private revelations and becoming guilty of various excesses. Second, when the initial exuberance was past, gradually the internal Word was robbed of its special, supernatural character, coming to be more and more identified with the natural light of reason and conscience. Abstract supra-naturalism was followed by rationalism. Because people despised the Word, they surrendered the criterion that alone enabled them to distinguish properly between nature and grace. The sharp contrast disappeared. What people initially thought they had learned only through special, internal revelation could later appear to be the exceedingly good fruit of God's revelation in reason. The internal light came gradually to be identified, as with the Quakers, for example, with the light of nature. In both instances, however, Scripture contained nothing other than what a person had already learned by God's Spirit.

In opposition to this tendency, the Reformed church and Reformed theology chose a position just as resolute as the one they had adopted

---

was the supreme representative at this time of modern theology in the Netherlands. The moderns wanted little to do with the past and were concerned to forge a new theology for the contemporary, modern era, especially given the triumph of modern science and the findings of historical criticism in relation to the Bible. They had unbounded confidence in human progress. Scholten's theology was subjectivistic, mystical, and pantheistic. The Ethical theology, represented by such men as N. Beets (1814–1903), J. H. Gunning (1829–1905), D. Chantepie de la Saussaye (1818–1874), and J.J. van Toorenenbergen (1821–1903), was the Dutch version of the German "Vermittlungstheologie" (mediating theology) and argued for a strong experiential form of Christianity in opposition to the intellectualism of rationalism, and for a heavy accent upon moral life in distinction from dogmatic theology. Moreover, ethical theology, though having sympathies to orthodox confessional theology, embraced a critical approach to Scripture, and was strongly influenced by Schleiermacher and modern German philosophy. Essentially, the "ethical" school sought to mediate between traditional orthodoxy and rationalist critiques of Christianity by focusing upon pious experience and ethical concerns. By disposition and conviction, the Ethicals promoted social responsibility and an irenical approach to theological and ecclesiastical controversy. However, they strongly opposed Abraham Kuyper's ecclesiastical reforms in the Dutch (State) Reformed Church in the latter half of the nineteenth century.

against Rome. They held firmly to the connection between Word and Spirit, between calling and regeneration. They were able to do that by means of their doctrine of the covenant of grace.

7.3 The Covenant of Grace and the Church

By means of their doctrine of the covenant of grace the Reformed were put in a position to maintain, against the Anabaptists, the connection between Word and Spirit, between calling and regeneration.

If, contrary to Rome's teaching, baptism does not accomplish regeneration in infants, but rather presupposes it, as the Anabaptists confessed, then it seemed logical that the Reformed would have agreed with the Anabaptists in denying any saving value to church and office, to Word and sacrament—or at least they would have agreed that these cannot lead the way as means of grace, but could merely come after grace, as signs and proofs of grace already experienced.

But the Reformed did not allow themselves to be seduced by this apparently logical line of reasoning. That would have been impossible and impermissible, even unnecessary, because they distinguished between the covenant of grace and the church.

7.3.1 *The coincidence of the covenant of grace and the church*

In a certain sense, and to a certain degree, there is not any great difference between the two. In its administration and its dispensation, the covenant of grace coincides with the church; the boundaries are the same for both. There is also agreement in the goods and benefits bestowed and enjoyed within both the covenant of grace and the church. Scripture, which is interpreted and explained, preached and applied by the church, is the book of the covenant. The sacraments administered by the church are signs and seals of the covenant. The benefits enjoyed by the church as the gathering of believers—regeneration and conversion, forgiveness and sanctification—are commodities belonging to the covenant. Finally, there is also a large measure of identity when the church is seen not exclusively as the institution of the church, but seen also as an organism.

7.3.1.1 Church as institute and organism

This last observation, however, points already to an important distinction that exists between the covenant of grace and the church. With respect to the church, we are able for a moment to abstract in our thinking the church from the institution that is manifest to our eyes. But this is nothing more than an abstraction, one which does not appear in reality. Historically the church has never existed, does never exist, and can never exist apart from any institutional identity. God established the church on earth, and preserved it until this very day, not simply and exclusively *as* an institution, but *with* its institution. In the time of the patriarchs, in the dispensations of Old and New Testaments, time and again that institution did have another shape; but an institution, a certain arrangement and organization, has always belonged properly to the church.

Therefore it is completely erroneous to place the church as organism and the church as institution in opposition to each other, to put the former high above the latter, and to play the former against the latter. The institution is particularly that organization, that one, necessary, indispensable organization undergirding the so-called church as organism. This latter has no other specific address than precisely that address of the institution. It comes to manifestation in no humanly invented society or corporation, but in its God-given institution.

Precisely for that reason, however, we always immediately and instinctively include within the notion of the church the concept of the institution. Within our thinking we logically and momentarily distinguish between the church as organism and the church as institution, and we must do that in order to think properly; for only those who distinguish well, teach well. But that does not at all diminish the fact that both of these are connected most intimately, both in thought and in reality. Even when we describe the church as the gathering of believers, we have immediately included the institutional character of the church in that description. For, in the first place, a gathering cannot be imagined apart from an organization and a government of some kind. Secondly, the word "gathering" used in this description possesses not merely a passive, but also an active sense; the church is not only the fellowship within which believers are gathered, but it is also as such particularly the organization called continually to gather believers.

Without such a precise understanding of the church, one risks the danger of following Rome, which argues that since the church in its concrete existence always includes the institution, salvation depends on the institution of the church, of the priest, and of the sacrament. Or one faces the danger of Anabaptism, which seeks to purify the church once and for all, and definitively severs all the operations of grace from Word and sacrament.

7.3.1.2 The Reformed remedy

Both of these extremes were able to be avoided by the Reformed, since they derived from Scripture the glorious doctrine of the covenant of grace. This covenant included two elements, notions that are not absent from the understanding of the church as consisting of believers, of course, but elements that nevertheless do not appear in the foreground.

The first element is that this covenant is between God and man. The church is a gathering of believers who look to Christ for all their deliverance and salvation, but a gathering which at the same time mutually constitutes a congregation, a communion, a body. The covenant of grace, however, places God's relationship with man at the forefront, and places it there as a gracious relationship. In that covenant, God is the first and the last, the beginning and the end. The entirety of salvation is His work, from its very beginning to its completion in eternity. God is the one, and He alone, who seeks man and calls man and brings him into His fellowship. He appears to man and out of grace imparts unto him all the benefits.

The second element included in the covenant is that this covenant continues from generation to generation. When God binds Himself to being our God, then at the same time He binds Himself to be the God of our seed. With His grace He follows the line of the generations. He executes election along the route and pathway of the covenant. As Father of all mercies He walks the path that He Himself, as Father of everything, has drawn.

7.3.2 *The difference between the covenant of grace and the church*

This covenant of grace therefore precedes the church, viewed as organism and institution together. Indeed, it would not be incorrect to say that the children of believers are born into the fellowship of the church, for the church in its definition includes all the elect, all believers, both those with the capacity for believing and those who in actuality believe. Within Reformed theology, however, a distinction is usually made. For example, in the Form for Baptism, we read that our children are without their knowledge received into grace by God; they are heirs of the kingdom of God and of His covenant; and they are sanctified in Christ.[3] The Canons of Dort say that our children are *holy*, not by nature, but by virtue of the covenant of grace, in which they together with their parents are included.[4] Therefore, because they are such, they ought to be baptized and to become engrafted into the *church* through their baptism. Because God, out of sheer grace, has received and included them with their parents in the covenant of grace, therefore the church receives from God the right and the authority to engraft them into its fellowship through baptism. In a certain sense the church is the fruit of faith; it is, namely, the gathering of believers, the having-been-gathered believers, in a passive sense, and because the church is this, it also becomes, and according to God's appointment must also be, in an active sense, the institution that gathers the believers.

But the covenant of grace precedes faith. Faith is not a condition *unto* the covenant, but a condition *within* the covenant: the route to be followed in order to become partaker and to enjoy all the other commodities of that covenant. Yet faith itself is already a fruit, a benefit of the covenant, a gift of God's grace and thus a proof that God has received us in

---

[3] Ed. note: See page 69, footnote 1, regarding an English translation of this Formulary.
[4] Ed. note: See Canons of Dort, I, art.17.

His covenant. For God bestows all the gifts of His grace in and along the pathway of the covenant.[5]

Still more, the covenant of grace not only precedes the gifts of grace and the operation of the Holy Spirit, but it also precedes even the person of Christ, namely, His incarnation and atonement. The covenant was established already in eternity with Christ as the Surety of His own.[6] It did not come into existence for the first time within history. The covenant is rooted in eternity. At that point it consisted not simply in the decree, like everything else can in that sense be said to have existed in eternity. Rather, the covenant existed at that point also in truth and in reality between the Father and the Son, and therefore immediately after the Fall the covenant could be made known to man and be established with man.

Therefore, that covenant of grace, existing from eternity to eternity, functions within history as the instrumentality of all redemption, the route along which God communicates all of His gracious benefits to man. In Reformed dogmatics, therefore, the chapter dealing with the covenant always comes before the chapter dealing with the doctrine of the church, whether this is located at the beginning of the doctrine of the order of salvation, or appears already before the discussion of the person and work of Christ.

---

[5] Ed. note: This paragraph is very germane to modern discussions about the covenant of grace.

[6] Ed. note: Here Bavinck is referring to the counsel of peace or the *pactum salutis*; he expounds this doctrine in his *Reformed Dogmatics*, III, 212–16.

8

Diverse Views Concerning the Moment of Regeneration

THE COVENANT of grace is the great commodity that God in His compassion bestows upon sinners; and He imparts the benefits of that covenant to believers who in their gathering together constitute the essence of the church. But with that covenant belongs the gospel, which is inseparable from the covenant. Just as the covenant of works is proclaimed in the law and does not exist apart from the law, so the covenant of grace is revealed and made known in the gospel, which has the person of Christ at its center. Both the covenant of grace and the gospel are connected indissolubly. Where the gospel is not known, the covenant of grace does not exist; but it is also true that everywhere the gospel is brought, God establishes His covenant and glorifies His grace.

From the foregoing one might suppose that somewhere the gospel could be known where no one yet accepts the gospel in faith; but in reality that does not happen. For God has bound Himself to work with His Spirit wherever His Word is proclaimed. His Word does not return void, but accomplishes everything that pleases Him and prospers in everything for which He sends it [Isa. 55:11]. It is always an aroma of life unto life or of death unto death [2 Cor. 2:16]. Where God's Word is, there is God Himself, there God's Spirit is at work, there God establishes His covenant, there He plants His church. On the basis of God's own promises we may believe that, as Luther put it, God's people cannot exist apart from God's Word and God's Word cannot exist apart from God's people. Small though their number may be and unknown though their reputation may be among people, there are nevertheless believers across the entire globe, wherever the gospel has been spread.

8.1 The Reformed Remedy to the Anabaptist Error

If this is the case, then it follows, in the first place, that the Anabaptists err when they detach the Holy Spirit from the Word. For they taught that God regenerates through the Holy Spirit alone, through the internal word, apart from making use at that point of the Word of Holy Scripture. The Holy Spirit and He alone was the true seed of regeneration. Therefore they also had to accept and indeed did accept that God's grace was common and was at work among pagans as well. The internal word that was detached from Holy Scripture is to be found everywhere, among those who never heard the gospel as well as among those who lived under the dispensation of grace. The Word of Scripture merely made known and declared what God had accomplished through the internal word within the hearts of people both pagan and Christian.

The Reformed confessed wholeheartedly that the Word alone was insufficient unto regeneration and conversion, and that a special, almighty, direct operation of the Holy Spirit must accompany the Word in order to bring the sinner from death to life. But that explanation did not lead them at all to join the Anabaptists in detaching the operation of the Holy Spirit entirely from the Word. They held to Scripture and were unwilling to be more wise than one ought to be. They therefore generally maintained that the Word was the seed of regeneration, the means of grace. According to their Scripture-based conviction, the Holy Spirit worked only with the boundaries drawn by acquaintance with the gospel. Even though among the Reformed there were a few who acknowledged the possibility of election and regeneration among pagans, they nonetheless left that possibility for what it was and did not orient their teaching in terms of this, but with their confession they held to the rule of Holy Scripture.

8.2 The Reformed Remedy to the Roman Catholic Error

From this convergence between the covenant of grace and the gospel it follows, in the second place, that grace is not, as with Rome, dependent upon the institutional church, upon priest and sacrament. Protestants construe the relationship between Scripture and church entirely differently than does Rome. According to the latter, the church precedes Scripture, the church was not built upon Scripture, but Scripture proceeded forth from the church. Therefore, the church in terms of its essence and existence does not need Scripture, but Scripture needs the church for its origin, collection, preservation, and interpretation. The Reformation reversed that relationship by placing the church upon the foundation of Scripture and by exalting Scripture above the church. Not the church, but Scripture as the Word of God became the means of grace *par excellence*. Even the sacrament was subordinated to the Word and apart from the Word it has no meaning or power. But that Word could and did work beyond the boundaries of the church as well. It is true that God has

entrusted that Word to His church, so that the Word would be interpreted, preached, and defended by the church. But that Word was not
bestowed upon the church in such a manner that it could not exist or exercise its power beyond the church. On the contrary, that Word is directed to all people; it has value in every circumstance and for every area
of life. Moreover, that Word does not in any sense derive its power and
operation strictly from being proclaimed by an office-bearer in the context of the gathering of believers. The Word does its work also when it is
read and studied within the home, when it is taught by parents and
teachers, when it is made known in one form or another. Every person,
no matter who or what or where he might be, who accepts that Word believingly partakes in God's promise, in God's grace in Christ, indeed, in
all of salvation. At that point he need not wait for any church, any minister, or any sacrament. Anyone who believes has eternal life.

In this way the individual Christian was delivered by the Reformation
from the domination of the priest. He was not set free from his context
and from all his historical past in the sense that apart from the external
Word he could partake in God's grace in Christ. But for his salvation he
was no longer dependent upon the institution of the church. The minister
of the church was not the one who bestowed salvation upon him, and the
sacrament was no longer indispensable for him. Rather, God granted him
salvation, directly, personally, in a certain sense apart from any interme-
diary of office or sacrament, so that nothing came to stand between God
and the believer's soul. All of this, however, did not at all overthrow the
conviction that God, according to his own testimony, imparts that grace
only along the route of the covenant.

8.3 The Work of Grace and Covenant Children

In the third place, it follows therefore from the relationship between
the covenant of grace and the gospel that both of these always precede
the working of the Holy Spirit and the believer's participation in the person of Christ and all his benefits.

It does seem that this imparting of the benefits of grace to children
occurs in a different way than with adults. To a certain extent this is true.
For all of the Reformed unanimously confess with gratitude that God is
not restricted to any instrument and also that apart from the external
preaching of the gospel God can plant the principle of eternal life within
the hearts of little children. No one among us doubts that. Holy Scripture
proves that with the examples of Jeremiah and John the Baptist.

But at this point we may never lose sight of the truth that applies only to those children who are covenant children, who are born under the
administration of the gospel, and who together with their parents have
been received by God in grace. God can dispense His benefits apart from
the means of the Word, and He does so with the little children of believers. But He does this nonetheless always through the internal call of that

very Spirit whom He poured out upon the church. He does this in the communion of the church, which He commissioned to preach the gospel to all creatures. He does this along the route of that covenant which has received the gospel as its content and the sacrament as its sign and seal.

So even though it is the case that children of believers are engrafted into the instituted church for the first time through baptism, already before that happens, yes, even before their birth, they are included with their parents in the covenant of grace. That covenant precedes the gospel by which it is revealed, and precedes the gift of the benefits of salvation, including regeneration.

For these reasons, in their explanation of the teaching of the truth, the Reformed remained faithful to the order wherein calling occupied the first place in the order of salvation. They were afraid that otherwise the Baptistic error would creep in, which made the Spirit independent from the Word, regeneration independent from calling, and the dispensing of grace independent from the administration of the gospel. The Reformed could maintain this order because they had derived it not from the individual, from the manner in which this or that individual person had come to conversion, but from the objective relationships that God had laid down in His Word and to which He bound Himself in history.

Viewed individualistically, in the case of little children it could appear as though regeneration precedes calling and the Spirit precedes the Word. The Formulary for Baptism states correctly that the children of believers cannot understand all those things proclaimed in the gospel and sealed in baptism, but they may not for this reason be excluded from baptism. For just as *without their knowledge* they share in the condemnation of Adam, so in the same way—that is, *without their knowledge*— they are received by God in grace. So it has the appearance as if, in the case of infant children of believers, regeneration precedes calling and that thus in their case regeneration is immediate *in this sense* that it occurs apart from and outside of the Word of the gospel.

But this judgment is incorrect. If without their knowledge little children are received by God in grace and are regenerated, then this always presupposes that the covenant of grace together with the gospel wherein it is proclaimed had already existed objectively and historically. According to the order that God has established in His sovereignty and that He keeps in view when He dispenses the benefits of His grace, they could not partake of regeneration unless they were born as covenant children. Precisely as covenant children they are called by God. Even though they themselves do not understand the things of the gospel, they are nevertheless called together with and in their parents. To them as children of believers together with their parents comes the promise, that is, the promise of the gospel, the promise made known and offered only in the gospel. As the seed of Christian parents, not detached from the dispensing of the Word but in connection with it, they are internally called by the Holy Spirit and thus engrafted into the regeneration of Christ. When a child is isolated from this context, which in this case means from the covenant of grace, then it appears that regeneration precedes calling, although then this means at the same time that every reason for believing in the salvation of little children has disappeared. If we view the matter objectively and historically, however, attending to the order established by God for the dispensing of the benefits of His grace, then calling precedes regeneration, and the administration of the gospel precedes the working of the Holy Spirit.

This is further confirmed for the infant children of believers by the fact that as children of the covenant and as heirs of the kingdom of God they have a right to be baptized.

Baptism is one of two sacraments ordained by Christ for His believers. The sacraments mean nothing and are not sacraments if they are isolated from the Word. Sacraments are seals of the Word, follow upon the Word, and are connected indissolubly to the Word. The baptism of infants would therefore have absolutely no power and would cease being a sacrament if it were not preceded by the Word and did not follow upon that Word in order to signify and seal that Word. So just as baptism is the seal of the Word, so too the regeneration in which infant children of believers partake forms the fulfillment of the promise that comes to us in the gospel alone, the promise that according to this very gospel applies not only to believers, but in and with them also to their children.

8.4 Covenant Children Who Die in Infancy

The doctrine of the covenant of grace was the reason why the Reformed, in opposition to the Anabaptists, could maintain the order of the Word preceding the Spirit and calling preceding regeneration. But this was not the only reason. A second reason derived from the factual situation in which the church of Christ continually dwells here upon earth.

With a view to covenant children who die in infancy, the Reformed unanimously confessed that without their knowledge and thus also apart from any external calling these children were regenerated by God's Spirit and so were received into heaven. The Synod of Dort expressed the uniform conviction of the Reformed when it said that godly parents must not doubt the election and salvation of their children whom God takes from this life in their infancy. But that uniform confession did not deny the fact that among the Reformed some difference of conviction had always existed with respect to such covenant children who died in infancy.

Some were of the opinion that among these infants as well, one should distinguish between those who were already elect and those who were not. Being included in the dispensation of the covenant could not in itself serve as a proof of one's election; for how many children were not born to believing parents who later became apostate and took up travel on the broad way? Moreover, Holy Scripture nowhere teaches that dying in infancy was automatically a sign of their election and salvation for those children born in the covenant. So those among the Reformed who reasoned this way thus acknowledged that the elect among covenant children dying in infancy were regenerated before their death by God's Spirit and so were received into heaven. But lacking any express declaration in God's Word, they did not dare to believe with full certainty that all covenant children dying in infancy belonged without exception to the elect.

Others adopted a somewhat broader position. They proceeded from the promise of God. To Abraham, the father of believers, God had once declared: I will establish my covenant between me and you and your seed after you throughout their generations, to be a God to you and to your seed (Gen. 17:7). According to God's Word, the promise was not only to the parents, but also to their children (Acts 2:39). To this one should hold firmly, until the opposite appeared. With covenant children whose life was spared it later became manifest in their words and deeds whether they desired to walk in the way of the covenant; and if that was not the case, they were removed from the midst of the church through ecclesiastical discipline. But with covenant children who through death were taken away early in life, this could not be manifested; thus they could not provide, either through words or through deeds, evidence contradicting the fact that they were covenant children. For that reason, one should consider such a child as having been received by God in grace, and as having become a partaker of salvation at death. Just as we presume a person innocent until proven guilty, so too we should view covenant children as elect. Thus there was no basis for considering some covenant children who died in infancy to be elect while considering other covenant children not to be elect.

The Synod of Dort adopted this gentle position. It deserves mention, however, that it described this position in a very delicate way. First, it did not proclaim this as a dogma that was objectively fixed, but rather the Synod spoke in a subjective manner by saying that parents must not doubt the election and salvation of their children who die in infancy. Second, the Synod did not extend this comfort to parents in general, but to godly parents. After all, parents who themselves have no interest in their own election and salvation cannot be genuinely concerned about the fate of their children, and neither need nor can enjoy such comfort. In order genuinely to believe that our deceased infants share in salvation, we ourselves ought to have accepted with upright faith the benefits of the covenant, and be assured of our own election and salvation.

For our purpose it is unnecessary to pursue this point any further, the less so because with all of our reasoning we would progress no further than issuing the humble judgment of charity which the Synod of Dort expressed. Moreover, we could never remove all the objections raised by people holding to the position mentioned.

Although many covenant children die in their infancy, and though this number is surely much higher than people in earlier times with their lack of statistical data could assume, there are nevertheless thousands upon thousands who grow up to reach the age of discretion and at that point come to stand personally before the choice of following Christ or serving the world. With a view to these covenant children, whose life is spared and who later are admitted to the Lord's Supper upon profession of faith, another twofold question arises.

The first question is whether all of those covenant children in fact belong to the elect and will therefore at some point infallibly and certainly become partakers of the heavenly salvation. This question need not detain us long, however, for upon careful reflection and with Scripture in hand, no one would be able or would dare to give an affirmative answer to that question. If on the basis of the Scriptural teaching that the church of Christ is to be viewed as a gathering of *believers*, here or there an individual deduces that therefore every member of the church is truly a sincere believer, then such reasoning rests upon a misunderstanding for which a brief word of clarification and warning is sufficient. For Scripture teaches as clearly as possible that not all who are descended from Israel belong to Israel (Rom. 9:6), and it is not the children of the flesh but the children of the promise who must be considered the seed. All of the confessions of all the churches agree with this. And everyday experience places the seal on this, for repeatedly it becomes manifest that in the church hypocrites are mixed in with the sincere believers, hypocrites who are not *of* the church although according to the body they are *in* the church. The most severe and most strict church discipline is incapable of separating the chaff from the grain, for the church cannot judge the heart and must deal only with confession and walk.

During various periods of history there was undoubtedly also variety in terms of the purity of the church. When the apostles preached the gospel and established churches in and beyond Palestine, the danger of many people joining the church without possessing upright heartfelt faith was minimal. The despising and persecution that the disciples of Christ had to expect from the world kept the insincere away. When in the period of the Reformation, confessing Christ exposed one to the danger of being burned at the stake or hung from a scaffold, underlying that confession with the mouth was by far and away in most instances a genuine heartfelt faith. By contrast, within a church that is exempt from persecution, that has become a significant force within a culture, and that neglects discipline, the number of merely external confessors usually increases. All of this is, however, merely a difference in degree. An absolutely pure church, all of whose members are believers in the true sense, does not exist on earth. For that reason, the seed must always be considered to be only the children of the promise and not the children of the flesh.

8.5 Voetius's View: Regeneration from Infancy

Another question is when and at what moment those covenant children, still living, who belong to the elect, become personally partakers in the promise which, in the covenant of grace, is addressed to them with their parents.

Concerning this matter difference of opinion has always existed among the Reformed churches.[1] The opinion of Voetius, which we mentioned earlier, comes down to this, that all the elect who are born to believing parents in the covenant are also regenerated in their infancy before baptism. He did find it a bit objectionable to take this position with respect to those elect persons who lived year after year in sin and came to conversion when they turned thirty, fifty, or seventy. But he accepted the possibility that the seed of regeneration, sown during the earliest days of life, could remain latent under the soil for that long.

He found this view preferable because, according to Holy Scripture, the children of believers together with their parents shared in the promises of God—otherwise circumcision and baptism would be reduced to empty signs—and only with this view could the arguments against the Anabaptists and the like retain their force. According to Voetius, not only such children as those who from their youth showed that they were partakers of the life of grace, but also others, like Abraham, Manasseh, the sinner in Luke 7, the murderer on the cross, Cornelius, Lydia, Augustine, Luther, all of whom were converted later in life, were most likely regenerated already in their youth. He even thought—although one could better refrain from rendering a firm judgment about this—that the conviction was not at all to be dismissed that an elect infant was regenerated at the very moment of conception.

Voetius was not alone in holding this view. Before and after him, various divines held the same view in broad outline. Today as well his opinion has found sympathy among many.

This view was then defended with the further observation that the deaf cannot hear. For that reason, according to their position, regeneration must precede calling through the Word. An elect person is first regenerated immediately by the Holy Spirit, apart from the Word, but then sooner or later becomes acquainted with the gospel and called by the gospel to faith and conversion. The administration of the Word does not serve to plant the new life within the heart, but rather to bring unto manifestation in deeds of faith and conversion the new life that has already come into existence apart from the Word. For the unregenerate, on the other hand, the administration of the Word serves to remove from him all excuse. Others did and do hold to a different view, however, and it is worth our trouble to become familiar with their opinion.

---

[1] Ed. note: A useful essay that explores the different views among Reformed theologians on this question is Herman Witsius, *Disquisitio Modesta et Placida de Efficacia et Utilitate Baptismi in Electis foederatorum Parentum Infantibus* (Utrecht, 1693), see xxiv–lv; translated into English by William Marshall, edited and revised translation, with an introduction by J. Mark Beach, "On the Efficacy and Utility of Baptism in the Case of Elect Infants Whose Parents Are under the Covenant of Grace," *Mid-America Journal of Theology* 17 (2006): 121–190; see especially pp. 142–168.

8.6 Opponents of the Voetian View

8.6.1 *Jesaias Hillenius*

The opinion of those who differed from Voetius was set forth very clearly by Jesaias Hillenius (1700–1759), minister in Drachten, who in 1751 and 1752 published *De Mensch beshouwt in de staat der elende, der genade en der heerlijkheit . . .* [Man viewed in the state of misery, of grace, and of glory]. In the second section of that work, he raised the question: Is there in every elect person, from the very first moment of life, a seed of regeneration that germinates at the appointed time? He answered this question as follows.[2]

1. It is certain that the elect have several advantages over the reprobate when it comes to their regeneration, such as the fact that God considers them to be those for whom His Son has made atonement and for whom He has obtained the right unto life. God considers them to be His elect, unto whom He grants the means of salvation, together with the aim of effectually changing them at a particular time through those means. God so preserves them that they do not become guilty of committing the unforgiveable sin against the Holy Spirit, and suffer its consequences.

2. That some elect are regenerated through the almighty power of God before they can use their understanding, we will not contest. But that every elect person from the first moment of life should possess a seed of regeneration, we judge that such is not taught in the Word of God, but much rather the opposite.

For in the first place, Holy Scripture clearly teaches us that they are dead in transgressions and sins, even as Paul says concerning the converted Ephesians, that they once were such, and they had once walked according to the ways of this world, according to the ruler of the power of the air, the spirit under which they had formerly walked according to the desires of the flesh, performing its will and thoughts (Eph. 2:1–3). What seed of regeneration would possibly have existed within them? Concerning the converted Corinthians the same Apostle says: and such were some of you, namely, what had been said in the preceding verses: sexually immoral, idolaters, adulterers, etc. But, he continues, "such were some of you: but ye are washed, but ye are sanctified, but ye are justified in the name of the Lord Jesus, and by the Spirit of God" (1 Cor. 6:11). Consider also Titus 3:3, cited earlier: "For we ourselves also were sometimes foolish, disobedient, deceived, serving divers lusts and pleasures, living in malice and envy, hateful, and hating one another." How can one say that such people possessed a seed of regeneration?

---

[2] Jesaias Hillenius, *De mensch beschouwt in de staat der elende, der genade, en der heerlikheit: of, Een uitvoerige verhandeling van eenige voorname leerstukken, welke die driederley staat des menschen vertonen . . .* (Leeuwarden: Pieter Koumans, 1751), 705.

Secondly, if every elect person possessed a seed of regeneration from the first moment of life, it could not be said concerning some of them that they were subsequently initially regenerated (1 Pet. 1:23, James 1:18). Thus, the beginning impulses of spiritual life are imparted through regeneration.

Thirdly, what else can this seed of regeneration consist of than a principle of the spiritual life? This being the case, we agree that it is not impossible that children who are not yet capable of using their reason nevertheless possess that principle on account of their capacity, apart from it being operative since they do not yet have use of their reason. For if innate depravity or a principle of depraved life can be present within an infant before the infant is capable of using reason, even as is truly the case, so too a principle of spiritual life can be present within that same infant.

But just as the principle of the depraved life manifests itself in the child when the child begins using reason, so too by way of analogy that principle of spiritual life will manifest itself, if such a principle is present within that child. It is an incomprehensible reality that this good principle would continue to be inoperative for many years, lying buried beneath the seductive desires of the flesh. Experience teaches that people who have lived a very impious life, after living many years in sin, to the point even of reviling godliness and everyone who is godly, opposing them with hostility, can be changed and converted; but could the seed of regeneration have been present within such a person as long as that person lived under the ruling power of depravity, hating God and the godly?

The Apostle John says that anyone born of God does not sin, for God's seed abides in him, and he cannot sin, for he is born of God (1 John 3:9). Can there be a disposition for loving God within a person who lives in hatred of God and of His truth? Can the seed of God and the seed of the devil be present in the same place, and in such a way that the seed of God hides in secret and remains quiet, while the seed of the devil displays its power and completely rules over that person? After all, what is that seed of regeneration? If it is a capacity, how then can this capacity reside in the soul, which is a spiritual entity, inert without any activity? We approve what the great Calvin said: "Those who dream of some seed of election implanted in their hearts from their birth, by the agency of which they are ever inclined to piety and the fear of God, are not supported by the authority of Scripture, but refuted by experience" (Inst. III.24.10).

People reply, however, by saying that Paul teaches that "anyone who does not have the Spirit of Christ does not belong to him" (Rom. 8:9). Now it is undeniable that the elect belong to Christ; from that, one must also infer that they have the Spirit of Christ. We reply by saying that the reality that the elect belong to Christ cannot be doubted, for they are elect in Him in order to be saved through Him (Eph. 1:4). They have been given unto Him by the Father (John 17:6). So these belong to Him already from eternity. They belong to Him because He has purchased them (Acts

20:23). So from that time forward they belong to Him by right, as His acquired and purchased possession, and thus they belong to Him before they are born; but they cannot possess the Spirit of Christ at that point, because they do not yet exist. From this it follows that there is nothing to the objection being raised.

One must note further, however, that having the Spirit of Christ is presented here by the Apostle as a mark that enables someone to know whether he shares in Christ, since having the Spirit of Christ is here understood as something in contrast to being in the flesh and subsequent to being in the flesh. Being in the flesh indicates beyond question that a person is under the powerful dominion of sin, and is not yet converted. Everyone who is still in the flesh, however, must not immediately be identified as reprobate, as someone for whom Christ did not atone, since God's Word and experience teach us that people who have lived very fleshly lives are able to be converted. But the person who continues living according to the flesh, even though he may be an elect person for whom Christ died, such a person receives no guarantee from this passage that such will happen—for a person who lives according to the flesh is not living according to the Spirit, since the Spirit of God does not dwell in him.

What then is more clear than that Paul identifies this reality of having the Spirit of Christ as a sure sign by which the Roman believers could know that they were partakers of Christ and that they belonged to Him? But how would a person be able to know this from a seed of regeneration that lay quiet and inert within him? It seems sufficiently evident that no proof at all can be derived from this passage for such a seed of regeneration.

Moreover, such marks are for adults, or at least for those who can use reason, but not for infants who are still unable to use reason. One can observer further that belonging to Christ can include being effectually united to Christ and having communion with Him; but no one is effectually united to Christ, though he belongs by right through the grant and purchase by Christ, if he does not have the Spirit of Christ; for there is no communion with Christ apart from His Spirit, since communion with Christ is spiritual, and there is no spiritual communion except through the Spirit. The Spirit is the one who regenerates a person and brings about faith within a person, whereby that person is united to Christ.

After having refuted the opinions of others, Hillenius explained his own understanding concerning the time of regeneration this way:

> As far as the time of regeneration is concerned, that is quite varied. The papists teach that it occurs in baptism, since they desire that baptism itself effects regeneration by virtue of the act performed, but we will not pause to refute that erroneous view. The theologians who composed the Augsburg Confession are of the opinion that regeneration is imparted commonly to children only in the administration of baptism, so that the grace of regeneration is connected so closely to baptism that each per-

son baptized in infancy is regenerated at the same moment, although they ascribe no regenerating power to the water of baptism.[3]

8.6.2 *The propriety of this view*

Some of our people are inclined to this view as well. Others of our people want to believe that elect infants are regenerated in their infancy before baptism, though the seed of regeneration remains hidden under the surface. Still others are of the judgment that God regenerates the elect at various times; some, in their infancy, whether before their baptism or during baptism or after baptism, when they acquire the use of their reason; others in their adolescence, others in adulthood; others (the fewest) in old age; a few even on their deathbeds and, as it were, immediately before the portal of death.

We are inclined to this view as well, considering that even as God merely according to His pleasure has chosen certain people unto salvation, He is also entirely free to regenerate them at whatever time pleases Him. Even as we have seen that the view of the divines, that a seed of regeneration supposedly lies within each elect person from the moment life begins, is not supported by any adequate basis, from this it follows that one cannot suppose that the elect in general are regenerated in their infancy before baptism. The view which identifies the moment of regeneration as the moment one is baptized is a claim that Holy Scripture nowhere teaches us, but on the contrary, Scripture teaches us about several people who were regenerated already before baptism, such as Paul (Acts 9:11, 17–18) and Cornelius (Acts 10:47). If God ordinarily regenerated a person during baptism, then parents would hasten or delay the regeneration of their children (to the extent there were elect among them) by choosing to present their children for baptism speedily or unhurriedly, thereby making the child's regeneration dependent on the parents—a position everyone can recognize as preposterous.

Moreover, experience teaches that many people are changed for the first time in their adolescence, or in their adult years, and some even in their old age, after having spent their earlier years living in sins and godlessness. How then would it be possible that these same persons had allegedly been changed already at such an early age of infancy, if for so many years they went on living as slaves of sin? The claim that the seed of regeneration can remain hidden under the surface for such a long time is entirely improbable, as we showed earlier.

8.6.3 *The Reformed pedigree of this view*

Hillenius was not alone in his view. The same opinion regarding the time of regeneration we find in Calvin, Musculus, Beza, Ursinus, Alsted, de Brès, Alting, Acronius, Gomarus, Walaeus, Maccovius, Cloppenburg,

---

[3] Hillenius, *De Mensch*, 727.

Comrie, and many others, all of them people of reputation among the Reformed church and in Reformed theology. They objected to binding God, with regard to the fulfilling of His promises and in the operation of His Spirit, to a moment in time that what not specified in His own Word. Therefore they viewed baptism not as a sign and proof that regeneration had already occurred in all elect infants, but as a seal of God's promises to believers and their seed, promises that He would certainly fulfill toward all of them in His own time. Therefore Calvin declared that the baptism he had received in his youth first became profitable to him at a subsequent age. The promise given at baptism is no vague, general, conditional address, but it contains nothing less than the truth that God will be the God of believers and their children. Such a promise, however, contains no specification of time in which this promise will be fulfilled for the elect seed of believers. God charts His own course in this matter and has spoken to us this word through His Son: the wind blows where it will and you hear its sound, but you do not know where it comes from and where it is going; so is everyone who is born of the Spirit of God.

8.7 Problems with the "Presupposed Regeneration" View

So among Reformed churches there always existed a difference of opinion about the time when God fulfilled, on behalf of the children of the covenant who remained alive after infancy and who belonged to the elect, the promises of grace granted to them in and with their parents.

People did not accuse one another of heresy, however, and never considered criticizing each other before the church public as being less Reformed. The difference of opinion existed within the boundaries of the confession, one that did no injury to brotherly love and one wherein unity in diversity came into its own. This is all the more reason to respect the opinions on both sides of the issue, since, as we wish to briefly recall later, Holy Scripture virtually leaves us in the dark concerning this moment of regeneration, so that apart from Scripture we are left with little more than guessing and stumbling about.

In the preceding we heard that all the elect are regenerated already before baptism, even that they enter the world as already regenerated, and even that they are regenerated at the moment of conception. Especially the view of creationism fits well with the idea that regeneration occurs at the moment when the soul is created and united to the body.

8.7.1 *Its speculative nature*

But everyone senses that here we are traveling through a terrain of guesswork, where Holy Scripture has been altogether abandoned, so that we are exposed every moment to various errors. The lesson to be recommended for the theologian and every Christian alike is that we should not be more wise than we ought, and we should not desire to know more than God has revealed in His Word. Even Voetius, when he was confronted with the question whether someone was regenerated at the moment of conception, preferred to refrain from making a firm judgment. It was pure guesswork to think that the elect children of the covenant are all regenerated at the very same moment in their lives. It has not been given to us to specify the moment of regeneration.

This applies in general to all the elect children of the covenant, whether they die early or continue living. But in the latter situation the theory is frequently contradicted in a sad way by reality itself. Voetius could not accept without objection the claim that such elect children of the covenant had been regenerated during their first days of life who later fell into various sins and came to conversion for the first time at the age of thirty, fifty, or seventy. He did maintain the possibility that the seed of regeneration could lie dormant within the human heart for so many years. So long as this is framed in terms of possibilities, no Reformed person anywhere would disagree with him, for who wants to draw the lines and limits for God's almighty power and the working of His Spirit? The church's confession of faith may not be composed of possibilities, but must contain established truths based clearly upon God's Word. Thus, one may grant the permissibility of Voetius's opinion within the boundaries of the confession, while no one would misconstrue the weight of the objections raised against his view, for example, by Hillenius. Life does not proceed with such regularity as logic requires. Life often mocks every system; it is richer and fuller than the deepest thinker in all his wisdom can imagine.

8.7.2 The problem of undetected hypocrites in the church

That remains the case even when discipline must be maintained so purely and strictly in the church. Occasionally it is proposed that the doctrine of regeneration before baptism would be translated into practice if only ecclesiastical discipline were maintained. But this conclusion is far too optimistic. There are hypocrites within the purest church, whom the church cannot uncover and oppose. Experience teaches repeatedly that many children of the covenant, even apart from later becoming guilty of ungodly doctrine or offensive living, have not the least understanding of guilt and not the least attraction to Christ. Of course, the church can not and may not exclude such persons from its fellowship; the church must officially testify concerning those members that they are "upright in doctrine and irreproachable in walk." The church must even consider them, according to the judgment of charity, to be believers, until the contrary becomes evident. All of this, however, does not contradict the reality that there is chaff among the wheat and that not all who are descended from Israel belong to Israel [Rom. 9:6]. Practice conflicts with theory; the number of those who must officially be considered regenerated is far greater than the number of those who are genuinely regenerated. Theoretically, baptism may well include the presumption of regeneration; but this presumption does not regulate life. Reality teaches us all too often that regeneration does not always precede baptism, unless one takes refuge in the hypothesis that the seed of regeneration can remain hidden beneath sinful desires, dormant and barren for years.

8.7.3 *No practical benefit*

Aside from the objections that are derived from the nature of spiritual life which Hillenius and others raised against this view, it is clear that this hypothesis has practically no benefit at all. For whether one presupposes that all the elect children of the covenant are regenerated before baptism, the fact is incontestable and is denied by no one that they do not all come to faith and conversion at the same moment. The preaching unto faith and conversion therefore continues to be an indispensable element of the administration of the Word in the gathering of believers. For everyone who lives under the gospel, the saying of Scripture applies: Whoever *believes* in the Son has eternal life, but whoever disobeys the Son will not see life, but the wrath of God remains upon him. Whoever will *believe* will be saved, but whoever *does not believe*, even though he was born in the church, baptized, and allowed to come to the Lord's Supper, will be condemned. No one has any advantage from any regeneration that might occur before baptism, unless he manifests that new life in faith and conversion.

8.7.4 *The practical harm of this view*

Whereas the doctrine of a regeneration that occurs before baptism has practically no advantage in all those cases where faith and conversion are not yet present, such a teaching can instead inflict different sorts of spiritual harm. Such a doctrine *need not* and *should not* do that, but it *can* easily do that.

First, this teaching can provide ready occasion for many to be lost who imagine they are headed for heaven. When the emphasis is shifted from faith to regeneration, one can quickly console oneself with the thought that a person is regenerated in youth and such new life will sooner or later manifest itself in faith and conversion; even if it does not manifest itself, that is not decisive, for regeneration is enough and leads infallibly unto eternal salvation. In this way one ends up with the same situations of spiritual superficiality that prevail among the Roman Catholic and Lutheran churches; generally speaking, anyone who is a member of the church and is baptized is saved. For whether regeneration occurs before or during baptism makes no difference. The opportunity for false security is in fact still greater in terms of the Reformed position than with the Roman Catholic or Lutheran positions, because with the latter, the grace of regeneration bestowed in baptism is able to be lost, but among Reformed churches such grace is viewed as unable to be lost. Fearing such false security, therefore, Reformed preaching was always distinguished by serious exhortation unto honest self-examination. Without any doubt Reformed preaching has been imbalanced in leaning toward this direction with its emphasis; the so-called sermon application has often pushed the explanation of the Scripture passage into the background and devoted far too much attention, even focused attention, on the exposition of the characteristic marks of the regenerate and the unregenerate states. In every age, however, Reformed preaching has excelled in carefully exposing the human heart, by unmasking every excuse of unbelief and worldliness, and by penetrating investigation of the smallest and most tender features of divine grace. This precious component that can be observed in all the printed sermons of our forefathers may not be lacking in any measure whatsoever in our own day.

Second, the doctrine of regeneration before baptism can easily engender the notion that the minister of the Word need extend the invitation to faith and conversion only to the regenerate. Since according to this teaching as a general rule the elect are regenerated in their infancy before baptism, it comes down to assuming that the preaching of the gospel applies only to the elect and for the others, nothing remains but a proclamation of their reprobation. We do not wish to place too strong an emphasis on what was presented earlier as the opinion of some people on this issue. An unfortunate expression can flow from anyone's mouth or pen. A sympathetic listener or reader will pay attention not only to the formulation, but also to the intention lying behind the formulation.

All of this notwithstanding, however, the teaching that the elect as a rule are regenerated before baptism easily gives rise to the opinion that the invitation to faith and conversion need be directed only to the regenerate. The others are deaf and cannot even hear; after all, they are spiritually dead and cannot arise. For them, the preaching of the gospel has no other purpose than to remove from them every excuse and to make known the truth of their reprobation.

This opinion, however, robs the preaching of the gospel of its seriousness and its power. For in the first place, with this view the eternal destiny of every person is really decided not at death but already at birth. Of course, we are not speaking of viewing things from God's perspective, for then everything, including the salvation and condemnation of people, has been determined in eternity in His decree; but we are speaking here about the human perspective. Given the human perspective, it becomes obvious that the elect who by virtue of their election were regenerated already in their earliest days of life, will surely and infallibly—even though it may ultimately be on their deathbed—come to faith and conversion, or in the other case, the hope of salvation is as good as cut off entirely. In both cases, the kind of preaching that supposes it can and may direct itself only to the regenerate results in a false passivity.

Third, the proclamation of the gospel is restricted by this teaching in a manner that conflicts with Scripture and the confession. In the Reformed church an intense struggle has been waged regarding the "offer of grace." Ultimately, however, the general character of that offer has always been maintained.

The promise of the gospel—that everyone who believes in Christ crucified will not perish but have eternal life—must, according to the Synod of Dort (Canons of Dort, II, art. 5), be proclaimed and presented *without discrimination* to *all* nations and people unto whom God in His good pleasure sends the gospel, along with the command of conversion and faith. As many as are called by that gospel are seriously called. For God shows seriously and genuinely in His Word what is acceptable to Him, namely, that those who are called come to Him. With all seriousness He also promises rest of soul and eternal life to those who come to Him and believe (Canons of Dort, III–IV, art. 8).

Whether we can harmonize this general offer of grace with the doctrine of particular atonement is another question. Scripture leaves no doubt, however, that the gospel must be preached to *all* creatures. For us this command means the end of all backtalk. The rule for our conduct, also in administering God's Word, is God's revealed will alone.

9

A Weighty Counter-Argument

AGAINST THE opinion generally presented by the Reformed, that calling precedes regeneration, one weighty objection can be registered that merits separate discussion.

9.1 The Objection Stated

It goes like this: calling cannot precede regeneration because deaf people cannot hear and dead people cannot come alive. In order genuinely to believe God's Word, the new life of regeneration must already have first been implanted in the human heart and within that new life the capacity to believe must already have been created. Saving hearing of the gospel presupposes regeneration, just as the act always presupposes the capacity. Therefore regeneration precedes calling, if not within time, then certainly always in the order of salvation.

9.2 Reformed Responses

We can grant this objection its full weight without necessarily accepting its logic or the conclusion people have drawn from it. It does not require too much effort to clarify this for everyone.

The teaching that *saving* hearing of the gospel presupposes regeneration has always been confessed in the Reformed church. No one doubts it or would be inclined to argue with it. Nowadays as well, no one among the Reformed churches has arisen to whom a different opinion has been ascribed in this respect. All of the Reformed have always held the conviction that whoever accepts the gospel with an upright faith must have received the capacity for that faith through regeneration (if not in a chronological sense, certainly in a logical sense). We could even add to this the observation that within the Reformed view no difference *may* exist on this matter, for this confession is most intimately related to the doctrine of sin and of spiritual inability.

9.2.1 *The English theologians at the Synod of Dort*

Apparently this confession came into conflict, however, at the Synod of Dort, with a construal of the order of salvation provided by several English theologians at that time. At the Synod of Dort the theologians from Great Britain argued, concerning the third and fourth article of the Canons, that the will of the fallen person is bereft of the supernatural and saving gifts with which he had been endowed in the state of innocence, and to that extent the will was incapable of rendering any sort of spiritual effort apart from the powers of grace.[1] This notwithstanding, they accepted that with those who were regenerated and converted at a later age, various things preceded regeneration, such as going to church, hearing the preaching of the gospel, learning the will of God together with a conviction of sin, the fear of punishment, the idea of salvation, and the hope of forgiveness.

Divine grace, they taught, ordinarily brings a person to the state of justification not by a swift divine inspiration, but by many preparatory acts, whereby through the ministry of the Word a person is subdued and prepared for regeneration. This is to be seen in those who, having heard the sermon of Peter, sensing the burden of their sin, were fearful and sorrowful, desired salvation and received the only hope of forgiveness (Acts 2:37). It is proven by the nature of the matter. For even as with natural birth, there are many preceding protocols, so too a person is spiritually regenerated along with many prior activities of grace. This appears also from the means that God employs to regenerate a person, for He uses the ministry of men and the instrument of the Word for that purpose (1 Cor. 4:15).

But these preceding operations that are accomplished within the human heart through the power of the Word and the Spirit are not infallibly and indissolubly connected to regeneration, according to the English theologians. Through the culpability of the rebellious will these operations can be suffocated and on occasion extinguished, such that some of those in whose conscience some knowledge of the truth, some sorrow for their sins, and some desire to be saved have been worked, nevertheless come to reject and hate the truth entirely, surrender themselves to their desires, and harden themselves in sin (Matt. 13:19; 2 Pet. 2:4; Heb. 6:4). Even the elect never act in response to these operations that precede regeneration in such a way that they might be abandoned by God on account of their negligence and rebelliousness. Rather, toward them the particular mercy of God is of such a nature that even though this awakening and illuminating grace may be resisted or suppressed for a period of

---

[1] *Acta of Handelingen der Nationale Synode,* 469.

time, God always prompts and stimulates them until at some point He brings them under the yoke of His grace and establishes them in the company of His regenerated children.

9.2.2 Ames's teaching

Everybody senses that this teaching of the English theologians, though in itself not wrong, nevertheless could easily be misunderstood and could give rise to the notion that a preparatory grace in a proper sense, whether positive or negative, precedes regeneration. That came to expression with William Ames, who was born in England in 1576, became a student of William Perkins at Cambridge, came to the Netherlands in 1610, and was appointed in 1622 as professor in Franeker. This theologian taught that various protocols precede the regeneration of adults, whereby the subject is made more receptive to partaking of regeneration. Just as wood is made more receptive to fire by having dried out, so the preparation of the sinner makes it easier later to light the fire of the torch of life. Preparation removes the barriers. Knowledge of the truth makes ignorance yield its sway; grief about one's sin removes the enjoyment brought about by the taste thereof; fear slays the boldness for sinning. On the other hand, these preparations impart things that are very important in conversion, namely, illumination, aversion to sin, and a desire for salvation.

9.2.3 Maccovius's corrective rebuttal

Maccovius took up the case against this presentation of the issue. If he could have mustered more sympathy for the intention of his opponent, he would surely have dealt less severely with his opponent. For Ames undoubtedly wished to teach nothing else than what was being taught by his master, William Perkins, and by the English delegates at the Synod of Dort. But it cannot be denied that Ames did not always formulate matters appropriately; and as usually happens, the polemic did not improve things, and he was backed into a corner he initially had wished to avoid.

To that extent Maccovius was entirely correct in his opposition of Ames. There is no state between death and life, between being unregenerate and being regenerate. The unregenerate person is a natural man who can do no spiritual good, who follows the things of the flesh and lives under the dominion of sin. The preparatory protocols leading to regeneration are actually not preparations unto, and even less a cause of, regeneration. For regeneration is a direct, almighty, and irresistible work of God under which a person remains entirely passive. If those so-called protocols and operations possess a spiritual character, they are a fruit and proof of regeneration; and if they do not possess that kind of character, then they remain natural, they belong at home under common grace, they neither lead to nor prepare for regeneration, and are not indissolubly connected to regeneration.

Although this is entirely correct, neither Maccovius nor any other Reformed theologian ever denied that with adults, the external calling through the Word, together with various additional experiences, preceded regeneration. This cannot be denied by anybody, in fact. Scripture teaches this and experience confirms it. Only if one harbors the notion that all the elect without exception were regenerated during the first days of life would one be able in a real sense to argue against this.

9.2.4 *Voetius, Comrie, and others*

Maccovius did not hold that view, however, nor did any Reformed theologian. Voetius distinguishes between the regeneration of children and that of adults, and in the latter case understands that an external calling through the Word precedes regeneration. Comrie, together with many other theologians, treats extensively the question whether there is such a thing as preparatory grace. The answer of all of them comes down to this: a preparatory grace that in one or another respect qualifies a person for regeneration does not exist. Regeneration, like creation, constitutes an absolute beginning. Therefore with adults various activities can precede regeneration, such as going to church, hearing God's Word, fear of punishment, some desire for salvation, and the like. These operations and experiences themselves do not include regeneration, but nevertheless according to God's leading they often precede regeneration—and thus constitute preceding, but not preparatory, operations!

Hence, in all of these cases, by both law and gospel, calling precedes regeneration. This calling presupposes nothing, and needs to presuppose nothing. According to Jesus' command, this calling is directed to all creatures, to all people without distinction, because they are all sinners and need salvation in Christ. Indeed, it is established beyond any doubt that no one hears the gospel *savingly*, which is to say: no one can believe the gospel uprightly, unless he is regenerated by God's Spirit and unless he has received the capacity of faith. From this, however, it does not at all follow that such regeneration must have occurred before the external calling, and that it always happens outside of and separate from the word of preaching. In fact, the one proclaiming the gospel has as such nothing to do with whether someone is elect or reprobate, whether or not a person is regenerated. He must merely hold firmly to Christ's command and bring the gospel to all creatures. God will then see to it that His Word does not return void but accomplishes everything that pleases Him.

9.2.5 *Gomarus*

For that reason, Gomarus also argued that through the Word God externally commands that man perform the act of faith, while through His Spirit He internally endows man with the capacity to believe and in this manner equips him for believing. The command of faith, then, indicates what man is obligated by God to do, but not what he can do, and the promise indicates whence that faith flows to him. It was that way with Lazarus when he had died. Christ had promised his resurrection, and although of himself he could not hear and could not arise, because he was dead, nevertheless Christ commanded him externally that he should come forth, and at the same time imparted to him internally the life and the powers whereby he could hear, rise up, and thereby obey Jesus' command.

Similarly Maccovius argued, although maintaining as strongly as possible that the *saving* hearing presupposed regeneration, and that in view of Ezekiel 37:4 and John 11:43, God does indeed thoroughly call such as are spiritually dead. He does that, and can do that, because He calls those things that are not as though they were, and particularly by means of this calling He brings them into being.

That is the common opinion of the whole Reformed church and all of Reformed theology. Deaf persons cannot hear, but under and in connection with the external calling, God can make them to hear. Dead persons cannot rise up, but by means of the Word, God can sow the seed of life in their hearts, so that with the prodigal son they rise up and return to the Father. In all these cases the connection between regeneration and calling is maintained, as is the connection between the operation of the Spirit and the administration of the Word.

10

The Anabaptist versus the Reformed Understanding of the Order of Salvation

IN ADDITION to the reasons derived from the doctrine of the covenant of grace and from the uncertainty of the moment of regeneration, there is yet a third reason why calling is given first place in the Reformed understanding of the order of salvation. This reason lies in the principled distinction that exists between the Baptistic and the Reformed understandings of the order of salvation.

10.1 The Reformed Consensus

Within the Reformed churches there were many who thought, along with Voetius, that the regeneration of the elect who were born in the covenant occurred as a rule before baptism. Others readily conceded the possibility of that being the case, and also acknowledged that regeneration often—for example, in the case of covenant children who died in infancy—happened in the first days of life, but for the rest they refrained from specifying the moment any further than that.

Everyone senses immediately that this is not a difference in principle; it is merely a matter of degree. For both positions accept the claim that regeneration often happens apart from and also often happens together with the Word. It is simply that people on one side think that the former describes the rule governing elect children of the covenant, whereas people on the other side prefer, for the sake of caution and with a view to experience, to refrain from further stipulating the moment of regeneration for elect covenant children whose lives are spared.

For the rest, the order of salvation was organized the same way by everyone. In dealing with the benefits belonging to the order of salvation, people generally assigned calling as the first step, before regeneration; beyond that, the existing difference of opinion in Reformed churches here and there was handled with charity and respect.

10.2 The Differences Stated and Defended

10.2.1 *The Anabaptists*

Something different would have happened if, on the basis of the view that regeneration as a rule occurred in covenant children apart from the Word, the claim had been defended that regeneration as such always excluded the instrument of the Word and characteristically preceded the external and the internal calling. Not that anyone in the Reformed churches ever defended this position. Rather, it was especially the Anabaptists who proclaimed this doctrine, and therefore were fiercely opposed on the point by the Reformed. Regeneration may be characterized as immediate—thus said the Reformed generally—insofar as it comes into existence neither through the external calling nor through an intermediate operation of the human will, but only through a direct, effectual, irresistible operation of the Holy Spirit. But regeneration is not immediate in the sense that, by virtue of its nature, it always and everywhere excludes calling and precedes the administration of the Word not only in a chronological but also in a logical sense.

For first of all, if that were the case, then every means of grace, both in the narrow sense and in the broader sense, at once lose their significance and value. If the grace of regeneration constitutes something in opposition to the administration of the Word, such that the latter cannot exist in any relation whatsoever to the former, then it becomes obvious that all grace excludes every instrumentality and can in no way be coupled with any visible sign.

This is how the Anabaptists reasoned, as explained earlier. They were the radical party of those committed to the Reformation. In seeking to avoid the one extreme, they in fact fell headlong into the other extreme. The misperceived nature, and had no understanding of the value of the relatively good, as distinct from the absolutely good. Because nature was not grace, they denigrated nature. Because the sacrament did not contain grace within itself and thus could not as such impart grace, they ascribed no power at all to the sacraments. Because the church was not the mediator of salvation, they denigrated every church institution. Because the ministers of the Word constituted no special priestly class, they rejected every office and all education for office. And because the Word alone could not regenerate, they pushed it aside as a dead letter and called the Holy Spirit the only seed of regeneration.

10.2.2 *The Reformed*

The Reformed, however, held a different view, because they honored God not only as the Re-creator in the kingdom of grace, but also as Creator in the kingdom of nature. Nature and grace are certainly to be distinguished, but because they both proceed from the same God they cannot contradict one another. Rather, nature is made serviceable to grace through His almighty power. The Word may well be unable to bring forth grace; it is nevertheless a means the Holy Spirit uses to work faith and to strengthen faith within the human heart. And although it is absolutely true that nobody can hear the Word of the gospel *savingly* unless he is regenerated and has received the capacity to believe, nevertheless the external hearing of the Word has not for that reason become empty and useless.

We must keep in mind that those who are not regenerated, and thus cannot hear the gospel savingly, can nevertheless hear with their physical ears. They can use the means of grace, and can receive a deep impression from the preaching of law and gospel. They can undergo various encounters and experiences that do not prepare for or result in spiritual life, but which are, nevertheless, according to God's leading often prior to spiritual life and therefore not without value and significance. Within God's decree, means and ends are bound to one another. In His sovereignty God has bound Himself to impart His grace not on account of our use of the means, but along the route of the means that He has prescribed for us.

Second, it is clear to all that the position of the Anabaptists leaves no room for Christ. If grace is of such a character that its imparting excludes every means, then that must be true of its acquisition as well. In that case, grace is not capable of being acquired through a Mediator. If regeneration is separated wholly and entirely from calling, from both the external and the internal, that is to say, from the Word, then grace is thereby also rendered independent of the person and work of Christ. For the Word is, after all, nothing else than the gospel of Christ. Christ is the content of the gospel, and He uses the gospel itself as an instrument for imparting to His church the benefits He has acquired.

10.2.3 *The Anabaptists*

But if regeneration in the Anabaptistic sense precedes calling through the Word, then, by virtue of its nature, it would thereby also precede the person and work of Christ. In its origin and essence, spiritual life would then not be the fruit of the merits of Christ, but a gift of God, a work of the Holy Spirit, wrought in the human heart immediately and directly, apart from the Word and apart from the historic instrumentality of Christ. To the question why after the Fall, God did not regenerate the elect simply and merely through His Spirit, but also sent Christ and delivered Him unto death, and thereafter instituted a church with word and sacrament—there could be no possible answer other than that God wanted to bring to manifestation outwardly and visibly in the world that which existed internally already through the immediate operation of His Spirit. Christ and His work, as also the church with its offices and ministries, thus would serve merely to make visible to the eye of the world and of the church itself the spiritual life that was sown in secret; merely to give voice to that inexpressible word written within the heart by the Holy Spirit, a voice that is understood in the world. Ascribing to grace an immediate, absolute character would not only reverse the order of the benefits of salvation, but even that of the person and work of Christ as well.

10.2.4 *The Reformed*

Once again the Reformed confession stands directly opposed to this view. It honored Christ not only as the Prophet who declares the Father, and as King who rules His church, but also as Priest who acquired every benefit through His perfect sacrifice on the cross, which sinners need for their complete salvation. Through His suffering and death He obtained the Spirit who alone is able to regenerate and renew and lead into all truth. That Spirit receives everything from Christ; He has come to glorify Christ, even as the Son came to earth to glorify the Father. The spiritual life that the Holy Spirit sows in the human heart He takes from the fullness of the merits of Christ. In a logical sense, regeneration does not precede the person and work of Christ and does not come into existence apart from Him, in order later to be brought into the open by Him. Rather, it is a fruit of His work, taken from Him by the Holy Spirit. Therefore regeneration is brought into existence by the Spirit only in connection with the Word of the gospel that proceeds from Christ. In terms of the range of historic Christianity, regeneration therefore occurs in the realm of the covenant of grace. The operation of the Holy Spirit extends as widely as the administration of the Word.

10.2.5 *The Anabaptists*

Finally, to mention no more, if the Anabaptists consider grace by its nature to be incapable of being imparted along the route of instruments, then that involves an entirely false contrast between spirit and matter, between God and the world, between creation and recreation, between believers and unbelievers. This comes out most clearly in their doctrine of Christ, according to which He did not receive His human nature from the flesh and blood of Mary, but brought it along from heaven. It also comes to expression in their doctrine of "shunning," according to which believers must separate themselves from the world not only in a spiritual sense, but also in an outward sense, in clothing, relationships, interaction, etc.

10.2.6 *The Reformed*

On this issue of principle the Reformed took a position directly opposite of the Anabaptists, because the Reformed replaced the physical contrast of matter and spirit, which the Anabaptists had taken over from the Middle Ages, with the contrast between sin and grace. Creation and nature and matter are not sinful and evil in themselves, but they are the handiwork of God the Father, the Almighty Creator of heaven and earth, and were only marred and devastated by human sin. For precisely this reason Christ came to destroy the work of the devil everywhere, but at the same time thereby to restore the Father's works in every area of life, and to exalt the Lord's name once again in glory and honor throughout the whole creation. Christ's human nature was therefore conceived by the Holy Spirit, but was received through Mary's own flesh and blood, and joined with the divine nature in the unity of His person. Believers are regenerated and renewed, but they are and remain partakers with all human beings of the same human nature. Grace does not destroy nature, but takes nature into its service and restores nature. The imparting of grace is tied, according to God's pleasure, to instruments taken from nature but sanctified unto God's service. When ministers go forth and preach, the Lord cooperates with and confirms the Word proclaimed by them.

10.3 Scripture on the Spiritual State of Covenant Children

If up to this point few references have been made to the words of Scripture, we were not intending thereby to construct a kind of framework apart from Scripture using materials supplied by human reasoning. On the contrary, even where explicit reference to Scripture was absent, Scripture nevertheless provided the basis on which all of the argumentation rested. This may be shown, not so much in breadth of argument as in several important strands of argument.

10.3.1 *The meagerness of biblical material on this subject*

The first observation worth mentioning is that Holy Scripture says very little about the spiritual state of children. It does indeed say enough about that, for it teaches that God is God not only of believers but also of their seed, that children are included together with their parents in the covenant of grace and therefore have the right to the sacrament of circumcision or baptism, and that as covenant children they must be nurtured in the fear of the Lord, etc. But all of this does not remove the fact that Holy Scripture does not supply a conclusive answer to many questions relating to the state and the destiny of infant children—in part of those within the covenant, but especially of those outside the boundaries of the covenant. This becomes sufficiently evident already from the fact that among theologians holding to the same confession significant differences of conviction have always existed.

10.3.2 *Jeremiah*

Even the two examples of Jeremiah and John the Baptist, who often serve in Reformed theology as proof of the claim that infants can be regenerated apart from the Word and only by the Spirit, do not serve beyond all doubt as valid proofs. According to Jeremiah 1:5 the Lord spoke to Jeremiah in the thirteenth year of the reign of Josiah, at the time when the Lord wanted to have Jeremiah serve as prophet: "Before I formed thee in the belly I knew thee; and before thou camest forth out of the womb I sanctified thee, and I ordained thee a prophet unto the nations."

Jeremiah is clearly speaking here of his calling to be a prophet. When the Lord wanted to appoint him as prophet in the thirteenth year of Josiah's reign, and when Jeremiah sensed many objections against this calling rising up within himself, the Lord encouraged him by telling him that He had appointed Jeremiah as prophet already before he was born. There is no mention here in this passage about regeneration or spiritual renewal, but rather about Jeremiah's foreordination to be a prophet already before he had been formed in his mother's womb and before he had been born. Jeremiah's prophetic office rested upon a decree of God that had been made already before his conception and birth. God decrees not only who we will be, but what we will be. He determines that before our birth; He determines that for all people; He determines that especially for those called to important service in His kingdom. Thus the angel of the Lord said to the wife of Manoah that she would become pregnant and bear a son who would be a Nazirite to God from his birth (Judges 13:5). Thus Paul testified later that God had set him apart before he was born and had called him by grace, which means, according to the explanation of the authorized Dutch annotations, that God had purposed and decided to set him apart from the universal mass of other people and in His own time to call him to be an apostle (Gal. 1:15; see also Isa. 44:2, 24; 49:1, 5).

Jeremiah speaks in the same way here about his calling to the prophetic office. He does not merely speak about what God did at the moment of his conception and birth; rather, he ascends still higher and confesses that the Lord knew him, sanctified him, and ordained him to be a prophet already before he had been formed in his mother's womb and before he had been born. Calvin interprets this verse correctly when he paraphrases it this way: Before I formed you in your mother's womb, I destined you to this ministry, so that you might serve among my people as teacher. I have not only formed you in your mother's womb as a human being, but at the same time appointed you for this particular ministry; and since it was not in your power to bring with you any qualification for the prophetic office, I formed you not only as a man, but also as a prophet. But those who think that the prophet was actually sanctified and renewed from the time of his mother's womb have inferred too much from this verse. For Jeremiah is confessing about himself only what Paul says in Galatians 1, that he was known by God before he was born. Jeremiah was thus not effectually sanctified in his mother's womb but in the foreordination of God and in His hidden counsel, because the Lord had at that point already chosen him to be a prophet. The explanatory notes of the authorized Dutch annotations agree with this explanation of Calvin.

10.3.3 *John the Baptist*

We can infer a bit more from Luke 1:15, where the angel tells Zachariah that the son which his wife Elizabeth would bear would be filled with the Holy Spirit from his mother's womb. Here as well regeneration is not being discussed in so many words; for there is an essential difference between the gifts of office and the gifts of salvation. For this reason Calvin says as well that with these words we are told that from the time of his birth, John would manifest such a disposition as would hold out hope of future greatness and correspond to the excellence of the office to which he was called. In any case, however, the possibility cannot be denied that among those gifts regeneration was also included. Still more to the point, the text establishes beyond any doubt that the Holy Spirit has access with His gifts to an unborn child. From a person's earliest day to his last years, as Calvin puts it, the operation of the Holy Spirit within a person is free. He imparts His gifts in the measure and moment that He wills.

10.3.4 *Holy children*

To this last passage we would add 1 Corinthians 7:14, since significant difference has always existed in the interpretation of this verse. In Corinth there were mixed marriages, due to the fact that one spouse became a believer while the other spouse rejected the gospel and remained loyal to paganism. The believing spouse raised objections on that account against continuing to live together with the unbelieving spouse. But Paul neutralizes that objection by saying that the unbelieving husband or wife is sanctified by the believing wife or husband, and for that reason their marriage is honorable among all and definitely does not need to be broken. Some have restricted this sanctification of the unbelieving spouse by the believing partner to the practice of sexual relations that would be sanctified by the prayer of the believing partner, but Paul is speaking in general terms about the entirety of married life. The believing spouse may live together with the unbelieving spouse, because marriage, which itself is already a divine institution and differs essentially from living a life of sexual immorality (1 Cor. 6:15), is sanctified by the faith of the one spouse in its full extent, which includes the other spouse. The unbelieving spouse is sanctified not in himself or herself but mediately, through marital communion with the believing spouse. The higher governs the lower;

where one of the spouses is a believer, there we are dealing with a Christian marriage and a Christian family.

This is what Paul is arguing when he says, "Otherwise your children would be unclean, but as it is, they are holy." This functioned in the church as an established truth, namely, that the children of believing parents were not unclean but holy. So if the children in a mixed marriage where one spouse was an unbeliever were viewed as holy, that was then proof that the marriage between that believer and that unbelieving spouse was a Christian marriage; for Christian children can be born only from a Christian marriage. The particular nature of that holy or Christian character of children born within such a marriage is not further specified by the Apostle. He states only that they are not unclean but holy. For that reason some people have supposed such holiness of the children to consist of subjective, spiritual renewal, whereas others thought it refers to an objective covenant relationship.

10.3.5 *The meaning of this holiness*

The latter opinion deserves preference, in our view, for these reasons. First, the Apostle does not say that the children of believers are sanctified in Christ. This may well be established on other grounds, but it finds no support in this text. Here Paul is saying only that they are holy and not unclean. Unclean is whatever is common (Acts 10:28; 11:8), whatever is not clean in a levitical, theocratic sense, whatever does not belong within the sphere of God's covenant. By contrast, holy is whatever belongs to that covenant, whatever has been taken over in service to revelation, whatever has been placed in a certain relationship to God. In this sense the New Testament often speaks of things that are holy; we are told of a holy city, a holy place, a holy covenant, a holy land, a holy writing, a holy mountain, holy prophets, and holy sacrifices. Concerning Christ we are told that He sanctified Himself because He sacrificed Himself to God in death. Believers are called saints (holy ones) because through their calling they have been placed in a special relationship toward God and now, in the place of ancient Israel, have been constituted the chosen race, the royal priesthood, His holy and purchased people. In Romans 9:11 all the children of Israel are called holy, despite their unbelief and hardening, because they were born of fathers with whom God had established His holy covenant.

Second, when it comes to children being holy, it is difficult to construe this any differently than when Paul says the unbelieving spouse is sanctified by the believing spouse. Even though Paul says of the children that they are *holy* and of the unbelieving husband that he is *sanctified* by his believing wife, the underlying Greek word in both instances is the same; there is no reason whatever to supply it a different meaning in one instance than in the other. In fact, the logic of the argument itself appears to contradict this. For if the children of believers are here being identified by Paul as holy in the sense that they were regenerated and renewed, then from that it would have to follow that the unbelieving husband was sanctified in that same sense by his believing wife, such that he would be regenerated and renewed as well. Otherwise the logic would be invalid and the argument would lose its force.

Third, concerning all the children of believers, without distinction, the Apostle says here that they are holy, even as he testifies in Romans 11:6 regarding all the children of Israel. But clearly Paul is teaching that not all who are descended from Israel belong to Israel, and that it is not the children of the flesh but the children of the promise who are reckoned as the seed. So the holiness that he ascribes here to the children of believers does not exclude that many of them would later fall away and thereby show that they had not partaken of the grace of regeneration. Therefore the explanation of the authorized Dutch annotations summarizes this holiness of the children of believers as being included in the outward covenant of God and having access to the signs and seals of God's grace. This is how the text has been understood by Calvin and by most Reformed theologians. The children of believers are called holy, even as the children of the Jews were, because they are heirs of the covenant and are set apart from the impure seed of idolaters,[1] or as Petrus van Mastricht formulated it: they are holy through a covenant holiness whereby in former times the *entire* people of the Jews were called holy, and now the children of believers are called holy, because they partake together with their parents of the same ecclesiastical privileges.[2]

10.4 Summary

All of this, however, does not contradict the truth that many covenant children are regenerated in their youth and even before baptism. Nor does it deny to godly parents the comfort that they must not doubt the election and salvation of their children whom God takes from this life in their infancy. For in addition to the fact that Luke 1:15 explicitly contains the possibility of such an early regeneration, this truth and this comfort are based upon the promises of the covenant of grace that God established with believers and their seed.

But all of this does prove that Holy Scripture says very little explicitly about the spiritual state of children. All of this does confirm what Voetius replied somewhere to a few questions in relation to elect children. In his *Disputations* Voetius raised the questions whether the perishing of elect children is equally serious in every case, whether between their birth and regeneration an identical span of time elapses for all of them, and whether the seed of regeneration sown in them is the same among all. His answer to those questions was this: because Holy Scripture which in

---

[1] Calvin, *Institutes,* IV.xvi.6, 31; and his commentary on 1 Cor. 7:14.
[2] Mastricht, *Theoretico-practica theologia,* IV.2.34.

a proper sense gives instruction to the adults, makes little mention concerning the state of children, and because children themselves are unable to communicate anything about their own spiritual condition, and because others cannot see into their hearts, therefore we must confess our ignorance at this point.[3]

Indeed, so it is. Scripture is of course appointed for the instruction of those who have come to years of discretion, but it treats the state of children hardly at all, nor was it given us for the purpose that we might discover answers to all sorts of questions arising from our curiosity. Therefore the route that God in His sovereignty travels with children cannot without any further qualification be fixed as the example and rule for the way God deals with adults. For this latter, Holy Scripture should be purposefully investigated.

---

[3] Voetius, *Selectae disputationes theologicae*, II.461.

11

Holy Scripture on the Spiritual State of Adults in the Covenant

AS WE investigate the manner in which Holy Scripture views and addresses adults in regard to spiritual things, we must immediately distinguish sharply between those who live outside and those who live inside the boundaries of the covenant of grace that God instituted with people after the Fall.

11.1 Missionary Preaching to the Gentiles

Already in the Old Testament this distinction is clearly demonstrable. There already we find an important difference in principle between the preaching directed to pagans and that directed to the people of Israel.

It is true that in the time of the Old Testament there was no foreign mission, in the proper sense, among pagans. Up to a certain point we may speak of the particularism of Israel's religion. The dispensation of the covenant of grace needed at that time, according to God's will, to have a national character and could not include the Gentiles at that point. Only in the time of the New Testament was the middle wall of partition broken down, when Jew and Gentile in Christ Jesus were made one new man, from which time forward anyone is accepted by God who, no matter what nationality, fears Him and acts in righteousness [see Eph. 2:14–21].

This particular character of Israel's religion, however, may not lead us to ignore the important fact that Israel was chosen not apart from the human race but precisely for the benefit of the human race. The mother promise of the covenant of grace in Genesis 3:15 was given to Adam's race. The tradition of Paradise lived on for a long time among the human race, as the examples of Melchizedek and Job and the testimonies of the nations abundantly demonstrate. The history of Abraham and of the nation that sprung up from him did not begin until the history of the human race had been told all the way to the time when the human race was divided into many peoples. Israel itself together with its religion was based on the foundation God had laid already centuries before.

For that reason, despite their distinctness, the people of Israel continued to have lively interaction with all the nations throughout all the centuries. Through circumcision those who belonged to another people could at any time be received into God's covenant with Israel. From Abraham's servants, who were circumcised along with Abraham's own family, there was always a smaller or larger number of proselytes throughout the centuries, people who were engrafted into the people of Israel and who received a share in the promises of the covenant of grace. Of still greater significance, however, was the fact that from the very outset prophecy among Israel included all the Gentiles in its scope and identified more and more clearly the salvation bestowed upon Israel as a commodity ordained for the entire human race. The promise granted to Abraham runs through all of Old Testament prophecy, namely that in his seed all the families of the earth would be blessed.

So in the Old Testament we find a rich, glorious mission concept, and even to a certain degree, as especially the history of Jonah shows, a "missionary preaching." This missionary preaching, however, was essentially different from that preaching which occurs among God's people and in the church of the Lord. For the Gentiles were not the people of the Lord; they walked according to their own ways; their gods were idols that do not exist and were merely lies and vanity. The condition in which the pagan world dwells outside of the special revelation is portrayed in Holy Scripture as darkness, ignorance, self-invented wisdom, and great unrighteousness. The preaching that addresses them is thus a calling to come out of darkness into the light; it is an invitation to be converted from idols and to serve the living and true God.

11.2 Preaching to the Church

By contrast, the preaching that occurs within the church, to the extent one may speak of this in the time of the Old Testament, had an entirely different character. We find the beginning of such preaching in Genesis 4:26, where it is said that in the days of Enosh, son of Seth, people began to call on the name of the Lord. The occasion for doing so was that among the Cainites, apostasy increased by leaps and bounds; they walked more and more on the broad way of destruction and surrendered themselves with all their powers and talents to the service of the world. In contrast to them we find the godly appearing as a community in the time of Enosh; they separated themselves, joined together, began together to call on the name of the Lord, and organized themselves as a church around the confession of the Lord's name. In distinction from and in contrast to the Cainites, they bore witness to the Lord's perfections; they came to the defense of His name, and preached and glorified that name. The first sermon in the church consisted of calling upon, confessing, proclaiming, praising, and thanking the Lord's name.

This element continued to be preserved in subsequent Old Testament worship. It came to expression in the thank offerings, the prayers and thanksgivings, and the psalms and songs of the Old Testament church. I will—so sang Israel's godly worshippers—tell of Thy name to my brothers; in the midst of the congregation I will praise Thee; from Thee comes my delight in the great congregation.

Even preaching in its narrower sense (referring to the preaching by the prophets of the people of Israel) always proceeded from the basic notion that Israel was the people of the Lord and therefore had to walk in the way of the covenant. Israel was the people, the field, the flock, the vineyard, the bride of the Lord—from this reality all prophetic preaching proceeded and to that reality it always returned. Modern criticism has from time to time expressed the view that Yahwism—which is the service of Yahweh, the God of the covenant—was introduced among Israel for the first time by the prophets. But this opinion is completely untenable. The prophets were not proclaiming a new religion; they were not seeking to lift the people of Israel up to a different, higher position than they originally occupied. But they proceeded from the reality that the entire people, together with the prophets themselves, were included in the Lord's covenant. They were to serve Him and Him alone, and serving other gods constituted apostasy, an act of infidelity, breaking the covenant, and committing spiritual adultery and whoredom.

That in part explains the power of prophetic preaching. Israel was not free in her choice. She had been accepted by the Lord in grace and through His great love she was obligated to reciprocate in love. Above the law according to which Israel's life was to be lived stood written: I am the Lord your God, who brought you out of Egypt. Salvation from misery was to have been Israel's motivation for serving the Lord and for walking before His face in faithfulness and uprightness. Sacrifices, priesthood, the entire Old Testament worship, the entire legislation, kingship, prophetism—all of this was built upon the great assumption that Israel was the people of God, the sheep of His pasture, who might enter His gates with praise and were called to praise His name.

Israel could fall only so deeply and stray only so far before the prophets' preaching unto repentance would proclaim again and again this benefit of God, namely, that He had accepted Israel in grace and chosen Israel above all the nations of the earth.

Coupled to this strong adherence to the foundation of the covenant, on which the prophets stood together with all the people, was the announcement of apostasy and punishment together with a summons to repentance and conversion that was as urgent and as pressing as possible. We have here no loose connection, much less any sharp contrast. Precisely because the prophets continued to see Israel, no matter how deeply she had fallen, as the chosen people of God, their preaching was so strict and intense. Israel's sin was not a sin of ignorance, as could be said in a certain sense about the sin of the Gentiles, since they did not know the law; but Israel's sin was a terrible apostasy, a transgression comparable to that of Adam in Paradise, an act of intentional and arrogant disobedience.

11.3 These Two Elements Always Present

Within Old Testament preaching, therefore, these two elements are always bound with one another: holding firmly to the unity of the entire people as people of God, while at the same time distinguishing within that one people between those who serve the Lord and those who do not serve the Lord. Not just the first, but the second as well constitute the unmistakable components of Old Testament prophecy. According to God's revealed will it was not supposed to be the case that some who were descended from Israel did not belong to Israel, insofar as the flesh was concerned. But it was nonetheless the fact that every day displayed the reality; Israel's history was a history of apostasy and infidelity. Sometimes it looked as though the entire people of the Lord fell away and went whoring after other gods. In his day, Elijah thought he was the only one left; although there were still seven thousand who had not bowed the knee to Baal, how few these were in comparison to the whole nation! Is it any wonder that the prophets sometimes complained that the entire land had gone whoring away from the Lord, that the Lord had a quarrel with His people, that Israel was a sinful people that had left the Lord, had profaned the Holy One of Israel, had transgressed His law, had broken His covenant, and that there was no knowledge of God, no fidelity, and no charity in the land any longer?

The psalmists spoke no differently. Throughout the ages no other people had enemies so powerful and numerous as those of Israel. Israel stood alone against all the surrounding pagan nations. Philistines, Edomites, Canaanites, Assyrians, Babylonians, Egyptians, etc., opposed Israel with threats, and by opposing the chosen people of God, they were opposing the God of heaven and earth Himself. Their struggle is portrayed in Psalm 2 as rebellion against the Lord and against His anointed.

These were not all of Israel's enemies, nor even the worst. Those lived within Israel itself. Among the people themselves were thousands who surrendered themselves to superstition or to unbelief. A mighty company of spies, persecutors, enemies, opponents, despisers, workers of unrighteousness, godless, or however else the Psalms designate them, opposed the few faithful, oppressed, miserable people who placed their trust in the God of Jacob. The godless spoke lies, they flattered each other, they enjoyed peace and multiplied their relationships with the world, and they were not in distress like other people and were not pestered along with the others. Therefore pride was their necklace and violence covered them like a garment (Ps. 73:6). From the heights they looked down upon the poor, simple godly folk and leapt in joy over their misery. Indeed, they set their mouths against the heavens and their tongue strutted throughout the earth (Ps. 73:9). They asked, Will God show us deliverance, will there be any knowledge with the Most High? All their foolish thoughts supposed that there was no God. With mocking they called out to the godly: Where now is your God, you who have relied upon the Lord looking to Him for help! They did not bother themselves about God's law, they shattered God's people, oppressed His inheritance, saying: The Lord does not see it, and the God of Jacob does not notice!

This differentiation existed among Israel. The preaching of the prophets took this difference into account. They were appointed as watchmen over the flock of the Lord, from whose hand the blood of the sheep would be required. Therefore they summoned the apostate, unfaithful people to confess their guilt and to be converted. They warned the entire people, without distinction, to return to the Lord and seek a new heart. For God took no pleasure in the death of sinners, but rather that these would be converted and live. But they proclaimed also to the godless that it would go badly for them, even as they proclaimed to the righteous that it would go well with them. They predicted a future day of judgment when the godless would be destroyed but when a poor and miserable remnant would continue serving the Lord, whom He would sanctify and preserve unto eternity.

So the preaching in the time of the Old Testament that was directed in the Lord's name to the people of Israel rested upon the foundation of the covenant to which the entire people belonged, and despite that, or rather precisely because of that, such preaching strictly differentiated between the true and the false participants in the covenant. Already then the Word of God was an aroma of life unto life for some, and an aroma of death unto death for others. Such was the case not only for pagans, but also for those included in the covenant as citizens of Israel.

11.4 The Preaching of John the Baptist and Jesus

The perspective we encounter in the New Testament regarding "missionary preaching" and regarding "congregational preaching" is essentially no different than what we found principally in the books of the Old Covenant.

When John the Baptist and later Jesus the Christ appeared among the people of Israel, they proceeded, on the one hand, from the idea that this people was the covenant people, whom the Lord in grace has elected and accepted as His inheritance. Zachariah saw in the birth of his son John a demonstration that God was visiting His people, that He was mindful of His holy covenant and of the oath He had sworn to Abraham, and he called his son a prophet of the Most High who would walk before the face of the Lord in order to prepare His paths and provide His people with the knowledge of salvation. Concerning Jesus it is said that He came to His own, that He would be called the Son of the Most High, to whom God would give the throne of His father David, and who would be king over the house of Jacob forever.

All of this notwithstanding, both of them appeared among the people preaching faith and conversion, never proceeding from the assumption that everyone was regenerated. When many of the Pharisees and Sadducees, who belonged to the people of Israel and were included in God's covenant with that people, came to John, the latter declared to them: You brood of vipers, who told you to flee from the wrath to come? Produce fruits worthy of repentance. And do not think to yourselves: We have Abraham as our father, for I tell you that God could bring forth Abraham's children even from these very stones. Although Jesus found many, especially among the simple people of the land, who were quietly awaiting the Messiah and who acknowledged Him as the Christ when He appeared, nevertheless Jesus traveled throughout the land preaching the gospel of the kingdom and calling people to faith and repentance. He did not come to call the righteous, but sinners to conversion. He was sent to the lost sheep of the house of Israel, in order to gather them like a hen gathers her chicks. He came preaching: You people must be born again, for unless a person is born again, he cannot see the kingdom of God.

In fact, the baptism with which John and Jesus came is already a proof that the people of Israel, having been accepted into God's covenant and having received its sign in circumcision, did not thereby have enough. For that baptism entailed that the Jews, despite all their privileges, were guilty and unclean, and needed a total renewal in order to enter the kingdom of heaven. Baptism, which God instituted already with John, was a condemnation of the Judaism of those days, and a resounding sermon declaring that outward circumcision by itself was profitable for nothing; that the true Jew was not the person who was a Jew outwardly, in the flesh, but a true Jew was a Jew inwardly by partaking in the circumcision of the heart.

11.5 The Fruit of this Preaching

This preaching of John and Jesus bore abundant fruit. The seed sown among Israel fell also upon good soil and bore fruit, some a hundredfold, other sixtyfold, still other thirtyfold. Nevertheless, the people of Israel as a whole rejected Jesus' gospel. To the degree that this hardening increased, the preaching of the gospel turned into the proclamation of judgment. Even though Israel was the Lord's people, eventually the terrifying woe was pronounced from Jesus' lips over the entire people; the woe upon the hypocrites who say "Lord, Lord," but who will not enter the kingdom; the woe upon the Pharisees and scribes who were blind guides of the blind and who made the evangelized fellow-Jew a child of hell, twice as condemned as they themselves; the woe upon Chorazin and Bethsaida, Capernaum and Jerusalem, who would be condemned by

Nineveh and Tyre and Sidon in the day of judgment; the woe upon this entire people whose hearts had become fat, who honored God with their lips but kept their hearts far from Him. The kingdom would be taken from them and given to a people who would bring forth its fruits.

And that is what happened. Already during His earthly ministry Jesus gathered around Himself a flock of men and women, disciples whom He referred to as the *church*. In the period of the Old Testament, the people of Israel had been identified by that name as the gathered people of God, as the gathering of the Lord. Now in the New Testament, Israel has exiled herself by putting the Messiah to death, so that the New Testament church has risen to take its place. The church is now the real, true people of God, as the Lord had said already through Hosea: I will call my people those who once were not my people, and I will call my beloved those who were not beloved.

In its earliest days this church was gathered mostly from the Gentiles. For that reason missionary preaching occupies the prominent place in the New Testament. Before His departure Jesus had given His disciples the command to be His witnesses, first in Jerusalem, in Judea and Samaria, but then beyond to the end of the earth, in order to make all the nations His disciples through the preaching of the gospel and the administration of baptism. This missionary preaching was directed to those people who were without Christ, alienated from the commonwealth of Israel, strangers to the covenants of promise, having no hope and without God in the world, who were therefore called out of darkness into the light, from serving dumb idols to serving the living God.

Alongside this missionary preaching, however, congregational preaching also appears in the New Testament. Jesus preached the gospel of the kingdom not only to those who did not yet belong to His disciples, but He set forth His instruction in the circle of His disciples as well, and gave them to understand the secrets of the kingdom of heaven. When He mandated His apostles, before His ascension, to make all nations His disciples through preaching and baptism, He immediately added that they were to teach all those who had been made His disciples in this way to keep everything He had commanded them.

Thereby congregational preaching was portrayed in its essential character and distinguished from missionary preaching. The one continued what the other had started. Congregational preaching builds further on the foundation laid in missionary preaching. Accordingly, we see the apostles deal very differently with the unbelieving Jews and the Gentiles who were still unfamiliar with the gospel of Christ, than how they deal with the members of the congregation who through faith had accepted that gospel and by their doctrine and life had professed that gospel.

11.6 The Church as God's Elect

According to the apostolic letters written to them, the churches of Christ consist of God's beloved, God's elect, called to be saints, believers, brothers in Christ Jesus; and they were not only addressed as such, but they were also viewed and treated as such. All of the apostles proceeded from the view that the members of the church, who had formerly walked in the darkness of superstition and unbelief, were now called out of that darkness to God's wonderful light. The apostles saw these church members as having been washed, sanctified, and justified in the name of the Lord Jesus and by the Spirit of our God, as having been transferred into the kingdom of the Son of God's love, and as those who would be preserved in the power of God unto heaven's salvation. Therefore there is in the letters of the apostles a more extended unfolding of the truth, a warning against various kinds of false doctrine, an exhortation to walk worthily of the calling and to be zealous in doing good works. But we find, properly speaking, no preaching unto faith and repentance, as we saw with the prophets, with John the Baptist, and with Jesus, and with the apostles when they brought the gospel to the Jews and the Gentiles. For the members of the congregation have been converted to God, they are believers and enjoy the anointing of the Holy Spirit, so that they do not need anyone to teach them.

Regardless of how definite all of this may be, the New Testament teaches additionally, with just as much firmness and clarity, that within the Christian churches from the very beginning and throughout their expansion, various kinds of error, heresy, and unrighteousness gradually crept in. Among the apostles there was a Judas; in the Jerusalem church we meet Ananias and Sapphira; in Samaria the heart of Simon, who had believed and had been baptized, was exposed as not being right before God. In general the writings of the New Testament teach that there is chaff among the grain, weeds among the wheat, bad fishes in the net, those called who are not elect, wicked branches on the vine, vessels for honor but also for dishonor, and that those who depart from the church did not belong to the church.

All such persons do not constitute the essence of the church, for the church, according to its nature, is a gathering of believers, the body and bride of Christ, the house and temple of God; despite that, such persons are present in the church as it comes to manifestation here on earth. Therefore preaching that is directed to the congregation always has room for the exhortation to examine and test oneself. When the apostle in 2 Corinthians 13:5 directed this exhortation to the Corinthians, he proceeded from the assumption that with such self-examination they would discover that they were in the faith, that Christ Jesus lived in them; but in spite of that, he considered it possible that they were somewhat blameworthy. All the more legitimacy and reason for such an exhortation existed to the extent that the church grew, or was relieved of persecution and distress, and believers had children and grandchildren. In such a situation various circumstances can arise, like those that arose among Israel, whereupon the requirement becomes more and more urgent to include the summons to faith and repentance in the preaching. For being included in the external covenant, being members in the church, having received baptism and Lord's Supper, and sharing in various ecclesiastical privileges do not grant entrance into the kingdom of heaven, which comes only through regeneration by water and Spirit, through the upright faith of the heart, and through true repentance toward God.

We see similar situations arising already in the Christian church during the apostolic age. In the letters of the apostles the exhortations and warnings multiply according to how late they were written; one need only read the letter of Paul to Timothy and Titus, the epistle of Jude, and the second epistle of Peter. More instructive in this regard than anything else are the letters sent by the glorified Savior through the apostle John to the seven churches in Asia Minor. All of those churches are acknowledged by Christ as His churches; they are the seven candlesticks among which He walks as the Son of Man. He also profusely praised everything in them that was praiseworthy; He knows their faith and their works and their suffering, and He will one day reward them for these. Notwithstanding all of this, He calls the church in Ephesus to repent, since she had left her first love, or else He would remove her candlestick from its place. The church in Pergamum He calls to repent because she tolerates those who hold to the teaching of the Nicolaitans, or else He will soon come to her in judgment. To the church in Thyatira Christ threatens to cast down all those who commit adultery with the false prophetess whose teaching was being tolerated, unless they repent. To the church in Sardis Christ declares that they have the name of being alive but they are dead. To the church in Laodicea Christ complains that she is neither cold nor hot, and that though she imagines herself to be rich, in reality she is miserable, pitiable, poor, blind, and naked, and therefore if she does not repent she will be spit out of His mouth.

These letters were originally directed by Christ to the seven churches of Asia Minor, but they reach beyond that region and are intended for the church of all ages. The circumstances that arose in those churches resurface repeatedly in the Christian church and in each of her parts. From these letters we see that a church of Christ can stray far and can surrender to various forms of error and unrighteousness, and still be acknowledged by Christ as His church. But we also learn from these letters that precisely for this reason He warns her all the more earnestly to believe and repent, and threatens her with judgment that is all the more awful.

12

Calling and Regeneration and Its Relation to Preaching

THE VARIOUS ways Scripture is understood in its view of the church of Christ affect the theory and practice of preaching. Two very distinct methods are opposed to one another at this point.

12.1 The Methodistic or Evangelistic Method of Preaching

On the one hand, there is the method of preaching in which the sermon culminates in a summons to faith and conversion. It takes no account of what precedes or what must follow. Such preaching acts as if there were no common grace, no leading through God's providence in natural life, no government by God the Almighty, the Creator of heaven and earth. Such preaching attaches no value to a person having been born into and included within the covenant of grace, to having been baptized in the name of the Triune God, to membership in the visible church, to experiences and operations that could precede genuine conversion to God; and such preaching denies the possibility that there could be a seed of regeneration that in its own time germinates, grows, and bears the fruit of faith and repentance.

Even as such preaching takes no account of what can precede conversion, so too it does not bother to see to it that the person who is brought to faith would grow in the grace and knowledge of the Lord Jesus Christ and move forward from the first principles to maturity. The only work to which the converted person is summoned consists in the need to go forth immediately in order to convert others. Everything else must give way to this practice. Evangelism and missions have a value far surpassing any other task in family and career, in state and society, in science and art. Every Christian should be a soldier, enlisted in the army of salvation that marches onward in desiring to overcome and subdue the world at the foot of the cross.

This approach to preaching arose during a time when the church of Christ was enamored of her successes registered in her struggle against the world. When that happened, the church was robbed of her radiance, and the administration of the Word and sacraments lost all its power for and relevance to the consciousness of believers. This happened in England, was transplanted to America, and from these countries it gradually gained influence throughout the continent of Europe, not only among the churches officially privileged by the state that had as a result become worldly, but still more among the free churches and sects that gradually reached an independent existence within Protestantism.

Even homiletics teachers came to prefer this approach to preaching and sought to defend it on Scriptural grounds as the only legitimate method. Preaching, they said, was always directed in both Old and New Testaments to unconverted people or at least to those parts of the person that were unconverted. If regeneration really occurred in a single moment and the whole person really was sanctified by faith all at once, then a person would no longer need preaching. But because this is not the case, the old nature within a person must continually be combated and subdued. For that purpose preaching was needed at the beginning and for the duration; but preaching must always be evangelistic preaching, calling to faith and repentance.

Despite its imbalance, this approach contains something useful that may not be ignored. In times of apostasy, when a spirit of deep sleep descends upon the church of Christ, preachers like John the Baptist who call people to repentance are needed to shake the people of the Lord awake from their slumber. With their powerful voice such preachers penetrate the heart and conscience; they cry out to the deeply affected multitude that what opens access to the kingdom of heaven is not having Abraham as father and not saying "Lord, Lord," not outward baptism and profession, but only saving faith and genuine repentance.

While gladly and gratefully acknowledging the excellent service that this Methodistic approach to preaching has rendered and continues to render, we may nevertheless not be blind to its darker side that characterizes this preaching or to the dangers to which it is prone. We are not criticizing this approach because it casts people down into the depths and summons them to genuine repentance; but it does err when it misconstrues the work of God that usually precedes the moment of regeneration and that by God's design must also follow regeneration. This approach erases the distinction that has always continued to exist between pagans and Christians; it misperceives the church with its offices and ministries; it denies everything that is referred to with the term common and preparatory grace; it ignores any distinction between evangelistic preaching and congregational preaching. When this method under the blessing of the Lord has brought someone to conversion, it separates that person from the environment wherein God has placed him, and it has no eye for the apostolic exhortation that each one after his conversion should remain in the calling entrusted to him. This approach appreciates the first part of Jesus' word: preach the gospel to every creature; but it neglects the second part: teach the nations that are made my disciples to keep all that I have commanded. This method does lay the foundation, but does not continue to build on that foundation, and therefore runs the danger that the entire foundation, constructed with little effort out of unstable materials, will later be washed away by the storms of unbelief and superstition.

12.2 The Edifying or Ethical Method of Preaching

Another approach stands in direct opposition to this one, a method that desires no discriminating preaching but only edifying preaching. Its advocates reason that the church consists of only believers. They are all Christians, distinguished essentially from pagans, born in the Christian church, baptized with Christian baptism, nurtured in the Christian truth and thereby formed in their understanding, souls, and consciences. The preacher standing before the church may therefore not act as though he has before him a multitude of unbelievers. He stands with his hearers on the same footing, and speaks with them from the same awareness. Therefore his preaching is not missionary preaching, but congregational preaching, putting into words what lives either wholly or partially subconsciously in the hearts of his hearers. This preaching is a formal exposition of the Christian faith that lives within one and all, intended merely in this way to strengthen their religious awareness. The goal of such preaching is not repentance and conversion in the narrow sense, but only encouragement and edification. Friedrich Schleiermacher once put it this way to a congregation: he wanted to speak as a brother to brothers, and he desired to introduce nothing new into their consciousness, but wished merely to develop the Christian consciousness already present within them, to purify, confirm, and clarify it for them.

In this approach as well we find elements of truth, which Scripture itself compels us to acknowledge. For no matter how deeply the church of the Old and New Testaments may have fallen, the preaching of prophets and apostles always proceeded from the conviction that they were the people of God. They never erased the boundary between Israel and the pagans, between the church and the world. They always drew a firm connection to what God had bestowed upon His people in distinction from the pagans. In our eyes this may be a tiny bit that does not mean much; it may be entirely inadequate for salvation. Nevertheless, the Lord requires of us in His Word that we do not despise that little bit, for it remains after all His work and it perhaps contains His blessing. The prophetic and apostolic preaching at that point was not intended, or at least not intended only, to summon to repentance, but beyond that it aimed at building further upon the foundation that had been laid, at maturing the hearers in the knowledge and grace of the Lord Jesus Christ, at supplementing faith with virtue, virtue with knowledge, knowledge with moderation, moderation with patience, patience with godliness, godliness with brotherly love, and brotherly love with love toward all.

So there is no doubt that "evangelistic preaching" and "congregational preaching" are essentially different, and this difference may never be lost from sight. But this does not mean, on the other hand, that there are no serious objections to this second approach. This approach appeals exclusively to the titles used in the New Testament when the apostles addressed the church in their epistles, but it fails to take into account the place these churches occupied, a place that was in many respects exceptional. Nor does it take adequate account of the circumstances of error and sin that appeared among the people of Israel and surfaced quickly in the apostolic churches as well, and later arose repeatedly within the Christian church. Proceeding from the ideal, this approach misperceives reality, and neglects the lesson of history that is supplied to us both within Scripture and beyond it.

This approach to preaching leads people gradually to confuse believing the confession with confessing belief, yielding a situation of dead orthodoxy that is satisfied with an intellectual assent to doctrine and that bothers itself very little with the disposition of the heart and purity of life. Indeed, why should these matters of heart and life be a concern at all? Such an approach teaches church members to think and talk this way: Are we not members of the church? Did we not receive baptism when we were young? Did we not make profession of our faith, and have we not participated in the covenant meal? Just as Israel exalted itself because of its descent from Abraham and because of the temple of the Lord in its midst, so too many New Testament church members often build their hope for eternity on the outward ecclesiastical privileges in which they share, and they surrender themselves to a false security. But the Word of the Lord testifies against all of this; it is not the one who says "Lord, Lord," but the one who does the will of the Father who will enter the kingdom of heaven.

12.3 Combining Both Methods

Whereas the methodistic and the ethical methods of preaching suffer from one-sidedness, a good administration of the Word always combines both elements, which are also always combined in Holy Scripture. These elements are (1) proceeding from the covenant, and (2) urging faith and repentance.

The difficulty of including both of these components in preaching and keeping them in balance is recognized by every minister of the Word according to his capacity. Even the ordinary members of the congregation sense immediately the disharmony when one constitutive part of the truth is sacrificed for the sake of the other, even though they themselves and others cannot explain their discomfort. For in relation to this matter, churches of Reformed confession have never been without examples of one-sidedness and overemphasis, even though they did not at that point fall directly into the methodistic or ethical extremes.

12.3.1 The one-sidedness of presupposed regeneration

On the one side there have always been those who reason this way: the congregation consists only of believers, and all of its members are to be viewed as regenerated, even the children head for head, who are included in the covenant of grace and have been presented for baptism. Accordingly, they are instructed in the truth, granted access to the Lord's Table after an adequate examination and after public profession of faith, unless, as happens occasionally, an exception occurs whereby a person guilty of heretical teaching or offensive conduct, after repeated admonition, is separated from the congregation by means of ecclesiastical discipline. For discipline is authorized in the church in order to remove the evil elements from the good and thus to keep the church on the right path as it develops and expands.

12.3.2 The one-sidedness of presupposed non-regeneration

But others look more at the reality of the situation and cannot bring themselves to believe that each child baptized and each member of the congregation head for head is elect and regenerated. Experience teaches wholly otherwise and reality contradicts this theory every day. Though clearly no one pretends to know hearts, it is incontrovertible that church leaders who visit with church members discover that many members of the congregation display no evidence of spiritual life, have no idea of the guilt of sin, and sense no need of a Savior for their souls. If for one moment these advocates forced themselves to believe that baptized children of the covenant are all regenerated, then they would eventually be disappointed upon seeing thousands of such baptized children grow up to fall in love with the world, serve sin, and die in unbelief. This viewpoint represents simply a kind of forced and invented belief designed to maintain seriously that all the members of a congregation are elect and regenerated by the Spirit, even those who are under church discipline.

In order to clear the path of any conflict arising from this way of thinking, conflicts between doctrine and life, between theory and practice, there are some who are willing to permit life to be governed by doctrine, and others who attempt to stylize doctrine to fit life. The former sacrifice the catholicity of the church for the sake of its holiness, taking firm hold of discipline to resist and exclude everything that shows no clear sign of spiritual life, hoping in this way to be able to establish and reproduce a church on earth consisting only of saints. The latter hold to the catholicity of the church at the cost of its holiness, and they advocate a national church that baptizes everyone inside its walls, basing the right to the sacrament merely on being included in an external covenant. The former proceed from the invisible side of the church and fail to carry that further to organizational form, to an established ecclesiastical institution; they fall into sectarianism and dissolve the gathering into innumerable, arbitrary groups of individuals. The latter proceed from the visible side of the church, seeking the essence of the church in its external organization, in its regulations and statutes, thereby running the risk that what is actually the essence of the church will be lost from their grasp; they make the church a skeleton whose life has flowed out of it.

These are the consequences that people encounter when they abandon the way of the Lord and seek by their own reasoning to solve difficulties that will always exist here on earth between the church's doctrine and life. For in His Word God desires precisely that we should *not* resolve these difficulties, but that we would accept them, and bring them to bear both in theory and in practice, upon ourselves and upon others. The truth is not to be found exclusively on one side or the other, but the truth is honored most fully only when we accept the *entire* Scripture and permit it to govern our personal and ecclesiastical life.

This problematic is analogous to the confession of God's immutable counsel and man's freedom and responsibility. One who at this point desires to maintain one truth at the expense of the other truth is left with neither, but loses them both. One who denies God's counsel in order to rescue man's freedom loses that freedom as well and surrenders it into the hands of human arbitrariness or brutal natural might. And one who denies human freedom in order to honor God's immutability exchanges the wisdom of this counsel for the foolish cruelty of fate. The one truth demands and presupposes precisely the other truth and without that other truth is immediately robbed of its particular character. As Scripture teaches it, human freedom is included within God's counsel. Human freedom cannot exist apart from the omniscient and immutable counsel of God.

12.4 Maintaining the Truth in Both Methods

So in the life of the church we must maintain both truths, namely that the church is a gathering of true Christ-believers and that, nonetheless, the appeal for faith and conversion must continually sound forth in her midst. We must confess in word and deed one *holy* and *catholic* church, and maintain that confession despite all the difficulties that it occasions. The church's holiness must not be sacrificed for its catholicity, and the church's catholicity may not be surrendered in favor of its holiness. For in denying either, we lose both. Both attributes by nature characterize the one Christian church.

12.4.1 *In way of the covenant*

On the one hand, we must proceed from, and as long as possible maintain, the covenant, not only as the Lord has established it in our own churches, but as He under the leading of His providence has seen to its continuation among the human race from generation to generation, insofar as one is baptized and bears the name of Christ. Anabaptism and Methodism, and movements associated with them, misperceive that covenant; they assign no value to the church, to baptism, to Christian nurture; because these are not everything, they mean nothing in their eyes. The Word of the Lord, however, does not teach us this. The preaching of the prophets proceeded from the assumption that Israel was the people of the Lord; and Christ Himself viewed the churches of Asia Minor as His congregations, even though they had already fallen into decay. The apostle Paul himself still confessed about Israel, after Israel had rejected its Messiah, that Israel had not been rejected by God, but that she continued to be loved for the sake of the fathers, and the apostle demonstrated this by pointing out that there were those from Israel who, like himself, were still continually being added to the church.

This manner of proceeding on the basis of the covenant is a powerful element in preaching and in all sorts of personal conversations. Being born in the Christian church, being baptized in the name of the Triune God, being nurtured in a Christian family—all of these are, as long as they are understood in the proper sense, points of contact for the preaching of the gospel. All of these realities place a claim upon the person. They sensitize a church member's conscience for the ministry of the Word; they supply the minister of the gospel a right to requisition the church member for the Lord's service. No matter how far away they have strayed, Christians are never in the same position as pagans. In terms of its starting point, congregational preaching is always distinguished essentially from missionary preaching.

12.4.2 *Covenant and catholicity*

Holy Scripture desires that we acknowledge and proceed on the basis of all of the elements of the truth. We must respect the catholicity of the church even to the extent that it has, according to God's purpose, spread among the human race in corrupted forms. Christendom in its entirety is the people of God that in the days of the New Testament has taken the place of Israel. Thereby Scripture also directly opposes all those who, in over-emphasizing principles and craving for consistency, would rather see those who bear the name of Christ while denying the Christ of Scripture surrender the name Christian and return to paganism, purely in the interest of consistency. There are people who seem to take delight, with the broom of "necessary consequence," in sweeping away the Ethicals into the company of the Modernists, and the Modernists into the company of the Socialists, and the Socialists into the company of the Nihilists and Anarchists. But the calling of the minister of the gospel is to rescue what can still be rescued, and to see people's manifold inconsistencies as a blessing and a demonstration of God's restraining grace.

12.4.3 *Covenant and holiness*

Even as on the one hand we must maintain the church's catholicity, nevertheless on the other hand we must confess its holiness. We may not, on the basis of practicalities, define the essence of the church differently than it exists in the truth of God's Word. The church is and remains the gathering of true Christ-believers, even if all the churches on earth fall away and degenerate; the church's being is determined by heartfelt faith. Thus the sacraments have been instituted only for true believers; on the basis of God's Word we may not confess anything else. Even were they to be administered a million times to people who do not belong among the true believers, their essence would not be, and may not be, changed for that reason. A true, Christian baptism is therefore administered only when together with the administration of the sign by the minister, Christ from heaven binds the working of His Spirit, and the thing signified is received and enjoyed by the one baptized.

12.4.4 *Covenantal summons to faith and repentance*

For this reason congregational preaching ought never to omit the serious summons to faith and repentance. Proceeding on the basis of the covenant does not exempt the preacher from that, but rather it is precisely this that obligates him to issue such a summons. That obligation is derived not first of all from the presumption that all elect persons already in their first days of life even before baptism have been regenerated, and this obligation applies not only with reference to those who in their childhood are supposedly regenerated. But this obligation is grounded in the covenant of grace, as it has spread historically throughout the human race under God's leading, and includes all Christians and their children, and it applies with reference to them all together, whether or not they were already regenerated in the earliest days of life. For no matter how inestimably great the blessings already are that God bestows upon us when from our birth we are included in the covenant, born in a Christian church to Christian parents, baptized with holy baptism, and nurtured in a Christian family—all these blessings are still not enough. Each person is confronted with the obligation of personal, saving faith; only one who believes in the Son has eternal life. Whether the church already presumes that all its members are believers, or, being unable to judge the human heart, the church must be satisfied with an outward confession and walk and base its response on these—all of this in no way detracts from the truth that each must examine and test himself, and that no one, whether inside or outside the church, will enter the kingdom of heaven unless he is born again of water and Spirit. Not the church, and not the minister of the Word, but only God in heaven brings about salvation.

12.4.5 *Congregational preaching*

Thus both elements belong together in congregational preaching. The preacher's sermons should connect to God's work that has preceded, to the gifts and blessings He has bestowed in His covenant, in His Word, and in His baptism. His sermons should continue building upon the foundation God Himself has laid, but then should also continue warning of the need for self-examination, so that people not deceive themselves for eternity. Biblical sermons seriously summon church members to faith and conversion both initially and continually, for only those who believe will be saved.

Neither of these elements may be omitted from preaching to the congregation—neither the element of discriminating examination nor the element of continual building on the foundation. Which one of these deserves priority in a given congregation and at a given time cannot be prescribed. That depends on the times and circumstances, on the situations and particularities of the congregation. In prophetic preaching the summons to conversion sounds the loudest; in apostolic admonition the emphasis lies on growing in the knowledge and grace of Christ, while in the letter of the exalted Savior to the seven churches, warning and threatening alternate with comfort and promise. In our churches the minister of the Word is not bound to any kind of lectionary system and is free in his choice of sermon text. But that choice is not therefore arbitrary. Choosing a preaching text ought to be determined by the knowledge that the minister of the Word, as a good and faithful shepherd, has of the flock and of each sheep. It should also be directed by the calling entrusted to him to administer not a part, but the entire Word—to preach the whole counsel of God.

With respect to a practical matter this double character of congregational preaching appears very clearly, namely, with regard to the administration of the Lord's Supper. On the one hand, all the confessing members of the congregation, without exception, are obligated by God to proclaim the Lord's death. On the other hand, only those may partake of the Lord's Supper who with true hearts have turned unto God. In reality time and again there are many painful conflicts between *must* and *may*, between obligation and permission. No human reasoning can solve this conflict; it exists and continues to exist despite all our theories. For it is incorrect, on the one hand, that the obligation to commemorate the Lord's Supper should not rest upon every confessing member of the church, yes, even upon every baptized member who has come to years of discretion. But it is no less true, on the other hand, that all those who, though they are members of the congregation, yet lack saving faith, nevertheless have free access to and the right to take the Lord's Supper.

Therefore preaching ought continually to keep together both the obligation of the "must" and the right of the "may." God requires that from us in His Word. He desires that we allow this conflict to exist and that we not try through our human reasoning to eliminate the problem.

But He Himself resolves the conflict, by granting grace to those who in their need look to Him, and by holding inexcusable all those who resist His calling. The covenant is the pathway along which the Lord carries out His decree.

PART IV

THE RELATION BETWEEN THE IMMEDIATE OPERATION OF THE HOLY SPIRIT AND THE MEANS OF GRACE

13

The Means of Grace in General

IN ORDER to see clearly the degree to which one may speak of immediate regeneration, there is one point that requires further elucidation as we conclude.

13.1 Review of the Distinct Questions

At the beginning of this treatment it was mentioned that when we discuss the doctrine of immediate regeneration it is most important to distinguish clearly and properly. In order to do that, three questions must be kept distinct.

The first question is this: In which way does the Holy Spirit work in the human heart? Does He remain outside and stand at a distance, working on a person merely along the ordinary routes to which we are bound as we deal with other people, the routes of intellect and will, by means of word and example? Or does the Holy Spirit descend into the human heart, so that nothing exists between Him and the inner being of the person, enabling Him to work directly and irresistibly within a person?

In answer to this first question we discovered that on the basis of Holy Scripture and following the lead of Augustine, the Reformed subscribed to the latter view. The Holy Spirit does connect His work to the Word, but does not bind His work within that Word, so that with His almighty power He penetrates the human heart, touches a person immediately in the innermost part of his being and thus renews him to conform in principle to the image of God, apart from a person's knowing and willing. The operation of the Holy Spirit in regeneration is thus absolutely independent from the consent of the intellect or an act of free will. Between regeneration and the person who is born again there stands nothing, no word, no sacrament, no church or priest, no act of the intellect or of the will. The Holy Spirit works the grace of regeneration within the heart of the elect person directly, irresistibly, and in this sense *immediately*.

The second question that came up for discussion was this: If these things are so, if the Holy Spirit is present within a person immediately and performs His work directly, then does not this direct operation exclude the use of means? If the operation of the Holy Spirit in the heart is immediate, does that not entail that the use of means is superfluous and futile, yes, even wrong and detrimental?

To this question our study has led us to respond that the Reformed have indeed called regeneration an internal, invincible, irresistible and in this sense immediate work of the Holy Spirit, in contrast to the Remonstrant doctrine that makes it dependent upon a free consent of the person involved. We also learned that the Reformed never called regeneration "immediate" in contrast with and to the exclusion of the Word as means of grace, to which the Holy Spirit joins His work. Rather, in response to various mystical groups the Reformed have continually maintained the connection between Word and Spirit; they uniformly taught that as a rule and ordinarily the Holy Spirit regenerates a person by means of the preaching of the Word. Therefore all of them without distinction also discussed calling before regeneration in their dogmatic treatments.

13.2 The Third Question[1]

13.2.1 *What is the relation between the Spirit's immediate operation and the use of means?*

Having discussed these two questions, a third and final question arises: If the immediate operation of the Holy Spirit in a person's heart does not render the use of means superfluous or detrimental, how then must we view the relation existing between the immediate operation of the Spirit and the operation of the means?

Everyone immediately senses the weight and difficulty of this question. The Synod of Dort confessed concerning regeneration that it certainly does not happen merely by outward teaching or by moral persuasion, but that it is an entirely supernatural, most powerful and most pleasing work, one that is at the same time a *marvelous, hidden, and inexpressible* work. In this life believers cannot fully comprehend the manner of this work; nevertheless they rest in this: that they know and experience that by God's grace they heartily believe and love their Savior (Canons of Dort, III–IV, art. 12, 13).

We may proceed on the basis of this beautiful confession as we investigate the relation in regeneration between the operation of the Spirit and the Word as means of grace. At the end of our investigation it will

---

[1] Ed. note: see pages 9–10, footnote 10.

become evident to us that we will need to return in all humility to this confession.

13.2.2 *The power of means in general*

This question, which we will consider for a few moments as we conclude this part of our discussion, involves, as everybody recognizes at once, the significance and power of the means of grace in general. Regeneration is but one of the many benefits God bestows upon His elect along the path of the covenant. All those benefits are granted by God not in an immediate way, but in relation to the means of Word and Sacrament, which He has ordained and instituted to that end in His sovereignty and favor. The Holy Spirit works faith in our hearts by the proclamation of the holy gospel and strengthens it through the use of the sacraments.

Moreover, the significance and power that people ascribe to the means of grace are closely related to the understanding people have of God's mediate working in the creation, preservation, and government of the world. God's relation to the world in general determines also the manner in which He makes use of means in His activity of re-creating in the realm of special grace. To the extent that a person erases the distinction between God and His creatures, whether one separates them from each other, assigning to the creature an independent existence, or whether one maintains the distinction and connection between God and the world, to that extent the value he ascribes to the means of grace will also differ. The connection formed between the relationship of the work of the Spirit and the power of the Word in regeneration to the doctrine of the means of grace in general, together with the doctrine of God's relationship to the world in creation and providence, make it most clear that the question now occupying our attention cannot be treated fully in a few paragraphs. So that is not our intention, and we will briefly set forth only those preeminent points that surface in the discussion of the aforementioned question.

To do this, we proceed from the magnificent Reformed idea that with God, means and ends always cooperate. In His decree the causes and the consequences, the pathways and outcomes are established in indissoluble connection with each other. His decree is no loose assembly of various incidental phenomena that exist on their own, but consists of a complex of decisions intimately related, forming an unbreakable whole and a system of divine ideas, one single arrangement of everything that will exist or occur within time.

God executes this decree within time. Therefore everything that happens within time is mutually related in the same unbreakable way as the ideas and decisions within God's eternal decree are related. Therefore we human beings are bound to means; anyone pursuing a goal must travel the path leading toward that goal. Anyone who does not work will not eat; anyone who labors with a deceitful hand becomes poor, but the hand of the industrious makes one rich. The Lord holds Himself to the means which He established in His counsel for attaining His ends. Predestination embraces not only the determination of the eternal state of rational creatures, but also the determination of the means and paths leading to that eternal state.

God always works this way—in creating and recreating, in the realm of general and that of special grace. He illuminates and warms the earth with the sun. He waters the plowed fields with the rain that He causes to fall from the clouds. He makes the field fruitful by means of the farmer's industry. He builds the house by means of the workmen. He brings forth children from and by means of parents. He nourishes by means of food. He quenches thirst by means of water. He heals the ill by means of medicine. He governs a person by means of that person's intellect and will. Always and everywhere the Lord binds outcomes to pathways, ends to means. He maintains and rules all things through and in relation to each other.

But no matter how true this may be, we may not forget for a moment that in His being and working God the Lord is never at any time separated from His creatures by all these means. There is nothing standing between God and His creature, whatever creature that may be. God is immediately and directly present with His being and power in all things. In Him all things live and move and have existence. He nourishes us by means of bread, but this is not to be understood as if the Lord Himself were outside of us with His power and merely delivered the bread from afar, as a mother distributes it among her children. No. Rather, He is present with His power in the bread itself. He maintains its nourishing power from moment to moment. He accompanies that bread with His power, when it enters our body and is changed into energy in our body. Therefore a person does not live by means of that bread alone but by means of the Word, the power, the blessing that proceeds from God's mouth and that He works and sustains in the bread from moment to moment. So if the Lord does not build the house, its builders labor in vain; if the Lord does not guard the city, its watchman watches in vain [Ps. 127:1].

The Lord maintains and rules all things *mediately*, but with His omnipresent and almighty power He Himself is *immediately* present in all of His creatures.

13.2.3 *The mystery of this relation*

Man does not live by bread alone, but by every word that proceeds from the mouth of God. This entails that man requires bread for the sustenance of his life; one who does not eat any food will die from starvation. And yet it is not that bread by itself that sustains a person but the word, which is the power and the blessing, that proceeds from the mouth of God, and is joined to the effectual working of the food. If necessary God can sustain a person equally well with or without food. Moses stayed forty days on the mountain and Jesus stayed forty days in the wilderness, both of them without eating. They were sustained and fed by means of God's power.

The divine power keeping a person alive is thus on the one hand related to food, for as a rule food is the means for sustaining life. On the other hand, however, that power is not so bound up with food that God is unable to feed a person and keep him alive without food. At this point we can identify errors on both sides of this path, errors we must guard against. But who will explain the actual relation between the nourishing power of food and the divine blessing—between the bread a person needs, even though he does not live by bread alone, and the word of power that proceeds from God's mouth? Even in the natural world, life is a mystery in terms of its origin and growth, its decay and deterioration, a mystery we must respect but which we cannot penetrate. Here, too, the confession applies that in this life we cannot fully understand the manner of God's working in creating and sustaining life.

If this now is the case in the natural realm, how much more will this apply to the spiritual realm? Who is to say in what way God conveys spiritual life and spiritual power to His elect through the means of grace? We can, here as well, perhaps trace the lines on either side, the boundaries within which we must think, just like the council of Chalcedon did with respect to the unity of the two natures of Christ. But we are unable to describe in fixed and clear formulations the relation established between God's grace and the means He uses in bestowing grace.

13.3 Views Developed in the Middle Ages

13.3.1 *The physical operation view*

In the Middle Ages, when people began to think more deeply about this relation, especially two sentiments developed. Some accepted a physical, others a moral operation of the means of grace, particularly of the sacraments.

The advocates of the former view reasoned this way: in the natural realm God embedded in the means themselves the power that He bestowed. The nourishing power lay in the bread, the thirst quenching power was in the water, the healing power resided in the medicine. This, then, was also the way that God, in the spiritual realm, embedded grace in the means of grace, so that God employed these as His tools to convey and communicate grace to the recipient. The grace that the recipient of the sacrament shared is thus a fruit of that sacrament, in the same way as being nourished is a fruit of using food, or to use another image frequently employed, in the same way as the cleaving of the wood is the product of the axe in the hand of the woodcutter. The woodcutter split the wood, but he did not do that immediately, but mediately by means of the axe. And the axe split the wood, though not by itself, but in the hand of the woodcutter. The splitting of the wood is an immediate consequence of the operation of the axe in the hand of the woodcutter.

Thus also God embeds the spiritual power of grace in the means that He used in its administration. Grace is the immediate fruit of the means of grace in the hand of God, who makes use of these means. Just as the paintbrush in the hand of the painter and the chisel in the hand of the sculptor in a certain sense contain within themselves their work which is brought about by them, so too the means of grace are elevated by God in the moment they are used to supernatural tools, so that they can transmit the grace contained within them to the recipient.

13.3.2 *The untenability of this view*

This perspective of the operation of the means of grace, however, was criticized by many. Indeed, there are objections one can raise that identify the untenability of this view.

For, in the first place, it is difficult to imagine that a supernatural spiritual grace lies deposited and confined within a physical sign. A paintbrush and a chisel produce no other work than what by nature they are capable of producing. Even the word we speak does not by itself somehow contain the thing it identifies, but is merely a sign and reference to that thing and thereby calls the thing to the memory of the one who hears it. How then could the means of grace be equipped with a spiritual, supernatural power to transmit and channel this power to the recipient?

Second, a tool operates only where it comes into contact with the object of its working. The axe of the woodcutter splits only the wood that it hits. Thus the means of grace can work only where they are applied and used, and nowhere else. The water of baptism, and the bread and wine of the Lord's Supper come into contact only with the body of the recipient and can thus never effectuate grace in his soul, of which they are the signs. Even the word is in itself nothing more than a sound penetrating our ears and as such is absolutely unable to generate within our spirit the idea to which it refers. In order to understand a word properly, something else is needed, namely, a clear understanding that is led by means of the sound of the word to the substance of which it is the sign.

Finally, to mention nothing else, grace would lose its spiritual character if it could be confined in that way within a physical sign. The preeminent benefit of grace is the forgiveness of sins, and this consists in the fact that God is no longer angry with us, but rather He shows us His favor and shines His friendly countenance upon us. How could this grace, this favor of God be separated from God Himself? How could it be confined to a physical sign and along this path be imparted as though it were channeled to the recipient of the means of grace?

These and similar considerations prevented many in the Middle Ages from lending their agreement to the physical operation of the means of grace. After the Council of Trent until the present day, some Roman Catholic theologians have continued to sense the weight of these objections so deeply that they proposed a view of the operation of the means of grace somewhat similar to the Reformed view.

It appears, however, that after Trent there is no longer any room in the Roman Catholic Church for such a modified view. For at that council it was established that the external sign in the sacrament does not merely signify grace, but quite definitely contains and imparts grace in itself. Thus with Rome the sacrament is the instrumental cause that effectuates grace in the recipient by virtue of the power of the work performed (*ex opere operato*). In response to the objections raised against this physical operation of the sacraments, the Roman Catholic catechism merely observes that the nature of the operation of the sacraments is inscrutable, and that a visible thing cannot by nature penetrate the human soul, but that the almighty God can impart to and bestow upon the sacraments a power whereby they can effectuate that for which they by nature have been designed.

13.3.3 *Moral operation view*

In addition to the opinion that a physical operation belonged to the means of grace, already in the Middle Ages there existed a view that ascribed to the means of grace a moral or ethical operation. Defenders of this view taught that the sacraments communicate grace not immediately, but mediately. God does not embed grace in the visible signs, nor does He transmit grace thereby into the soul of the one using the sacraments as though through a channel. Not the sacrament, but God Himself communicates grace from His fullness to the one who uses the sacrament according to its instituted purpose.

Thus, the means of grace work in the way a contract works, a contract that God has voluntarily entered with a person. When the sacrament is administered according to His instituted purpose, then God in His great goodness has bound Himself to impart the grace signified in the sacrament to everyone who receives and uses the means of grace in faith.

People attempted to clarify this operation of the means of grace with the use of various metaphors. Thus, people suggested that the sacraments impart grace in the same way that handing over the royal scepter grants royal prerogatives, and that giving someone a key to a building grants authority over that building. The sacraments were signs of the grace that God imparted through them—and then not only signs, but also conditions under which and occasions in which grace was imparted.

Just as the word of Elisha and bathing in the Jordan were not the cause of Naaman's healing, but rather God's power, so too grace was bestowed not by the sacraments, but by God alone. Therefore sacraments, in a proper sense, could not be termed causes, instruments, or tools of grace; such terms were merely figurative, insofar as God has obligated Himself according to His promise to the communicating of His grace to each person who uses the sacraments according to His instituted purposes.

13.3.4 Rome's rejection of this view

In the centuries preceding the Reformation, not a few theologians embraced this opinion. Even the theologian Bonaventure acknowledged that this view did not conflict at all with the exalted faith and was quite probably correct. But as already mentioned, after the Council of Trent there appeared to be no room in the Roman Catholic Church for this sentiment. Still there were theologians after this period who endorsed this opinion and sought to bring it into conformity with the church's teaching in one way or another. But they continued to hear the accusation leveled against them from their opponents that by ascribing to the sacraments a mere moral operation, they were reducing the means of grace to signs, conditions, or occasions, without being able to ascribe any instrumental or causative character to them. Thus, the Roman Catholic Church turned the sacraments into bearers and conveyors of grace, and to the degree they proceeded down this path they externalized grace, robbed the Word of its power, and elevated the church to the position of mediator of salvation.

For Rome, grace serves in the first place not to rescue a person from the situation of guilt and misery into which he has fallen. But before everything else, grace sought to elevate a person above the state of pure naturalness, and by imparting supernatural powers grace puts the individual in a position to merit a supernatural salvation. Genuine grace is a supernatural gift added to a person's nature; it consists not so much in the forgiveness of sins as in the infusing of a supernatural power. Although it is spiritual, it comes to be viewed more and more as a kind of independent power contained in the sacrament, as in a vessel, and imparted through the sacrament, as through a utensil.

With this view of grace it is obvious that the Word as means of grace must gradually lose its significance and value. After all, by the nature of the case this kind of grace is not capable of being imparted through the Word. With Rome, therefore, the gospel is not essentially different from the law; in fact, it is a new law: it contains only commands and counsels, and is not at all capable of imparting power whereby one can keep those commands and counsels. The Word therefore belongs merely to those preparatory means that precede the reception of the real, supernatural grace. The Word is merely the source of knowing the laws and commands, and is directed only to human intellect; a historical faith is sufficient to receive it and to prepare a person for the reception of grace, which is imparted in baptism by the priest.

Therefore the Roman Catholic is absolutely bound to the church for his salvation. If the Word is the proper means of grace, a person can be saved without being dependent on the church and the priest. For the Word comes to him along various routes, not only officially by the minister of the church, but also through the instrumentality of parents and teachers in the form of admonition and address, as an audible and as a legible word. But if grace is imparted only by the sacrament, then a person must be directed to the priest in order to receive this grace, and is dependent on the priest for the salvation of his soul.

13.3.5 *The Reformed endorsement of this view*

One element is always tied to the others. When the Reformation contended against the Roman Catholic Church on one of the points, e.g., the doctrine of the Lord's Supper, they were compelled to formulate an entirely different view of law and gospel, of Word and sacrament, and of church and office. Specifically they were compelled to reject the physical operation of the means of grace and to return to the sentiment that had been defended already in the Middle Ages by many theologians, but which had been gradually surrendered by the Roman Catholic Church. Word and sacrament perform no other operation than a *moral* operation. They operate in the same way as a contract. God has bound Himself to impart His grace to everyone who receives and enjoys these divinely instituted means in faith according to His ordained purpose. In those means He has, so to speak, indebted Himself to us. Whenever we use them in the proper way, in childlike obedience, then He gives us the right to plead with Him and to expect everything from Him on the basis of them; and then He binds Himself through His covenant, through His promises, to provide everything our spiritual and physical indigence requires.

Thus grace is indeed joined to the means, but it is not thereby infused and is not confined to them. Nor is this grace under the authority and in the control of the minister who proclaims the Word and administers the sacrament. But it remains the property of God who bestows grace in Christ through the Holy Spirit according to His sovereign good pleasure.

Whenever the means of grace are administered, therefore, properly speaking, no union between the external, visible signs and the spiritual, invisible grace comes into existence, as if both of these in any manner were locally bound and united together. Rather, there comes about a union between grace and the soul of him who uses the means of grace in faith.

This is how, already in the Middle Ages, the profound and pious theologian Bonaventure spoke. The sacraments, he declared, do not contain grace within themselves like a cup holds water or a pill contains medicine, but they signify grace and point to grace. And if it is claimed that grace is imparted by the sacraments, then this is to be understood thus, that grace is bestowed not to the visible signs but to the soul of the recipient.

Among the Reformed in a later period, Gomarus expressed himself in the same sense when he argued that it was more correct to say that the thing signified is united to *us* rather than that the thing signified is united to the *signs*. The mystical union arises between Christ and our souls; and of that the means of grace function as sign and seal.

14

The Word as Means of Grace in Particular

14.1 Recapitulation

THE MEANS of grace as such and viewed in themselves possess nothing else than a moral operation. In themselves they possess no power to re-create, for God's grace is not infused in the means but accompanies them. Even though God in His great goodness employs means and works through means, He Himself remains independent of those means; He descends into the heart of the sinner, and there works with His grace and Spirit in a direct, invincible, though also gentle and lovely manner.

Concerning the sacraments, however, we need speak no further in this connection. Our interest in raising them for discussion was merely to clarify briefly the nature and operation of the means of grace in general. At this point we will restrict our attention to the Word as means of grace, and attempt to answer the question: What operation is to be ascribed to the Word in connection with regeneration and conversion?

Since the means of grace in general, viewed as such, can perform merely a moral operation, it seems clear that this applies to the Word as well. At least we have full authority on the basis of the Reformed view-point to draw this conclusion. This is different with Rome, since Rome makes a substantive distinction between the means of grace, ascribing to the Word merely a preparatory, nurturing operation, and to the sacra-ments a grace-infusing operation. The Reformed, however, treat Word and sacraments together under the heading of means of grace. They sub-ordinate the sacraments to the Word, such that apart from the Word they cease to be sacraments. In both instances it is the Word that is pro-claimed to us—the one audibly and the other visibly. Both direct us to the same Christ and both point to the same benefits. If then the means of grace in general possess merely a moral operation, it is evident that the same is true of the Word as means of grace.

Naturally at this point one must then view the Word as the external call, coming to us through law and gospel.

14.2 Various Senses of "Word" of God

14.2.1 *The Word as the divine* Logos

One can speak of the Word of God in Holy Scripture in more than one sense. First, the term "Word" refers, especially in the Gospel of John, to the Son of God who became incarnate in Christ. As the Word He was in the beginning with God and was Himself God, the radiance of God's glory and the exact imprint of His nature. He bears the name of the Word, of the Logos, because the Father eternally declares His entire being in Him and thus has given Him to have life in Himself.

Obviously the Word of God in this sense possesses not merely a moral but a creating and recreating operation. For we read that all things have been made through that Word, and that without that Word nothing was made that has been made. In that Word was the life and light of the human race. As Logos, according to His divine nature, Christ was the image of the invisible God, the beginning of His creation, the firstborn of all creatures, through whom all things together exist. Just as together with the Father and the Spirit He shares divine omnipotence in the creation and preservation of all things, so too He possesses and exercises this omnipotence in fellowship with the Father and Spirit in re-creation. Just as the Father raises the dead and makes them alive, so too the Son quickens whom He wills. The hour has already come when the dead hear the voice of the Son of God, and those who have heard will live. And the hour is coming when all who are in the grave will hear His voice and will arise, those who have done good unto the resurrection of life, and those who have done evil unto the resurrection of condemnation. This is enough to show that Holy Scripture ascribes to the Word of God, referring to His only begotten Son, a creating and re-creating power whereby all things that are not are called as though they were [1 Cor. 1:28].

14.2.2 *The Word as God speaking*

In the second place, the term "Word" often refers in Holy Scripture to that which proceeds from God when He creates and preserves, and re-creates and renews things. The eternal generation of the Son by the Father is likened to speaking, and therefore the Son is called the Word, the Logos of God. But similarly creating and recreating are frequently presented in Scripture as the speaking of God. By speaking, He calls things into existence, both in the realm of nature and in the realm of grace.

In the beginning God said, "Let there be light," and there was light. This divine speaking preceded the bringing forth of all subsequent creatures. When He speaks, then things appear, and when He calls, then they stand before Him. He call the things that are not as if they were. This power of divine speaking is inscrutable; it has never arisen in the heart of any creature; only through faith do we understand that the world was prepared through the word of God, and thus that the things people see did not emerge from things that are visible.

This is also how all things are maintained and governed through the Word proceeding from God's mouth. Jesus Himself said that man does not live by bread alone, but by every word that proceeds from the mouth of God. Hebrews 1:3 confesses concerning the Son that as the radiance of the glory of God and the exact imprint of His nature, He upholds all things by the word of His power. When God sends His word of command across the earth, then the ice melts and the storm winds blow (Ps. 147:15, 18; 148:8). His word is the messenger running swiftly, performing His will in nature and in history (Ps. 105:19; 107:20; Isa. 55:10–11). In this sense, the word is the hidden, internal power proceeding from God, maintaining and governing all things. As quickly as God makes known His will and sends forth His command, so quickly do all creatures obey it.

Everyone can see clearly that in this sense, the Word possesses not a moral, advisory, persuasive power, but an effectual, creating, and sustaining operation. It is the almighty God who causes this word to proceed from Himself, and does so through the Word and the Spirit who share with Him the same essence and the same authority. Therefore the word sent forth by God in connection with creation and providence is no mere sound that flies upon the breath of the wind, no mere wish that creatures may obey at their whim, but a hidden, internal, almighty power that operates with or without means and accomplishes everything that pleases God.

When Holy Scripture identifies this power with the term *word*, such nomenclature is not without cause. The word spoken by a human being presupposes that such a human being is equipped with intellect and will; this is the highest expression of a human personality, the most complete revelation of a person's internal life, and therefore also the greatest power a person possesses, its strength far surpassing the power of weapons.

The word we speak supplies us with an obtuse analogy of the significance and power of the word proceeding from God's mouth. It presupposes that God is a person who eternally defines Himself with absolute freedom. And because it is a word spoken by God, it is almighty power which summons all things into existence and sustains their existence. His word never returns to Him void, but accomplishes everything that pleases Him and succeeds in everything for which He sends it.

14.3 The Word as the Law and the Gospel

If in connection with the Word we think of the Son of God, or also of the power proceeding from God in connection with all His works, then what is involved is not merely a moral, persuasive power, but a creating, irresistible operation.

But Holy Scripture speaks of the Word also in a third sense, namely, the word of the law and the gospel, whereby God addresses people, makes known His will, and invites them to obey that will. This word is directed to all who live under the administration of the covenant of grace and comes to them along the pathway of the so-called external call, whether this word is read or heard by them, whether it is brought to their awareness by Scripture itself or by any other book or tract.

14.3.1 *The nature of human words in relation to God's word*

When we take the Word in this sense, then it is clear that just as to the means of grace in general, so to the Word we may also ascribe a power that is moral, appealing, admonishing, and persuading. This can be inferred already from the significance and power possessed by human language in general. After all, the word that we speak or write is nothing else than a collection of syllables and letters that are in themselves merely physical phenomena and hardly the conveyors of the things they portray. The syllables and letters as such contain absolutely no spiritual power capable of arousing knowledge in the consciousness of another person of those objects, ideas, or events being referred to by those sounds or signs. For if this were the case, if the sign of the spoken or written Word and the thing signified were so united that the thing were imparted by the sign itself, then the word would always supply someone knowledge, even though it were a word spoken in a foreign language. The word heard in syllables or seen in letters is thus in itself nothing but a sign that arouses within another person an idea of the thing being referred to. Therefore the word presupposes in the person to whom it is addressed a certain awareness, and operates within that consciousness merely in a moral manner. The sound of the word *father* makes the child think of the person he knows by that word, the person who gradually has become related in his consciousness with this sound and, as it were, united with this sound. For, although as a sound or a sign, the word stands merely in a certain contractual relation to the thing signified, that relation is nonetheless very intimate and close.

In the eighteenth and late-nineteenth centuries, many scholars indeed thought that the relation between the word and the idea was purely accidental and arbitrary. But that opinion is surely untenable. Just as no society or state came into existence through a free act of the will proceeding from a so-called social contract, so too no language depends upon an agreement made by people in a former time.

Bilderdijk correctly opposed the form of Pelagianism in the realm of language. Just as God brings to manifestation His virtues and perfections in that which was created, so also the human spirit expresses itself in all its works, especially in its words. And just as all of nature is an image and likeness of invisible, spiritual things, so too language in all its richness is a reflection and manifestation of man's spirit, the imprint of his soul, the expression of his being.

In this connection, Bilderdijk went to the other extreme. In his view, there was nothing accidental in language; every sound, every letter, every word has and must have its specific power and significance, and none other. This would not have been entirely incorrect if Bilderdijk had meant this in a historical sense. But the etymology that he gave to words bore not a historiographical, but a philosophical character and therefore often led to crass arbitrariness.

The claim that each letter and each word has its own necessary meaning would probably be valid if a language existed that had developed in a perfectly normal way, that is, apart from the influence of sin. But this is not true of any language spoken among human beings. Word and essence no longer correspond. Signs and things signified frequently appear in a relation that is hardly fixed by nature and therefore can hardly be called necessary.

From this it does not at all follow, however, that this relation is arbitrary and accidental, that it rests on a treaty or an agreement. For, in the first place, that relation began in history; it was not manufactured or agreed upon, and does not rest upon human will; rather, it came to be so and grew to be so. It came into existence organically, not mechanically. Therefore, in the second place, a certain secret, hidden relation exists between them, for history is God's work. He rules and governs all things. Under the leading of His providence various languages also came into existence, the development of languages occurred, and between word and idea a union came into being whose foundation is found in the awareness of every person. To mention but one example: there is apparently nothing more arbitrary and accidental than the name each of us has. Personal names have thoroughly lost all their meaning and significance. They have become nothing more than unintelligible sounds, whose original meaning can seldom be identified and is hardly recognized any longer. Nevertheless, between the person and his name there exists such an intimate relation that the person can be injured and denigrated in his name. Nobody likes to have his name spelled or pronounced incorrectly.

That relation between word and idea, between sign and substance, finds its foundation, certainty, and continued existence in the notion of a rational, thinking human being. That notion is aroused and nurtured in a person from youth onward. It is strengthened by the environment in which one lives, by the society of which one is a member, by the history within which one grows up. Every word and language thus presupposes a certain notion, a minimal awareness, that is gradually developed and clarified by that language itself. A foreign language does not penetrate our awareness; it is merely sounds that we do not understand and that cannot direct us to those things being referred to. The word presupposes that we can hear and understand at a certain level. The word influences us, by means of pointing us to, and making us think of, the thing being signified by the word. It works in a moral manner. The word possesses no creating power, but a moral effect.

14.3.2 *The external call of the Word*

All of this applies as well with regard to the word of God that addresses us in the external call through law and gospel. For it is indeed a word of God and thus powerful and living, but it nevertheless comes in our human language, it has assumed the form, nature, and shape of the human word, and has become like us in every way, except for the error and lies that have crept into our language. Just as the Word, that is, the Logos, has assumed genuine human nature in Christ, so too the word of God's will has become flesh in law and gospel in our human language and therefore has also become subject to the laws and rules of that language.

Because the Reformed understood this, they also insisted that the external call was neither sufficient nor effectual. For the external call was simply a call by the word and could thus perform merely a moral, persuasive operation. In this they agreed with the Remonstrants. But whereas the latter thought that such a moral persuasion was sufficient, the Reformed taught on the basis of God's Word that an effectual, invincible, direct operation of the Holy Spirit must accompany the word if the external call was to be heeded and obeyed.

The Reformed also correctly inferred from this moral operation of the external call that nobody can hear the word *savingly* unless a person is previously regenerated—not in time, but in sequence—by water and Spirit. The *saving* hearing of the Word of God presupposes regeneration. For no one can come to Christ unless the Father draws him. And everyone who has heard and learned the Word of the Father comes to Christ.

15

The Work of God's Word in Regeneration, Faith, and Conversion

BECAUSE THE Word by itself, according to its character and nature, can exercise nothing other than a moral operation, regeneration precedes the saving hearing of that Word, if not always within time, certainly in terms of sequence. And because the Word of God can be heard savingly only by one who is regenerated (for the natural man does not understand the things of the Spirit of God), therefore a distinction must be made between the operation of the Word in regeneration and its operation in connection with faith and conversion.

15.1 Regeneration Distinguished from Faith and Conversion

To prevent misunderstanding, however, we must first emphasize that making this distinction does not yet settle this other question as to whether regeneration and faith always or as a rule coincide, or whether they can occur years apart, even separated by a life of serving the world and living in sin.

On the one hand, no one will disagree that with adults regeneration and faith can occur simultaneously, and that a person savingly hears and accepts the Word at the same moment he is regenerated under the preaching of that Word. On the other hand, no one will dispute that our infants can be regenerated by God's Spirit without being in a position, on account of their age, to manifest that new life in acts of faith and repentance.[1]

---

[1] Ed. note: The "act" or "acts of faith" is a technical locution as used in Reformed theology to refer to the perfecting or actualizing operation of faith, i.e., faith as it occurs in the human, believing subject, in which the intellect and will appropriate the object of faith—

Both of these truths were always held firmly by the Reformed. Therefore, although in opposition against all Pelagianizing interpretations they
insisted on the one hand that the Word alone was insufficient and required a direct, invincible operation of the Holy Spirit in the sinner's
heart to accompany it, on the other hand they always affirmed that as a
rule such an operation of the Spirit was paired with the administration of
the Word. So to acknowledge that the operation of the Word in regeneration is different than in faith and conversion is not thereby to say that the
Word is completely excluded from regeneration in every way whatsoever.

15.2 The Word in Relation to Regeneration

It was shown earlier that Reformed theologians did indeed frequently
call regeneration immediate, but never thereby to suggest that regeneration always occurs apart from or outside the Word, but to indicate that
the preaching of the Word must be paired with an operation of the Holy
Spirit in the sinner's heart that is direct, independent of the human will,
and irresistible.

Even those theologians who emphasized as strongly as Maccovius
that the saving hearing of the gospel presupposes regeneration, and thus
that the significance ascribed to the Word in connection with regeneration differed essentially from the significance that it bears in connection
with faith and conversion, hardly intended to sever all connection between regeneration and the Word. This comes out most clearly in the
teaching articulated by Reformed theology regarding internal and external calling.

15.3 Internal and External Calling

The distinction between this twofold calling was first deduced from
Holy Scripture by Augustine, and then later elevated by Calvin to a most
important article in Reformed theology. Whenever Reformed theologians
treated this distinction within the divine call, however, they continually
emphasized that this distinction does not involve two kinds of calling.

Internal and external calling are actually one. The distinction is not
the classification of genus into kinds, but the description of a whole by its
parts. Just as the church's visible and invisible dimensions are distinguished, and just as the internal and external dimensions of the covenant

---

namely Christ and all his benefits. The *act* of faith does not refer to an activity that achieves
a saving knowledge of and trust in Christ, for this would turn faith into a "good work" and
deny justification by grace alone. The capacity or disposition for faith and the act of faith
must be distinguished: the former refers to a potency for faith that can be actualized as
faith; the latter, the act of faith, "although it may be defined as an operation, is not an activity in the sense of a deed or a work, but an operation in the sense of an actualization in
which faith comes to be faith or, in other words, moves from potency to actuality" (Richard
A. Muller, *Dictionary of Latin and Greek Theological Terms: Drawn Principally from
Protestant Scholastic Sources* [Grand Rapids: Baker, 1985], 22; see Muller further for a
discussion of *actus fidei*, and related terms).

of grace are distinguished, so too with calling. Calling is one, just as the church is one and the covenant of grace is one, but it has two sides, it consists of two parts. The Word that God causes to be proclaimed by the external call is the same Word that He causes, in the internal call by the Holy Spirit, to be inscribed on the heart. It is one call, whose two parts are continually connected to each other.

This connection between the external and the internal with respect to the church, the covenant, calling, and the means of grace, the Reformed maintained specifically in opposition to the Anabaptists, the Quakers, and various Enthusiasts, who with their doctrine of the internal word undermined God's entire special revelation, leading ultimately to rationalism.

It is true that both dimensions of these distinctions never coincide. The visible and the invisible church are not coterminous. According to the saying of Augustine, there are sheep outside and wolves inside the sheepfold of the church of Christ upon earth. The external and internal sides of the covenant of grace do not correspond fully to each other. There are many who according to our estimate belong within the dispensation of the covenant of grace and nevertheless do not share in the essence and the spiritual benefits of that covenant. In connection with the means of grace, the sign and the thing signified are not always united with each other. There are many who have been baptized and who partake of the Lord's Supper without ever having received by a true faith the thing signified in these sacraments.

So, too, external and internal calling are not always united. On the one hand, many are called who are not chosen; and on the other hand, it is possible that some are internally called who were never able self-consciously to hear the preaching of the Word. This latter occurs in the case of children of believers who die in infancy, in reference to whom the Synod of Dort confessed that believing parents ought not doubt their election and salvation [Canons of Dort, I, art. 17].

Despite all of this, however, the Reformed were always careful to keep external and internal calling connected to each other. As a rule the Spirit of Christ works only where His Word and sacrament are administered in accord with His ordinance. And to the extent that this Spirit might work savingly outside of this sphere, such a working is infrequent, extraordinary, and unknown to us.[2]

Therefore it is incorrect to argue that the Reformed have severed regeneration (as exclusively the work of the Holy Spirit) from any connection with the Word. At most this was done by a few theologians, and then only in a certain sense and to a limited degree. With much more accuracy the uniform position of the Reformed churches and theologians can be described this way: *regeneration, as a rule, is a fruit of the*

---

[2] Johannes Polyander, "De hominum vocatione ad salutem," *Synopsis purioris theologiae*, XXX. 33.

operation of the Holy Spirit, connected to the proclamation of the gospel. They did not even hesitate to call the Word the means and the seed of regeneration.

No matter how one evaluates this matter, this much is sure in any case, namely, that the operation of the Holy Spirit, because it can only be a moral working, works differently in connection with regeneration than with faith and conversion.

15.4 The Word of God in Relation to Faith and Conversion

Although regeneration is connected to the Word (since as a rule the Holy Spirit works savingly only where the gospel is proclaimed), a distinction must be made between the operation exercised by the Word in connection with regeneration, and the operation occurring thereby in connection with faith and conversion.

This flows forth naturally from the moral operation of the Word, and proceeds then whenever regeneration and faith differ not in the time of occurrence but merely in the order of their occurrence.

15.4.1 *The act of faith*

For arousing faith, that is, the act of faith, the Word is absolutely necessary. Naturally this is so not in the sense that God could have made use of no other instruments to work effectual faith in His elect. But it is necessary when we take into account the revealed will of God. For this informs us that faith comes from hearing, and hearing from the Word of God. For how shall they call on the name of the Lord unless they have believed? And how will they believe in Him whom they have not heard? And how shall they hear unless someone preach to them? [Rom. 10:14] For bringing into existence this act of faith and of repentance, the Word is an instrument in the proper sense. The Word is a means whereby God makes the capacity for faith progress genuinely into the act of faith. The Word is an effectual cause that, in God's hand and under the leading of the Holy Spirit, produces that for which it is designed and equipped. Even as the eye alone is insufficient but genuinely sees only when rays of light pass through it from the outside, and as the ear by itself is insufficient but hears only when it receives sounds from outside, so too the capacity for faith that is sown in regeneration cannot progress to the act of faith apart from encountering the Word of the gospel from the outside. Just as light is suited to the eye and sound is suited to the ear, so the object of faith offered in Holy Scripture fits and is suited to the new life that the Holy Spirit infuses into the heart in regeneration. Like the deer pants for water streams, so the soul of the regenerated person thirsts for God, who in Christ has revealed Himself as his Father, and finds refreshment only from the fountain opened for him in the Holy Scripture [Ps. 42:1].

15.4.2 *The agency of the Holy Spirit and the act of faith*

Of course, one may not infer from this that through the operation of the Word alone the capacity for faith either progresses or can progress to the act of faith. Even if a person is regenerated, the external calling of the Word is nonetheless inadequate for that. For God works both the willing and the working according to His good pleasure [Phil. 2:13]. Not only from Him, but also through Him and unto Him are all things [Rom. 11:36]. The external calling is never sufficient, neither at the beginning nor with the progress of faith and conversion. The internal calling must always be connected to the external calling in order to make the capacity for faith to progress initially and continually to acts of faith. Just as the seed does not germinate, sprout, and bear fruit apart from having been sown in a field prepared for it, and apart from being continually nourished and supplied by rain and sunshine, so too the Word remains fruitless unless God continually supply the growth. The Holy Spirit must join Himself to the preached Word if the capacity for faith is to progress to the act of faith. Presupposed regeneration does not render this special, accompanying operation of the Spirit superfluous, nor does it make the Word alone to be sufficient. One who has the capacity to believe cannot genuinely believe if the Holy Spirit does not sanctify and bless the Word to that person's heart by internal calling. The capacity to hear savingly is bestowed in regeneration—but this saving hearing itself, in its actuality and its genuineness, is just as much a fruit of a special operation of the Holy Spirit. Even if one presupposes that those to whom the gospel is proclaimed are regenerated, such in no way obviates the need for the Holy Spirit to accompany the proclamation of the Word and to make the capacity for faith progress to the act of faith.

15.4.3 *The instrumentality of the Word and the act of faith*

Only when this is given proper attention can one say that the Holy Spirit employs the Word as an instrument in connection with this operation. In this way the Word is a genuine means, a moral instrument, but nonetheless a means in the proper sense, effectuating and working that for which it is equipped and designed. It bestows upon faith its object and content, just as language supplies a child with ideas for which that child is suited in terms of the child's capacities for thought and speech.

The operation of the Word possesses a rather different character, however, in relation to regeneration. Although with adults, regeneration and faith occasionally occur simultaneously, nevertheless, in a logical sense the Word presupposes regeneration if it is to be heard and accepted savingly. For a natural human being can hear the Word physically. By virtue of various influences of nurture and environment, such a person can with a historical faith acknowledge it as truth. Such a person can also hear the Word and immediately receive it with joy and rejoice in it for a time. But such a person cannot believe savingly unless he be born again of water and Spirit beforehand, perhaps not in terms of time but certainly in terms of order. If the Word is to bear the fruits of faith and conversion, it must fall in good soil that has been prepared by the operation of the Holy Spirit [Matt. 13:23; Luke 8:15].

One who insists on denying this would thereby be abandoning the Reformed position and be moving over to the Remonstrant position. Such a person would be erasing the boundary line drawn in Holy Scripture between one who is spiritually dead and one who is spiritually alive, and would be exchanging the essential difference between both for a gradual transition.

From this it also follows, however, that with the coming into existence of regeneration, the Word can exercise no moral operation. For in order to exercise such an operation, the capacity for believing would need to be sown beforehand. By the nature of the case, the Word can work only when it is understood. But the Word can be understood only by the person who has been regenerated. As long as a person is in his natural state he does not understand the things of the Spirit of God [1 Cor. 2:14]. The saving operation of the Word begins and can begin only at the moment when a person is furnished by the Holy Spirit in regeneration in order to understand what is spiritual and receive it believingly.

So regeneration occurs *under* the Word, *by* the Word, *with* the Word, but it does not occur *through* the Word in the sense that the Holy Spirit could work with the human heart only through that Word. For the Holy Spirit has indeed bound Himself to creating fellowship with Christ and His benefits where the Word of Christ is proclaimed; but He has neither imprisoned nor enclosed Himself and His operation within the Word. No more than the sacrament is the Word a magical instrument that imparts grace by its supernaturally infused power; rather, it supplies the condition under which, the occasion when, and the path along which God exalts His grace to the sinner and makes the sinner to share in Christ and all His benefits.

15.5 Preaching Still Necessary

If regeneration comes about under, with, and by, but not through the Word, the objection can be raised that then the preaching of the Word becomes rather unnecessary and superfluous. The Remonstrants, in their time, raised this objection against the Reformed doctrine of effectual and irresistible calling—and that objection has been repeated ever since that time, including today. It would therefore be useful to examine this objection for a few moments.

15.5.1 *The mandate of preaching*

We can immediately meet this objection with the observation that the command to preach the gospel is so clearly contained in Holy Scripture as to remove all doubt or objection. Even if we were unable in any way to envision the profitability and necessity of the proclamation of the gospel, even if we could hardly explain the connection between the proclamation and imparting of God's grace in Christ to the sinner, even then we would not be permitted, either directly or indirectly, to render God's command impotent by means of our reasoning and considerations, and we would be obligated to do nothing less than submit ourselves in childlike obedience to His will. If Christ mandates us to preach His gospel to all creatures, then that means for His disciples that every objection evaporates. Not seeing the future, we focus on the command—that is every Christian's motto.

15.5.2 *The parable of the sower*

There is more to be said, however, in order to strip the Remonstrants' objection of its force. In the first place, even where it does not result in true faith and genuine conversion, the preaching of the Word of God is not superfluous and futile. The sower certainly sows with the intention of casting the seed upon good soil, so that it will germinate and sprout and bear fruit. But in the sowing, some seed falls along the path and on stony ground and among the thorns. Even there it is not entirely inoperative. For even though in each of these three instances the seed does not fall in good soil and does not bear fruit, nevertheless, it does come into contact with the earth and manifests its nature and properties. All those whom Jesus describes in His parable of the sower with the metaphors of the path, the stony ground, and the weed patch, are hearers of the gospel. They may well hear the gospel with apathy and indifference, or receive the gospel with some awakened though superficial interest, or even be moved by the gospel to a partial though not heartfelt conversion—everyone nevertheless hears the gospel and adopts a certain posture toward it.

These responses are far from insignificant. By them we are shown, first, that God's truth revealed in Christ makes an impression upon the consciousness of everyone who comes into contact with it; it makes manifest the thoughts of the hearts of many people. Second, historical faith, temporary faith, and miraculous faith are completely different from saving faith, and none of these other kinds of faith is a preparation unto saving faith in any way; but given that, this is not to say they are without any value for this life. For preaching does restrain unrighteousness from bursting forth, lays claim upon the evil thoughts and counsels of those who live under the gospel, and makes possible to a certain degree the existence of a Christian society. It makes it possible for the church to be able to lead a quiet and tranquil life in society.

Third, preaching renders inexcusable every person who hears the gospel but rejects it, since the person rejecting the gospel acts contrary to the testimony of his own conscience, which in the midst of a Christian context has been, to a lesser or larger degree, illuminated by the Holy

Spirit. Fourth, the counsel of the Lord is also fulfilled through the external calling that is not accepted in genuine faith. For Christ came not only for the rise of many but also for the fall of many. The gospel that did not become a savor of life unto life becomes an odor of death unto death [2 Cor. 2:16]. Election has reprobation as its counterpart.

15.5.3 *The promise of God*

In the second place, the preaching of the gospel is neither superfluous nor futile because the Lord has promised in this way to exalt His grace and to impart the benefits of Christ. This involves not only faith and conversion, justification and sanctification, but also regeneration. Without doubt, properly speaking there are no preparations for regeneration, for there is no communion between death and life. Regeneration is a completely new beginning in which a person is passive, doing nothing yet undergoing something.

Despite this, however, the Reformed have maintained that under and through the preaching of the Word various operations could precede regeneration. Nature and grace are distinct, yet they do not stand detached from one another. The same God who regenerates His elect in Christ through the Holy Spirit is the one who, as Creator and Sustainer, cares for them and leads them also to the moment when He visits them with His grace.

Therefore the means of grace are not superfluous; and how we make use of them is not an insignificant matter. This is part of the reason why Reformed theologians have insisted on the connection between external and internal calling. The one divine call which comes to the elect through Word and Spirit is simultaneously effectual and moral. It is so powerful that it cannot be overcome, and at the same time it is so lovely that it excludes every form of compulsion. Its power is so excellent that the depraved nature is renewed by it, and, at the same time, so friendly and winsome that it fully respects a person's rational and moral nature.

The Synod of Dort confessed, wholly in this sense, that God's supernatural working by which He regenerates us in no way excludes or subverts the use of the gospel, which the most wise God has ordained to be the seed of regeneration and food of the soul. Therefore, then, just as the apostles and the teachers who followed them piously taught the people about this grace unto the honor of God and the humbling of all pride, and further did not omit to keep the same, by means of sacred gospel warnings, under the exercise of the Word, the sacraments, and discipline; so may it be far from those who today are taught or instructed in the church to arrogantly tempt God by separating those things that God desires to be closely united, according to His good pleasure. For grace is imparted by means of warnings; and to the degree that we perform our obligation readily, to that degree will the benefit of God who works in us be the more excellent.

15.5.4 *Assurance of salvation through the preaching of the gospel*

In the third place, the preaching of the gospel is necessary and profitable so that those who are regenerated become, by these means, conscious and assured of the new life that God has bestowed upon them. Regeneration is a work of the Holy Spirit in the innermost being of a person. As the wind blows where it will and no one know whence it comes and where it goes, so is it with everyone born of the Spirit [John 3:8]. Little can be determined with regard to time and manner of regeneration. But whether we are regenerated becomes manifest to ourselves and to others in the fact that we accept with genuine faith the Word preached to us, and in the fact that we with a true heart repent toward God. It will benefit us very little if we presume regeneration—in others or in ourselves—if the new life does not transform us in terms of acts of faith and repentance.

For that reason, the apostle Paul summoned the Corinthians this way: Examine yourselves, whether you are in the faith; test yourselves! [2 Cor. 13:5] We can examine ourselves only according to the standard of God's Word. That Word is our measure. According to that Word everyone who has heard it will be judged. According to the testimony of that Word, those persons will enter the kingdom of heaven, not who call out "Lord! Lord!," but who do the will of the heavenly Father, who in faith and conversion show that they have been born again of water and Spirit [Matt. 7:21].

15.5.5 *Two additional advantages*

So it is completely true that the Reformed doctrine of God's supernatural operation in regeneration in no sense excludes or banishes the use of the gospel. In addition to maintaining this usage unabridged, this view offers two additional significant advantages.

On the one hand, the Reformed view of regeneration maintains the person's rational and moral nature and preserves his responsibility unabated. For external calling and internal calling go together; the effectual operation of the Holy Spirit is coupled with the moral operation of the Word. The one calling is simultaneously irresistible and lovely. The Word does not work magically, as it would if God were to infuse grace in the manner that Rome teaches with regard to the sacraments. But the Word works morally upon the heart and conscience, upon human understanding and reason. No one then will be able to excuse himself for his unbelief by saying: I was not regenerated and therefore could not believe. No one will be condemned because he could not regenerate himself, for God does not demand that from any person. But each unbeliever will ultimately be condemned because he has spurned the testimony of his conscience in the gospel, and in hard-hearted unbelief has resisted the moral operation that proceeded from the Word.

That is the first great advantage flowing from the Reformed doctrine of the relationship between Word and Spirit, of external and internal calling.

The second is no less significant. Because the Reformed continually guarded against identifying both distinctions, they could confess with confidence, on the basis of God's Word, that our children could also be received by God in grace. For as a rule, the Holy Spirit works *with* and *under*, but not *through* the Word. He is not indissolubly tied to means. He can bring the elect to life where and when and how He wills.

In the Reformed doctrine of the relationship between Word and Spirit, respect for God's revealed will is coupled with the full acknowledgement of the sovereignty of His hidden will.

15.6 The Confirmation of Scripture

There remains, in conclusion, the task of explaining briefly how the relationship between calling and regeneration which we have developed thus far comports fully with what Holy Scripture teaches about this.

15.6.1 *The power of the Word*

In this connection we find, in the first place, that when it comes to the application of the benefits of salvation, Scripture ascribes an exalted significance and an excellent power to the Word. Just as by His speaking God calls all things into existence and continually maintains and rules all things, so too He brings into existence the work of recreation by means of the Word. The first thing God did for Adam after the Fall was to search him out and call out to him. Along the route of this calling God brought him again, in grace, back to His side and restored him back into His fellowship. Afterwards, God Himself brought the word of calling directly and in an extraordinary manner to Abraham, Israel, and the prophets— or He had that word of calling brought to people through the mouth of His servants. Jesus Himself appeared on the scene preaching that the time is fulfilled and the kingdom of God has come near, repent and believe the gospel. He also gave His apostles and servants the task of preaching that same gospel to every creature. The calling through law and gospel is the route whereby God glorifies His grace unto sinners and communicates fellowship in Christ and His benefits. That which the apostles had seen and heard, they proclaim to us, so that we would have fellowship with them, and together we would have fellowship with the Father and with His Son, Jesus Christ. No voice of conscience, no inward light, but the Word is the means whereby God imparts and applies to people the salvation obtained by Christ.

For that very purpose, according to Scripture, the Word is most excellently suited. For that purpose the Word was chosen far less arbitrarily than the signs given in baptism and the Lord's Supper. With greater effectiveness, the Word is the instrument ordained and equipped by God

Himself to make known His intentions, also His reconciling intentions in Christ, to manifest the power of His grace and to cause people, in agreement with their rational and moral nature, and yet effectually, to share in the benefits of the covenant of grace.

For that Word, spoken according to the Lord's mandate by His servants, is like a fire that consumes every human work, and like a hammer that breaks the rock in pieces and destroys every opposition (Jer. 23:29). The mouth of one who is equipped with that Word is like a sharp sword, and like an arrow that penetrates hearts (Isa. 49:2). That Word, therefore, does not return void, but it does everything that pleases God, and prospers in that for which He sends it. Even as the rain waters the earth and makes it fruitful, so the Word does the same with respect to the human heart (Isa. 55:11). The Word has within itself the power to fulfill its content and to transform that content into reality; the Word of prediction creates, as it were, the future, and the Word itself constitutes the beginning of the fulfillment of God's counsel.

Similarly in the New Testament, the Word of the gospel is described for us as a seed that sends forth roots in human hearts and yields the fruits of faith and repentance (Luke 8:11). It is a power of God unto salvation, a power proceeding from God wherein He manifests Himself at work as the One who accomplishes salvation (Rom. 1:16). When it is sown in people, it possesses the power to save their souls (John 1:21). Since it is not a dead letter but a living word, it is powerful, sharper than any two-edged sword, piercing to the dividing between soul and spirit, between joints and marrow, to the innermost being of a person, such that it judges all his intentions and uncovers all the thoughts of his heart (Heb. 4:12).

15.6.2 *God, not the Word, the agent of salvation*

And yet, this same Bible, which ascribes such great power to the Word, on the other hand teaches just as decisively and clearly that this Word alone is not sufficient, that it is but an instrument in the hand of the almighty God. Salvation, both in its acquisition and in its application, is God's work and His alone.

This is declared repeatedly in the Old Testament, even though, given the contrast with the then-operative legal dispensation, the Old Testament most often describes human regeneration and renewal as a benefit of the New Covenant. The Lord is the One who gives ears to hear, eyes to see, and a heart to understand (Deut. 29:4); He is the One who sets the heart free (Deut. 30:6); He it is who writes His law upon the inner heart (Jer. 31:32), and who removes the heart of stone and replaces it with a new heart and a new spirit (Ezek. 36:26).

But all of this is taught with greater clarity and distinctness in the New Testament. No one can enter the kingdom of God unless he is regenerated, and that regeneration comes from God, for it is the fruit of the operation of the Holy Spirit (John 3:3, 5). If therefore someone comes to Christ and believes in Him, that is due to the Father having drawn and instructed that person (John 6:44–45), for no one can say that Jesus is Lord except by the Holy Spirit (1 Cor. 12:3). When Peter confesses Jesus to be the Christ, that was revealed to him not by flesh and blood, but by the Father in heaven (Matt. 16:17). When Paul fell down in worship before Jesus on the road to Damascus, that is to be ascribed to the good pleasure of God who desired to reveal His Son in him (Gal. 1:16). When Lydia listened to the word spoken by Paul, her heart was opened for that purpose by the Lord (Acts 16:14). When God keeps the things of His kingdom hidden from the wise and understanding, and reveals them to children, the cause thereof lies solely in the good pleasure of God (Matt. 11:25–26).

15.6.3 *The limitations of the Word*

Thus, the Word is a living, fruit-bearing seed, but in order to demonstrate its power and bring forth its fruits of faith and repentance, it must fall in good soil, the kind that has been prepared by the operation of the Holy Spirit. The Word is indeed a power of God unto salvation, but only for those who believe; and this faith is a gift (Eph. 2:8). The Word is indeed a sword, but a sword of the Spirit (Eph. 6:17), one that is effective only when He is using it. Paul and Apollos could merely plant the seed and water it, being no more than servants, but God gives the growth (1 Cor. 3:6). They carry the treasure of administering the gospel in earthen vessels, so that the excellency of its power may be of God and not of them (2 Cor. 4:7). In those who believe, the excellent greatness of God's power is revealed, and that power is according to the working of the strength of His might, which He has wrought in Christ when He raised Him from the dead and sat Him at His right hand in heaven (Eph. 1:19–20). The gospel exercises its saving operation only when it is accompanied with the power of the Holy Spirit, who makes people know through faith the things that God bestows (Rom. 15:19; 1 Cor. 2:4, 12; 1 Thess. 1:5; 4:8; 1 Pet. 1:12). Believers are therefore new creatures (2 Cor. 5:17); they are God's handiwork, created in Christ Jesus (Eph. 2:10).

15.6.4 *The gracious content of the Word*

God imparts all these benefits of grace and brings about this entire application of the work of redemption along the path of the covenant, by means of the Word, which He causes to go forth to people in various ways and in various forms. In that Word He holds before us what we must do, but along the route of the proclamation of that Word He Himself fulfills through His grace what He holds before us as our duty. As the well-known saying of Augustine puts it: "Give what Thou dost command, and command what Thou wilt." Ezekiel received the task of prophesying over the bones in the valley and saying to them: O ye dry bones, hear the word of the Lord! (Ezek. 37:4). And when he prophesied as he had been commanded, there was a noise and a shaking, and the bones came together, each bone to another bone, and the sinews and the flesh covered them, and the Spirit came into them and they came alive and stood on their feet. The word Ezekiel spoke was not the cause of all that. For thus said the Lord: I will put my spirit in them and they will come alive. But the preaching of the prophet was nevertheless the route whereby and the occasion when God revealed His life-giving power in the dry and dead bones. Similarly, it was not the outward sound of Jesus' voice that made Lazarus rise from the dead; nonetheless, the dead Lazarus came forth at the moment when Jesus called with a loud voice, "Lazarus, come forth!"

The same manner obtains with respect to the spiritual process. Holy Scripture says relatively little about children; it merely provides believers sufficient basis for not doubting the election and salvation of their children who die in infancy. For the rest, Scripture deals only with adults, with those who have reached the age of discretion. For them what is decisive is not whether they presuppose that they were regenerated in their youth, but whether they now with upright faith receive Christ and all His benefits and turn to God with a true heart. In order that they should do this, the gospel is proclaimed to them. And along the path of this proclamation God imparts the benefits of His grace and reveals the power of His Spirit. When Paul preached, the Lord opened Lydia's heart, so that she listened to his word. When Paul planted and Apollos watered, God supplied the growth. When the disciples went forth preaching everywhere, the Lord was working alongside. Through miracles and signs He gave testimony to the Word of His grace.

16

Solution to the Controversy

ACCORDING TO Scripture, regeneration belongs to those benefits that God bestows upon His elect along the path of the covenant and by means of His Word. Nevertheless, there exist not only doctrinal but also exegetical differences of opinion about this. Everyone agrees that faith and repentance come about in no other way than by means of the Word. Romans 10:14–17 puts this beyond all doubt; faith comes from hearing, and hearing comes through the Word of God. But concerning regeneration in its narrower sense there exists difference of opinion among exegetes.

16.1 The Non-Pauline Treatment of Regeneration

In order to resolve this difference, it is of course inadequate to quote a few verses that mention regeneration. For the word "regeneration" hardly has a uniform meaning, either in our own linguistic usage or in the language of Scripture. For example, when in Matthew 19:28 Jesus promises His disciples that in the regeneration, when the Son of Man will have sat down on His throne of glory, they too will sit on twelve thrones to judge the twelve tribes of Israel, everyone understands that Jesus is not talking about the regeneration we have been discussing, but He is talking about the renewal of heaven and earth that will occur at the end of time. Thus, some texts where the word "regeneration" appears are not relevant to our discussion, while other texts that mention not the word but the subject itself are very significant for our discussion.

16.1.1 Regeneration in the broad sense

This rule is applicable to 1 Peter 1:3. There the apostle thanks and praises the God and Father of our Lord Jesus Christ, who according to His great mercy has begotten us again unto a living hope, through the resurrection of Jesus Christ from the dead, unto an inheritance that is incorruptible and undefiled, reserved in heaven. Although Peter here uses the word for regeneration, he does not thereby have in view the benefit that we usually describe with this term. For he is speaking here not of regeneration in its narrower sense, as the infusion of the principle of new life, but of being regenerated unto a living hope and an imperishable inheritance. This regeneration unto a living hope appears here to be a unified concept for the apostle. His idea is this: the believers to whom he is writing were formerly without Christ, without God, and therefore also without hope in the world. But since they had heard the gospel from those who proclaimed it to them through the Holy Spirit (1 Pet. 1:12), they have been rescued from this situation of being without hope and comfort, and have become partakers of an incorruptible inheritance. They have been regenerated unto a living hope. This hope is the new life unto which God has begotten them again; it is no idle or disappointing hope but one that is genuine, fruitful, and renews all of life. They have become new people, because they have become partakers in a particular hope that will not deceive them but that assures them of an incorruptible inheritance and therefore makes them live. They owe that new life of hope to God through the resurrection of Jesus Christ, for that resurrection is the foundation and the power, the source and the nourishment, of that hope. After the believers addressed in Peter's epistle heard of that resurrection of Christ and received that gospel with an upright faith, they who formerly had lived life without comfort and without hope were regenerated unto a living hope. The proclamation of the gospel and the believing acceptance of that gospel preceded *this* regeneration.

16.1.2 *"The Seed" and "the Word" in relation to regeneration*

In a different, less specific sense Peter speaks of regeneration in verse 23 of the same chapter. There he admonishes believers to love one another fervently and from a pure heart. And he presses the admonition with the observation that ultimately they had together all been regenerated not from perishable seed, but from imperishable seed, through the living and abiding Word of God. Without doubt this Word refers to the gospel, for in verse 25 Peter states emphatically that the Word of the Lord that abides forever is precisely that Word which was proclaimed among them. The regeneration that had occurred in them thus occurred by means of the proclaimed gospel.

But the apostle describes that regeneration in still another way. He states that these believers have been regenerated, not from perishable but from imperishable seed, by means of the living and abiding Word of God. Among exegetes there is a significant difference of opinion as to whether "the seed" from which and "the Word" through which believers have been regenerated refers here in each instance to a different thing, or both times to the same thing. Many understand the seed to refer to the Holy Spirit, or to the regenerating power of the Holy Spirit, or to the principle of new life planted by the Holy Spirit through the proclamation of the gospel. In support of this they appeal especially to 1 John 3:9: "Whosoever is born of God doth not commit sin; for His seed remaineth in him: and he cannot sin, because he is born of God."

This interpretation is indeed preferable to the view that understands the seed to refer to the same thing as the Word. That a difference exists between seed and Word is shown by the difference in prepositions. Believers are regenerated *from* imperishable seed, but *through* (or by means of) the living and abiding Word of God. Thus the Word is understood as the means whereby regeneration occurs, but the seed is viewed as the principle from which regeneration comes forth. A person who believes in Christ is born "not of blood nor of the will of the flesh nor of the will of man, but of God" (John 1:13). He comes forth from a creative act of God, from a power, from a new principle of life that God through His Spirit has planted within the heart.

But even though seed and Word are not the same, nevertheless they are placed in close relation to one another. That appears, first, from the fact that Peter says of these believers that they have been born again from an imperishable seed by means of the Word preached among them. Regeneration from imperishable seed occurred in them when the Word of God was proclaimed among them, and by means of that Word of God. Second, the close relation between seed and Word appears from the adjectives used to describe both of them. The seed is called imperishable, and the Word is called living and abiding.

The apostle has good reasons for describing seed and Word in those ways. For he is admonishing Christians to love each other fervently and uprightly. And he emphasizes that admonition with the observation that they have been born again from an imperishable seed and through a living and abiding Word of God. As those regenerated from this kind of seed and through that kind of Word, they are particularly obliged to show steadfast and upright love toward one another. Thus, Peter emphasizes not so much that they have been regenerated as that they have been regenerated *from an imperishable seed and through a living and abiding Word of God*. That Word to which they owe the instrumentality of their regeneration, and that seed from which they were regenerated, are both imperishable and abiding, and therefore obligate them to practice a fervent, steadfast, intimate love. To that Word, which the servants of the gospel have proclaimed to them through the Holy Spirit (1:12) and which in that manner was planted in their hearts through faith (James 1:21), they owe their new life, and through that same Word, which is living and abiding, they are continually obligated to show upright and fervent love toward each other.

16.1.3 *Regeneration in James*

James also is not dealing with regeneration in its narrower sense when he states, in 1:18, that God has brought us forth of His own will through the word of truth. In the original we read: "According to His will God brought us forth through the word of truth." That word is one of the extraordinary gifts that has come down from the Father of lights (1:17), for it is the perfect law, the law of liberty (1:25). And when that word is received with an upright faith, when in accordance with God's own promise (Jer. 31:33) it is planted in the heart by God Himself (1:21), we are thereby brought forth as different people, and come into an entirely new situation.

That this is the idea being communicated by the apostle appears from the addition of the words: "that we should be a kind of firstfruits of his creatures" (1:18). God has brought us forth as new people through the Word in such a way so that we, like Israel of old, should be consecrated to God and sanctified, so that we might appear in the place of ancient Israel, and should be God's special possession, manifesting ourselves as such in the world—not only as hearers but also as doers of the word (James 1:22).

In all these passages Scripture has in view with regeneration the new state and situation that has arisen with Christians when the gospel was proclaimed to them in the power of the Holy Spirit and they have received that gospel with an upright faith. Regeneration in the narrower sense, as the infusion of the new principle of life, is not excluded here; but the texts mentioned above nevertheless ascribe a much broader meaning to regeneration. The comprehensive renewal to which they give expression and which has its beginning with regeneration in our narrower sense was preceded by the proclamation of the gospel and by the effectual calling of the Holy Spirit.

16.2 The Pauline Treatment of Regeneration

It is the same with the apostle Paul, who uses the word "regeneration" only once, in Titus 3:5, but who repeatedly mentions the subject itself.

16.2.1 *Regeneration and baptism*

Upon first reading, one receives the impression that Paul ties this spiritual renewal of a person to baptism. Titus 3:4 need not come into view at this point, since it is highly doubtful that with the words, "washing of regeneration and renewal of the Holy Spirit," Paul was referring to baptism. It is more cogent to understand that the apostle used the imagery of bathing in connection with regeneration and renewal of the Holy Spirit in order to indicate thereby that believers are cleansed by that regeneration and renewal as through a spiritual bathing, and are thus saved.

But even though Titus 3:5 is thus probably not speaking about baptism, in many other passages Paul connects the regeneration and renewal of a person most closely to baptism. In Romans 6:3–4, for instance, he states that those who are baptized into Christ Jesus are baptized into His death and through baptism are buried with Him in His death, so that they, even as Christ is raised from the dead, may walk in newness of life. This idea is not only developed in the subsequent verses, but also reappears elsewhere (Gal. 3:27; Eph. 4:5; Col. 2:11–12). Baptism, which in Paul's time always occurred in the mode of immersion, is a grafting into the fellowship of Christ's death and resurrection, and thus is indeed a washing of regeneration and of the renewal of the Holy Spirit.

Nevertheless, Paul's intention cannot be to tie the mortification of the old man and the resurrection of the new man, namely, regeneration, so closely to baptism that these come into existence for the first time through baptism. For the apostle teaches clearly that baptism presupposes faith. According to the command of Christ no one was baptized in the time of Paul unless he had first heard the gospel, received it in faith, and made profession of that faith (Acts 16:31–33; 19:5; 1 Cor. 1:17).

Now the faith that precedes baptism is, for Paul, the means of partaking in Christ and in all His benefits. By that faith a person is justified (Rom. 3:26), becomes a child of God (Gal. 3:26), receives a new life (Gal. 2:20), shares in salvation (Rom. 10:9; Eph. 2:8), and shares in Christ (Gal. 2:20; 2 Cor. 13:5; Eph. 3:17). That faith is even an effectual principle, a source of joy and delight, of love and good works (Rom. 15:13; Gal. 5:6). In that way one who possesses faith is thereby a partaker of all the benefits of salvation.

For this reason Paul cannot have tied regeneration and the new life so closely to baptism, as if baptism were the cause or the instrument. But when Paul wanted to stimulate the Christians in Rome to walk in newness of life, he reminded them of their baptism, of the act that had clearly demonstrated, to themselves and to all those around them, that they had broken with the world and had gone over to the fellowship of Christ and His disciples. That break with the world and that entrance into fellowship with Christ had indeed already begun, at the point when they had received with upright faith the gospel that was preached to them. But that faith had proven its veracity and genuineness when it was completed in the act of baptism. Undergoing baptism was the immediate, visible expression of their faith. And their baptism imprinted a sign and seal upon that faith in the name of the Lord. Through baptism, believers were assured of the benefits of the covenant that they had accepted by faith. Therefore, faith and baptism are most intimately related in this sense, and it was for that reason that Paul can ascribe the same benefits one time to faith and another time to baptism. In Galatians

3:26–27 both stand alongside each other: believers are children of God only by faith in Christ Jesus, and yet by having been baptized into Christ they had put on Christ.

16.2.2 *Regeneration and the gift of faith*

From all of this we see that the mortification of the old man and the resurrection of the new man, namely, the regeneration and renewal of the Holy Spirit, together with justification, are described by Paul as a fruit of faith. But that faith itself, although it comes from hearing, is a work of the Holy Spirit, who performs it in the context of the proclamation of the gospel by effectual calling. The proclamation of the gospel occurs in the Holy Spirit, in demonstration of spirit and power (1 Cor. 2:4, 4:20, 1 Thess. 1:5). Calling, which comes to the elect, is an effectual power whose consequence is faith (Rom. 8:28, 30). That faith is a gift of God (Eph. 2:8). No one can say Jesus is Lord except by the Holy Spirit (1 Cor. 12:3). So for Paul, as the means of justification and as the principle of new life saving faith is a fruit of the working of the Holy Spirit. And the Holy Spirit works that faith in the context of the proclamation of the Word, by the external and internal call together. If Paul plants and Apollos waters, then God gives the increase.

16.3 John's Treatment of Regeneration

Although difference exists in the manner of expression, the teaching of John agrees substantially with this teaching of Paul. Whereas Paul ascribes the origin of faith to God's effectual call, to the operation of the Holy Spirit, John answers the question, "Who are those who come to Christ and believe in Him?" this way: Only those who are born of God. Even as Paul declares that the natural man does not understand the things of the Spirit of God, so in John we read that the darkness does not apprehend the light, that the people who live in darkness prefer the darkness rather than the light, that apart from regeneration no one can see the kingdom of God, etc. Thus only those come to Christ who have an upright faith, who have been given by the Father to the Son (John 6:37, 39; 17:2–3; 18:9), who by virtue of that gift can be said to have already been included in the purpose of God as being children of God (11:52) and belonging to Jesus' sheep (10:16), who therefore within time are born of God, by His Spirit (1:13; 3:3, 5–6; 8:47; 1 John 2:29; 3:9; 4:7; 5:1, 4, 18), who are of the truth (18:37), who do the truth (3:21), who desire to perform God's will (7:17), who are drawn by the Father and have heard and learned it from the Father (6:44–45; 8:47; 10:27).

Undoubtedly included among these people who came to Jesus with upright faith because they had been born of God were first of all those Israelites who had been nurtured in the truth of the Old Testament revelation, who loved this truth and walked according to it, and who all therefore gradually came to acknowledge Jesus as the Christ and accepted Him with unfeigned faith (1:11–12). We find examples of this with Andrew, John, Simon, Philip, Nathanael (1:35–36), Nicodemus (3:1–2), Joseph of Arimathea (19:38), and others. Although they were upright believers, such Israelites nevertheless could have doubted for a shorter or longer period whether Jesus really was the Messiah promised to the fathers. But since they were really born of God, knew and loved the truth, sooner or later they all also came to Jesus and confessed Him as the Christ. Because they had been given by the Father to the Son and thus belonged to His sheep, they knew His voice when it came to them (10:26–27).

This coming to Christ, believing in His name, was a proof from the opposite direction that they had been born of God. Each one who believes is born of God (1 John 5:1), and demonstrates by his faith that he is born of God. Faith is the consequence and fruit, but therefore also the sign and seal of being born of God. Being born of God becomes evident, to ourselves and to others, first of all, in that very faith. Therefore John connects salvation and life with faith just as strongly as the other apostles do. One who believes in the Son has eternal life (3:16, 36; 5:24; 6:47; 11:25; etc.), but one who does not believe remains under God's wrath, has already been condemned, and will not see life (3:16, 18, 36; etc.).

Wherever Scripture treats regeneration and faith, they appear in the closest possible connection. In his commentary on John 1:13, John Calvin writes with beauty and veracity: the evangelist seems to reverse the sequence when he has regeneration precede faith, since it is much more a fruit and result of faith. But to this we must reply that the one agrees so closely with the other, for through faith we receive an imperishable seed whereby we are regenerated unto a new, divine life. And yet that faith itself is also a work of the Holy Spirit, who dwells in no one but God's children.

16.4 What God Has Joined Together

What God has thus joined together let us not separate. Regeneration in the ethical sense of Paul's usage may not be severed from regeneration in the metaphysical sense with which John frequently speaks of it.

Leaving aside for a moment children who have not yet reached the age of discretion, we may say that wherever regeneration in the narrower sense is present, it becomes manifest in regeneration in the broader sense, in upright faith, in genuine repentance, and in living according to God's testimony. Wherever true faith and repentance are present, we may conclude on the basis of God's Word that a preceding operation of the Holy Spirit has occurred in ourselves and in others.

God imparts all these benefits along the pathway of the covenant, in the context of the administration of the means of grace, which He has ordained. The means of grace do not themselves contain those benefits within themselves, and therefore they cannot communicate or effectuate them. But yet God in His great goodness has bound Himself to impart all the benefits of the covenant of grace where that covenant is administered according to His institution.

That provides courage and hope for going forward with the proclamation of God's Word and the administration of His sacraments. God's Word does not return void, but accomplishes everything that pleases Him. For some it may be a savor of death unto death, for others a savor of life unto life. Along the path of the covenant God executes the decree of His eternal election. But that also entails the duty to preach the gospel to all creatures, not only to the elect and regenerate, who after all are unknown to us, but to all people without exception. There is distinction between the administration of the Word in the gathering of believers, and the preaching of the gospel among pagans, and that distinction may not be erased. For all who have heard the gospel, however, this principle applies: whoever believes in the Son has eternal life, but whoever disobeys the Son will not see life, but the wrath of God abides upon him.

Appendix

The Conclusions of Utrecht[1]

I. INFRA– OR SUPRALAPSARIANISM

In regard to the first point, infra- or supralapsarianism, Synod declares:

that our Confessional Standards admittedly follow the infralapsarian presentation in respect to the doctrine of election, but that it is evident both from the wording of Chapter I, Article 7, of the Canons of Dort and from the deliberations of the Synod of Dort, that this is in no wise intended to exclude or condemn the supralapsarian presentation;

that it is hence not permitted to present the supralapsarian view as *the* doctrine of the Reformed Churches in the Netherlands, but neither, to molest anyone who personally holds the supralapsarian view, inasmuch as the Synod of Dort has made no pronouncement upon this disputed point.

Furthermore, Synod adds the warning that such profound doctrines, which are far beyond the understanding of the common people, should be discussed as little as possible in the pulpit, and that one should adhere in the preaching of the Word and in catechetical instruction to the presentation offered in our Confessional Standards.

II. ETERNAL JUSTIFICATION

In regard to the second point, eternal justification, Synod declares:

---

[1] This English translation of the Conclusions of Utrecht (the Dutch original had been adopted in 1905 by the Reformed Churches in the Netherlands) is reproduced from *Acts of Synod 1942 of the Christian Reformed Church* (Grand Rapids: n.p., [1942], Supplement XVII, pages 352–54.

that the term itself does not occur in our Confessional Standards
but that it is not for this reason to be disapproved, any more than
we would be justified in disapproving the term Covenant of
Works and similar terms which have been adopted through theological usage;

that it is incorrect to say that our Confessional Standards know
only of a justification by and through faith, since both God's
Word (Rom. 4:25) and our Confession (Art. XX) speak explicitly
of an objective justification sealed by the resurrection of Christ,
which in point of time precedes the subjective justification;

that, moreover, as far as the matter itself is concerned, all our
Churches sincerely believe and confess that Christ from eternity
in the Counsel of Peace undertook to be the Surety of His people;
taking their guilt upon Himself as also that afterward He by His
suffering and death on Calvary actually paid the ransom for us,
reconciling us to God while we were yet enemies; but that on the
basis of God's Word and in harmony with our Confession it must
be maintained with equal firmness that we personally become
partakers of this benefit only by a sincere faith.

Wherefore Synod earnestly warns against any view that would do violence either to Christ's eternal suretyship for His elect, or to the requirement of a sincere faith to be justified before God in the tribunal of conscience.

III. IMMEDIATE REGENERATION

In regard to the third point, immediate regeneration, Synod declares:

that this term may be used in a good sense, insofar as our
Churches have, over against the Lutheran and Roman Catholic
Churches, always professed that regeneration is not effected
through the Word or the Sacraments as such, but through the
Almighty and regenerating operation of the Holy Spirit;

that this regenerating operation of the Holy Spirit, however,
should not be in such a way divorced from the preaching of the
Word as if these two were separate from each other. For though
the Confession teaches that we should have no doubt concerning
the salvation of our children dying in infancy despite the fact that
they have not heard the preaching of the Gospel, and though our
Confessional Standards nowhere express themselves about the
manner in which such regeneration takes place in these and
other children, it is, on the other hand, no less certain that the

Gospel is a power of God unto salvation to everyone that believeth, and that in the case of adults the regenerating operation of the Holy Spirit accompanies the preaching of the Gospel.

Even though Synod does not dispute that God is able also apart from the preaching of the Word—as, for instance, in the pagan world—to regenerate those whom He will, yet Synod judges that on the basis of the Word of God we are not able to make any declaration in respect to the question whether this actually occurs, and that, therefore, we should adhere to the rule which the revealed Word offers us, and should leave the hidden things to the Lord our God.

IV. PRESUMPTIVE REGENERATION

And finally, in regard to the fourth point, presumptive regeneration, Synod declares:

that according to the Confession of our Churches the seed of the covenant, by virtue of the promise of God, must be held to be regenerated and sanctified in Christ, until upon growing up they should manifest the contrary in their way of life or in doctrine;

that it is, however, less correct to say that baptism is administered to the children of believers on the ground of their presumed regeneration, since the ground of baptism is found in the command and the promise of God;

that, furthermore, the judgment of charity with which the Church regards the seed of the covenant as regenerated, does not at all imply that each child is actually born again, seeing that God's Word teaches that they are not all Israel that are of Israel, and of Isaac it is said: in him shall thy seed be called (Rom. 9:6, 7), so that it is imperative in the preaching constantly to urge earnest self-examination, since only he that believeth and is baptized shall be saved.

Moreover, Synod in agreement with our Confession maintains that "the sacraments are not empty or meaningless signs, so as to deceive us, but visible signs and seals of an inward and invisible thing, by means of which God works in us by the power of the Holy Spirit" (Article XXXIII), and that more particularly baptism is called "the washing of regeneration" and "the washing away of sins" because God would "assure us by this divine pledge and sign that we are spiritually cleansed from our sins as really as we are outwardly washed with water"; wherefore our Church in the prayer after baptism "thanks and praises God that He has forgiven us and our children all our sins, through the blood of His beloved Son

Jesus Christ, and received us through His Holy Spirit as members of His only begotten Son, and so adopted us to be His children, and sealed and confirmed the same unto us by holy baptism"; so that our Confessional Standards clearly teach that the sacrament of baptism signifies and seals the washing away of our sins by the blood and the Spirit of Jesus Christ, that is, the justification and the renewal by the Holy Spirit as benefits which God has bestowed upon our seed.

Synod is of the opinion that the representation that every elect child is on that account already in fact regenerated even before baptism, can be proved neither on scriptural nor on confessional grounds, seeing that God fulfils His promise sovereignly in His own time, whether before, during, or after baptism. It is hence imperative to be circumspect in one's utterances on this matter, so as not to desire to be wise beyond that which God has revealed.

Scripture and Confession Index

INDEX OF CONFESSIONS

Person and Subject Index